v + vl

ECONOMIES
IN
TRANSITION

STRUCTURAL
ADJUSTMENT IN OECD
COUNTRIES

ORGANISATION FOR ECONOMIC CO-OPERATION AND DEVELOPMENT

HD
82
E39
1989

Pursuant to article 1 of the Convention signed in Paris on 14th December 1960, and which came into force on 30th September 1961, the Organisation for Economic Co-operation and Development (OECD) shall promote policies designed:

- to achieve the highest sustainable economic growth and employment and a rising standard of living in Member countries, while maintaining financial stability, and thus to contribute to the development of the world economy;
- to contribute to sound economic expansion in Member as well as non-member countries in the process of economic development; and
- to contribute to the expansion of world trade on a multilateral, non-discriminatory basis in accordance with international obligations.

The original Member countries of the OECD are Austria, Belgium, Canada, Denmark, France, the Federal Republic of Germany, Greece, Iceland, Ireland, Italy, Luxembourg, the Netherlands, Norway, Portugal, Spain, Sweden, Switzerland, Turkey, the United Kingdom and the United States. The following countries acceded subsequently through accession at the dates indicated hereafter: Japan (28th April 1964), Finland (28th January 1969), Australia (7th June 1971) and New Zealand (29th May 1973).

The Socialist Federal Republic of Yugoslavia takes part in some of the work of the OECD (agreement of 28th October 1961).

Publié en français sous le titre:

ECONOMIES EN TRANSITION
L'ajustement structurel dans les pays de l'OCDE

The studies behind this Report were carried out by economists of the Country Studies and Economic Prospects Branch in the Economics and Statistics Department from 1984 to autumn 1988, in the context of the OECD Economic and Development Review Committee's (EDRC) annual reviews of Member countries' economic performance and policies, the results of which are published as the *OECD Economic Surveys*. In May 1984, the OECD Council at Ministerial level had called on the Organisation to strengthen its review and appraisal of adjustment policies in an overall economic perspective. This task meant putting into practice the broad policy orientations that had been elaborated by an OECD Special Group on Positive Adjustment Policies *(Positive Adjustment Policies – Managing Structural Change, Paris, 1983)*.

To ensure comparable analysis across countries, the Committee selected four key areas – labour markets, financial markets, industrial adjustment and the public sector. Structural analyses of one or the other of these themes have subsequently been included in all Surveys, resulting in over 70 structural studies so far. This Report provides a synthesis of these studies. The Report benefited from comments by members of the Secretariat and discussions with Committee members. However, the views expressed here do not necessarily correspond to those of the national authorities concerned. The Report is published on the responsibility of the Secretary-General.

Table of contents

Chapter 1

Structural Adjustment – What we have learnt   9

Chapter 2

Greater Flexibility in the Labour Market   24

The experience of unemployment   26
Measuring real labour cost gaps   33
The wage formation process   42
Structural aspects of labour market performance   52
Other measures affecting unemployment   63
Conclusions   64

Chapter 3

Financial Markets: The Challenges of Modernisation   77

Pressures for change   78
General overview of change in financial markets   85
Some implications of change   96
Conclusions   111

Chapter 4

Industrial Adjustment: Freeing Initiative   118

The evolving OECD economies   119
The process of industrial adjustment   130
A new thrust to industrial policies   137
Macro-economic consequences of policies to strengthen competition   147
Conclusions   151

Chapter 5

The Public Sector: Restoring the Balance 156
Public expenditure: containing the expansion 157
Tax reform: motivation and design 168
Medium-term strategy: controlling government indebtedness 191
Conclusions 208

Tables

2.1.	Growth and labour market performance	28
2.2.	Wages, prices and unemployment	30
2.3.	Characteristics of unemployment	32
2.4.	Real wages, productivity and the terms of trade	35
2.5.	Labour productivity and factor substitution	37
2.6.	Measuring wage flexibility	44
2.7.	Estimates of NAIRUs	47
2.8.	Estimates of the NAWRU	50
2.9.	Unemployment benefit replacement ratios	57
2.10.	Non-wage labour costs	60
2.11.	Changes in labour market practices	66
3.1.	Corporate sector self-financing ratio	82
3.2.	Foreign business of the banking sector	84
3.3.	Size of financial markets and degree of intermediation	90
3.4.	Issues of securities in domestic credit flows	91
3.5.	Issues of securities as percentage of investment	91
3.6.	Debt/equity ratios of the non-financial corporate sector	92
3.7.	Nature and motives of financial innovation	93
3.8.	International comparison of bank concentration	97
3.9.	Income and cost margins in banking	100
3.10.	Cost of bond issues in domestic markets	101
3.11.	Marginal tax rates on capital attributable to the corporate tax system	106
3.12.	Main features of capital-income taxation	107
4.1.	Employment trends in services and manufacturing	123
4.2.	Labour productivity and real growth in market services and manufacturing	124
4.3.	Nature of service activities	124
4.4.	Business-sector and manufacturing total factor productivity	127

4.5.	Import/export elasticity differentials	129
4.6.	Shares of manufactures and services in foreign trade	130
4.7.	Index of structural change	131
4.8.	Output structure: relationship to world demand structure and import penetration	132
4.9.	Relative production, import and export patterns	133
4.10.	Intensity of intra-industry trade	135
4.11.	Constant market share analysis	136
4.12.	Direct subsidy payments	138
4.13.	Structure of R & D expenditure	139
4.14.	Extent of non-tariff barriers in OECD countries	140
4.15.	Employment in three ailing sectors	142
4.16.	Price and real-wage sensitivity to market conditions	149
5.1.	Structure and growth of general government outlays	158
5.2.	General government claims on resources	159
5.3.	Change in the relative price of public services	162
5.4.	Social security transfers	164
5.5.	Determinants of the growth of state retirement pensions	165
5.6.	Structure and growth of general government tax receipts	171
5.7.	General government current receipts	172
5.8.	Fiscal drag and inflation	174
5.9.	Total marginal tax rates on labour income	175
5.10.	Indexation provisions in OECD Countries	176
5.11.	Changes in personal income tax rates	177
5.12.	General consumption taxes	181
5.13.	Changes in corporate income tax rates	182
5.14.	Corporate tax allowances	183
5.15.	Effects of interest rate on personal saving	188
5.16.	General government financial balances	192
5.17.	Gross public debt	194
5.18.	Structural budget balances net of debt interest payments	195
5.19.	Seigniorage and tax revenues	197
5.20.	Government deficits and interest rates	198
5.21.	General government deficits and private saving	199
5.22.	Gross interest paid on public debt	201
5.23.	Stabilizing general government debt/GNP ratios	203
5.24.	Age dependency ratios	206
5.25.	The influence of demographic change on the share of pension expenditure in national income	207

Diagrams

2.1.	Wages, prices and unemployment	25
2.2.	Wages, prices and unemployment in the OECD	31
2.3.	Relative price of labour in seven major OECD countries	38
2.4.	Profitability	39
2.5.	Unemployment rates and capacity use	41
2.6.	Real wage rigidity	45
2.7.	Real wage flexibility and employment adaptability	46
3.1.	Sector financial balances	80
3.2.	Inflation, interest and exchange rates	83
3.3.	Relative importance of foreign-owned financial institutions	88
3.4.	Composition of household assets	94
3.5.	Gross liabilities by sector	95
3.6.	Share of financial activities in GDP	99
3.7.	Spain: implicit subsidies through compulsory financial ratios	103
3.8.	Credit controls and resource allocation in Italy	104
4.1.	Structure of nominal GDP: an international comparison	120
4.2.	Rates of return differentials: overall business sector and manufacturing	126
5.1.	Total public sector expenditure	157
5.2.	Public expenditure excluding interest payments	160
5.3.	General government receipts	170
5.4.	The effects of inflation on income tax rates and allowances in the United States	173
5.5.	General government financial balances	191
5.6.	Gross public debt	193
5.7.	Real rate of return on government debt and the "inflation tax" in the United States	196

Chapter 1

STRUCTURAL ADJUSTMENT – WHAT WE HAVE LEARNT

This volume is a synthesis of the structural work carried out by the OECD Secretariat for the Economic and Development Review Committee (EDRC) of the OECD over the period 1984 to 1988. Given the mandate of this Committee, the work has been country-specific. One objective in undertaking it was to explore more broadly the potential of micro-economic policy changes for improving economic performance. To gain insights into desirable directions of policy change, a common question runs through these country structural analyses: to what extent have the cumulative effects of policies that have tried to modify the functioning of a market, or to influence economic developments in "key" areas, resulted in a lasting improvement of conditions, or in a deterioration?

This broad orientation suggested the following specific questions:

- What are the key features of OECD countries' microeconomic policies, and what changes in them have occurred over the past five years or so? Have there been preferred instruments of intervention in factor and product markets? What inter-connections have been observed between microeconomic policies and their effects? What lessons have been learnt from the use of the policy instruments (including the control of public sector expenditure) and how transferable are the results from one economy to another?
- Which theoretical concepts and operational criteria could be employed in assessing the effects of a change in particular microeconomic policies, subject to constraints imposed by the requirements of cross-country comparability and by data limitations? Can micro-structural indicators be devised to gauge the size of distortions similar to the indicators familiar to macroeconomists such as real-wage gaps or non-accelerating inflation rates of unemployment?

- How have the pressures for change in a given field varied across OECD economies over time? Which forces have stimulated structural change in OECD economies; has change been policy-induced or market-led? And has structural change accelerated, as many observers believe, or not?
- More generally, how should structural change, and the impact on it of micro-economic policies, be thought about in relation to aggregate economic performance? By which channels do micro phenomena interact with key macroeconomic characteristics of an economy? In turn, has the macroeconomic environment affected specific channels of micro/macroeconomic inter-action?

This introductory chapter firstly sketches out the approaches to the analysis of structural adjustment taken in the country studies; second sets out key features of the international economy of the 1980s that have shaped the common environment and conditioned the structural adjustment experiences of individual countries; and third summarises the main findings from the four following subject area chapters. Finally, it draws some tentative conclusions from the overall evaluation of the adjustment process.

Different approaches to structural adjustment

While the general attitude towards structural change became more supportive in the course of the 1980s, the reliance put by individual governments on market forces differed. The OECD Council of Ministers had adopted a set of broad criteria on "positive adjustment policies" in 1982; and this subsequently served to orientate the EDRC's discussion of microeconomic policy issues (*Positive Adjustment Policies – Managing Structural Change*, OECD, Paris 1983). This document classified different approaches of governments to structural adjustment according to *preventive, anticipatory, defensive* and *interventionist* strategies, which broadly reflected the spectrum of government thinking at that time about intermediate objectives with respect to the *intended* direct effects of their sector-specific and horizontal policies. The overall evaluation of microeconomic policies in the country analyses sought to go beyond this, by taking into account also indirect effects including possible economy-wide repercussions on incentives, as well as dynamic effects on long-run efficiency.

The approach adopted

The approach adopted restricted the subject matter by choosing to focus on four themes: *i)* labour market problems; *ii)* financial market change and reform; *iii)* industrial adjustment and *iv)* public sector imbalances. These were selected on the basis of their policy relevance and applicability in a large number of countries. Broadly speaking, the methodology adopted for each theme was comparable:

  i) A case study approach was followed which, being country specific and in-depth, highlighted the micro-structural environment of a given country (including in particular its institutions);

  ii) A fact-finding approach which would generate over time a "structural data bank" of micro-policy measures and performance indicators, broadly comparable across OECD countries;

  iii) A qualitative/quantitative analysis which sought to identify the micro/macroeconomic interaction, identifying key intermediate variables.

In synthesizing findings, this Report has gone one step further: it has sought to build-in cross-country comparability by using many common analytical tools and evaluation criteria, so far as data limitations and country differences permit. All quantitative estimates, however, are open to the objection that they do not capture the possible consequences of reform in full.

Crucial to the methodology was the widespread use of quantitative measures which, given the subject matter, have often been termed *structural indicators*. It is important to bear in mind that they have been used in different ways corresponding to the three headings listed above:

  i) To characterise the micro-structural environment (in Chapter 2, for example, an indicator of the degree of corporatism is used to summarise the institutional structure);

  ii) As indicators of policy measures and performance (e.g. structural budget balances, Chapter 5, and an intra-industry trade index, Chapter 4);

  iii) As measures of micro/macroeconomic interaction (e.g. real wage gaps, Chapter 2).

Within each category several different indicators have been utilised, reflecting the diversity of country experience, the ambiguity of theoretical measures and the differing availability of information.

As between themes or subject areas there is a marked difference in the nature of the indicators that have been developed. For example, whereas micro/macro linkages are examined in the Chapters on labour markets and public sector issues, this is much less the case with respect to the industrial adjustment and financial market themes. To an extent, this difference in coverage reflects the uneven development of economic

11

analysis for the different areas. But it also reflects the great difficulties in making the existing body of analysis operational. Thus, for example, the links between financial intermediation and economic efficiency are well known but an adequate quantitative framework integrating the two concepts is far from self-evident.

The productivity slowdown – a shared experience

Government policies toward structural adjustment have been influenced both by domestic developments and by events external to each country. Most OECD economies had experienced a slowdown in productivity growth, albeit to varying degrees, through the late 1960s, the 1970s and into the early 1980s. As this proved to be a lasting phenomenon in most economies, the shared experience became an important factor contributing to re-focus OECD governments' attention on the micro-structural foundations of growth and the policies needed to enhance them. The slowdown was associated with a slowing of capital accumulation, reduced capacity utilisation, smaller opportunities for technology transfer and catch-up, and possibly a slowing of new technology generation (*OECD Economic Studies*, Spring 1988). Growth of the productive potential of key OECD economies had fallen off in the 1970s and subsequent to the second oil shock, and conditions for private-sector capital investment became a key area of policy concern. Thus, OECD governments had a strong common interest in reassessing the impact of micro-economic policies on the business sector's financial position and its investment decisions. Their aim was to invigorate private sector performance, by improving the functioning of labour, product and financial markets and to reform the corporate tax system.

The global economic environment

Among the *external* forces that conditioned governments' attitudes to structural adjustment of the economy featured the advent of the Newly Industrializing Economies (NIEs), the pronounced exchange rate movements of the dollar in the 1980s and the 1986 oil price fall. The rise of new suppliers from the NIEs lastingly influenced the governments' perception with respect to the need to facilitate actively the process of structural change. The consequent increase in competitive pressures has varied across industries and therefore has a very strong structural aspect. For example, in 1973, the share of NIEs in OECD labour-intensive imports was around 8 per cent but by 1985 this had reached around 20 per cent. By contrast, for total manufacturing, the figures were 4 and 8 per cent respectively (*Structural Adjustment and Economic Performance,* OECD, Paris, 1987, page 288). However, there are indications that this process is spreading to other non-traditional industries, thereby furthering the interest in future structural adjustment.

The sustained rise of the dollar until early 1985 and its subsequent fall up to early 1988 had substantial effects on the allocation of resources, both within the tradeables sector and relative to the non-tradeables sector of the OECD economies, through shifts in relative prices and hence in relative profitability. Because of the large exchange-rate movements, growth of output was enhanced in the first half of the 1980s in *Europe* and *Japan*, while progress in the process of disinflation was made more difficult. The reverse was true of the *United States*, where domestic demand grew strongly, and faster than output though growth rates of output and employment were high. During this period concern for the economic and social consequences of structural change was somewhat muted in Europe. Yet the strong commitment to lower inflation motivated policy-makers in OECD countries generally to reduce rigidities in the price and wage formation process, to dismantle price controls and to review the way in which administered prices were set.

From 1985 onwards, the required unwinding of the international current-account imbalances that had built up over the first part of the 1980s implied a sustained reversal of the global pattern of differential demand growth across OECD economies. This in turn required a stronger contribution from domestic relative to foreign sources in *Japan* and the European surplus countries in particular (OECD Council of Ministers; Communiqué, paragraph 8; Press/A(86)17). In both *Europe* and *Japan* this new orientation for macroeconomic policy gave a fresh impetus to reassessing the role of micro-economic policies. In *Europe* there was increasing concern with the poor job-creating record of many countries, so that a review of the way in which markets worked became a matter of urgency, together with a reassessment of the potential of new technologies and a reappraisal of the role of social policies.

Another pertinent event was the fall in oil and non-oil commodity prices by 15 per cent in 1986, as the effects contributed to improving supply-side conditions in most OECD economies. As many European governments were concerned about the continued sluggishness of investment, their policies to influence the direction of the income gains implied by the change in the terms of trade aimed at benefiting the business sector (in the form of higher profits), thus seeking to facilitate the restructuring of industry. Where governments appropriated most of the terms-of-trade gains for themselves by raising energy taxes, more progress was thereby made possible in cutting back public deficits; where the controlled or state-owned energy sector was allowed to keep most of the gains by not lowering prices, this improved its financial position. For several OECD economies with a large energy sector, particularly oil, the implied shift in the inter-sectoral terms of trade led to a significant redistribution of income which set in train and/or accentuated a change in relative output shares, thus exacerbating adjustment pressures. For most OECD economies, however, the real income gains induced by the fall in commodity and oil prices cushioned the short-run detrimental effects on output and income of the improvement of U.S competitiveness as the dollar depreciated through 1986, 1987 and early 1988.

Finally, in several of the smaller European countries – notably in Scandinavia – which had faced external problems in the early 1980s, the interest of the authorities in micro-structural reforms was reinforced by the difficulties their governments had met in consolidating the gains in international competitiveness subsequent to a depreciation of the exchange rate. Though the shift in relative prices was generally flanked by a tightening of macro-economic policies, the compression of demand was typically not long sustained for fear of jeopardizing the low levels of unemployment that prevailed. Thus, the high priority attaching in several of these countries to the goal of full employment, together with a strong preference for a more egalitarian income distribution, meant that these economies tended to be run at stronger demand pressures than warranted by their underlying external position, i.e. their production structure. This hampered the intended switch of resources away from the sheltered sectors as did strong wage-wage links which prevented the emergence of sufficiently large and sustainable profitability differentials in favour of the open sectors, as would have been needed to shift the investment pattern. When from the mid-1980s the underlying weakness of the exposed sectors of these economies seemed likely to resurface, governments increasingly chose to aim at alleviating external pressures through micro-economic policy reforms, rather than resorting to further currency depreciation combined with a stronger dose of demand compression which seemed to bring only temporary relief.

Limitations of the approach

In interpreting the changes observed and the likely forces that are driving the adjustment process, the various limitations, outlined above, together with the nature of the review exercise itself call for a fair measure of caution. Firstly, the choice of subject area for structural analysis resided *de facto* with the country concerned. Second, the policy priorities of the authorities concerned were taken as given. Third, for each country, considerable effort went into investigating the process of policy formulation in order to explore the institutional constraints. Fourth, the assessments given in the subject chapters, in addition to standard empirical analysis, relied on a large measure of judgement which has, however, been importantly informed by the *collective* experience of the EDRC. In any case, the country structural analyses are a continuing exercise, and fresh evidence should come to light from them. Hence, this Report provides a preliminary overview from a "workshop" perspective, rather than a comprehensive survey of recent comparative economic history of the structural adaptation of the OECD economies.

An overview of the analysis by topic

Chapter 2, which addresses *labour market problems*, begins by reviewing the experience of unemployment across OECD countries, highlighting differences. In the early 1970s, these differences could be largely attributed to the evolution of real wages. The second section explores this aspect, using the concept of "real wage gaps", and discusses how behaviour changed between the first and second oil shocks and then into the 1980s. The third section reviews the evidence that the "natural" rate of unemployment may have drifted higher in many countries during the last decade or so. The following sections then review the main structural features of labour market performance. Many countries have sought to improve performance: the measures taken are examined as also are their limitations.

The chapter concludes that, although part of the worsened employment performance may be associated with the slowdown in demand growth, other elements also contributed, while persistent demand weakness itself can be explained in part by inflationary pressures arising in labour markets:

– High levels of unemployment have persisted in many countries, even after the OECD economies recovered from the effects of the second oil shock and despite real wage growth in general being more moderate than after the first oil shock. Attention has thus shifted in the early 1980s to the appropriate *level* of real wages. In many countries, the absence of profitable opportunities at prevailing cost/price ratios seems to have discouraged both investment and employment;

– Real wages were found to respond less to labour market conditions in most European countries than in the *United States*, *Canada* and *Japan*. Policies have sought to improve the wage-formation process in order to promote the real wage adjustment that seemed to be required after the second oil shock. There is some evidence that countries with greater aggregate real wage flexibility do have wider wage differentials between sectors. Again, for a given degree of flexibility, countries with higher adaptability of employment

15

experience a stronger moderating influence on wages. Even though the responsiveness of wages to unemployment may only be average, by experiencing a quicker and greater rise in unemployment after a negative supply shock, the process of returning the economy to equilibrium is speeded up. This may contribute to preventing the emergence of sustained unemployment;

- The main impediments to better functioning of labour markets arise from specific wage-bargaining institutions, tax and social spending policies, and over-protective legislation. In particular, in many countries the interaction of the income tax and social transfer systems, especially unemployment benefits, exacerbated the unemployment problem.

Chapter 3, which deals with selected developments in *financial markets* in recent years, first appraises the factors both internal and external to the sector which have exerted pressures for structural change. The second section reviews developments, including those in policy and regulatory reform and in the functioning of financial markets, and examines the effect of these developments on savings, investment and the allocation of credit. The third section draws out some implications of these developments for economic performance in respect to the efficiency of intermediation, for the operation and effectiveness of monetary policy, and for the supervisory framework.

The speed and extent of change – greater than in most other sectors – have had important effects on financial flows and the efficiency of the financial system, while at the same time raising concerns for systemic soundness. Innovation and continuing trends towards internationalisation of financial activities in an era of around-the-clock trading, have significantly broadened the "menu" of instruments available for portfolio allocation and for financing capital formation, but has also led to increased anxiety over the potential for the global transmission of disturbances, as underscored by the October 1987 stock-market crisis. The main features noted in the chapter are the following:

- While countries had extremely varied initial conditions and their actual policies differed, policy orientation has converged to an appreciable extent. Greater freedom of capital movements across borders, the complete or partial abolition of price and quantity controls on domestic financial flows, and stimulation of increased domestic and international competition have been characteristic across the OECD area. As a result, markets have "deepened", allocative mechanisms have improved, and efficiency has been enhanced;

- The degree of competition now prevailing in financial markets is generally much greater than in the past, with markedly less official intervention in the credit-allocation process. The scale of financial operations has expanded, sometimes dramatically, with new markets and instruments emerging. The conduct of monetary policy has at times been made more difficult, while the degree of systemic risk may have increased. Greater instability of markets as a result of innovations and growing integration has become a matter of concern, highlighting the need for vigilance and greater international coordination of prudential supervision. Steps have been taken in this direction by monetary authorities and regulators around the world;
- The role of market forces is likely to be reinforced in the future, as countries pursue the process of integration and liberalisation. Further efficiency gains may be expected; however, increased international coordination of domestic policies affecting financial markets remains an important priority, particularly in the field of taxation of financial assets and prudential supervision.

Chapter 4 reviews the adjustment of the *industrial structure* to the changes and shocks of the 1970s and 1980s, together with the role and effect of policies. Reflecting governments' concerns, emphasis has been placed on manufacturing industry, given its growing importance in the foreign trade of many countries and its weight in R & D activities, though this choice also reflected practical considerations with respect to data availability. The first section deals with the course of events. The changes that have taken place in industrial structures since 1970 differ greatly across countries as regards their intensity and underlying causes as well as their consequences. The adjustments that have taken place are then examined from the standpoint of external performance, placing special emphasis on international comparison of country experiences. Then follows an analysis of the effects of traditional industrial policies and the recent change in the rationale and thrust of policies. Finally, the macroeconomic implications of strengthening competitive forces in OECD countries are explored.

The main findings from the synthesis can be summarised as follows:

- Manufacturing is clearly giving place to the service sectors, although the extent varies from one country to another. In large measure, this is a normal development characteristic of economies which have reached an advanced stage of development. However, within the context of slower growth, adjustment has been accompanied by serious transitional problems since the 1970s. Manufacturing employment has fallen almost everywhere, most noticeably in the EC countries, though in the more recent past this trend has reversed or weakened in a few of the larger countries, with some small countries continuing to experience employment gains. The decline in the relative weight of manufacturing has contributed in part to the observed slowdown in growth of total factor productivity, as measured productivity growth is higher in manufacturing than in the other sectors;

- Faced with rapid pace of structural change, governments in the 1970s responded in different ways. Interventionist policies that affected product markets have been practised in a large number of countries – whether as targeted or defensive industrial policies, or as sets of measures affecting the competitive environment or the rules of the game of international trade. Yet, very little evidence points to the initial objectives having been attained. Rather, the results of these policies have often had broader ramifications than originally envisaged; direct budgetary costs have been higher than estimated, and it has been difficult to ensure control over terms and conditions of subsidies or other sector-related forms of assistance;

- Since the early 1980s, a broad convergence of views and policy actions has been observed in most OECD countries, in line with the evolution of the OECD medium-term economic strategy. Increased emphasis is now placed on the stimulation of competitive forces through deregulation, at times accompanied by privatisation of public enterprises or by the adoption of criteria of increased efficiency. In addition, sectoral plans have increasingly been viewed as useful mainly in order to facilitate adjustment in crisis sectors thereby alleviating any social costs. This requires clarity of objectives, aid whose period is strictly limited, and diversification away from customary ranges of products and industries;

- The strengthening of competitive forces in OECD countries has macroeconomic implications. It will reinforce economies' capacity to respond to adverse shocks. As prices and wages become more sensitive to market conditions, they should adjust faster than in the past, reducing cumulative losses in output and employment over the medium term which may be associated with the adjustment process. As a result, the deterioration in human capital – associated with sustained unemployment – may be more limited, and the incentive for investment – a key vehicle of technical progress – may be strengthened. It is therefore to be hoped that, in the face of similar external shocks to those in the past, the trend growth of the OECD economies, especially the European countries, would in the future be more resilient.

Chapter 5, which reviews the *public sector*, concentrates on the progress of budgetary reform, as the consolidation of public finances was seen as a crucial element in the medium-term OECD strategy for sustainable, non-inflationary growth[1]. A first section discusses public spending issues and the progress made towards better public expenditure control. There follows a section reviewing issues arising from the development of the tax system: the rationale for, and progress towards, reform. Issues arising from government debt are discussed in the third section.

Several interesting lessons emerge from the review of these issues. The experiences of the 1970s, when there was a coincidence of slowing economic growth, rising unemployment and accelerating inflation, persuaded governments that the usual goals of economic policy were no longer being served by a continuing expansion of the public sector. Evidence has accumulated that higher taxes and/or deficits may have contributed to allocative distortions whose costs outweigh the short-term benefits of higher government spending. Powerful constraints have emerged in the form of growing debt interest payments, which have threatened to make debt expansion explosive. Where governments resorted to importing capital to finance budget deficits the snowball-effect associated with debt accumulation has often been compounded by adverse changes of the exchange rate. Thus governments have turned increasingly towards greater self-restraint, and the 1980s have been characterised by a lowering of marginal tax burdens, greater tax neutrality and better control of government expenditure. The principal features have been:

- While public expenditure has continued to grow in relation to GNP, the rate of increase has slowed and in some cases stabilized; some of the factors which made for a faster-than-average public-sector growth in earlier years have been checked as public sector pay and recruitment have been more closely controlled and greater efficiency imposed on public sector operations;
- The overall tax burden has continued to rise. But tax reforms, implemented and proposed, have meant that important progress has been made towards a more neutral, and allocatively more efficient, tax structure in many countries, reducing marginal rates of income tax, harmonising post-tax yields on different sources of income, and widening the base of indirect taxes;
- Fiscal restraint has succeeded in reducing budget deficits relative to GNP from their peaks in the early 1980s. However, debt/GNP ratios continue to rise in many economies, and even in those economies where the ratios have stabilized, pressures may build up in the future because of prospective deficits in social security funds.

The rationale for tax reform is rather similar across countries: to reduce economic distortions, to broaden the tax base, and to lower disincentives to work and saving. However, there have been differences in priorities, in particular between the *United States* and the rest of the OECD countries over the relative urgency of tax cuts and deficit reductions. Though progress has been made towards better overall budgetary control and the importance of planning the annual budget in a medium-term setting has been widely recognised, average tax rates remain high in many economies and real rates of interest may remain above prospective growth rates. In these conditions debt interest payments will continue to remain a heavy burden, restricting the scope for further reductions in taxation and making the financing of the government sector difficult for some time to come.

Evaluation – some broader lessons

The above summary overview of the subject chapters indicates that reforms have been taken in all of the areas examined and that micro-policy changes led to modifications at a sectoral level and to visible gains in flexibility in many instances. More importantly, however, for many countries the examination of structural issues for at least two or three subject areas – through a series of EDRC reviews that stretched from 1984 to 1988 – has generated a body of circumstantial evidence that lends support to the supposition that strong inter-industry linkages and marked product/factor market inter-actions have been at work. One of the salient examples frequently observed was in the field of *industrial policies*. First, protecting particular sectors affects not only individual prices and output, but may also have profound repercussions on the structure of the economy more generally. The most noticeable instances include public procurement, subsidies, financial relief through the tax system and the use of tariffs, quotas and other trade barriers. Second, protection in one sector may induce labour to appropriate part of the rents thus conferred in higher wages which, in turn, may stimulate high wage demands elsewhere, or causing a deterioration of labour market conditions more generally. Third, financial support for a sector may not only distort the composition of its investment, with possible adverse effects on employment growth, but also create increasing budgetary problems. In particular, off-budget financing subsequently tends to exacerbate problems of control over public expenditure.

By the same token, removal of distortions to resource allocation may be expected to confer benefits to the economy at large. At the aggregate level, budget consolidation including policies aiming at a better control of public expenditure have had favourable macroeconomic repercussions, notably by reducing pressures on interest rates and freeing resources for the private sector, enhancing overall conditions for successful structural adaptation. Governments have in many cases taken the view that the full potential benefits of the reforms undertaken in product and factor markets as well as in the public sector in recent years have not yet been fully realised. The overall impression from the key manifestations of structural adjustment summarised in this report may to some extent justify such an attitude.

The principal findings reported here, together with the analytical experience gained through a large number of structural studies, suggest three sets of observations: one on the impact of microeconomic policies on aggregate economic performance; another on the scope for improving governments' approach to structural reforms; and a third on the potential role of indicators in the monitoring of structural adjustment.

Though it has been possible to represent the channels of interaction between the micro sphere (i.e. microeconomic policy measures) and the broader relationships characterising macroeconomic performance and to evaluate their likely relative importance for a specific country, it has not proved generally possible to quantify these direct links. This is hardly surprising for two inter-connected reasons, one related to the nature of policy and the other to the tools of economic analysis. With respect to microeconomic policy, it is clear that an individual measure may not have a very large overall effect whereas a coherent programme of micro-policy reforms which takes account of interdependencies may be highly effective. But the reality of microeconomic policy is neither one extreme nor the other but a series of measures extending over time and often related to one another as the consequences of earlier action show the need for a further response. Moreover, experience has shown that credibility of the reform effort is important and that this often relates as much to determined implementation, based on a sustained medium-term commitment of the government, as to its coherence and perceived social equity. Hence, quantification involves not just the representation of a given measure but consideration of the overall policy stance and how this is evolving over time. Even so, benefits may not be realised quickly, as it takes time for business, labour and individuals to reassess and respond to changing opportunities. To become effective, a policy of encouraging structural change often requires substantial changes in sometimes long-ingrained attitudes (e.g. risk-taking) and behaviour (e.g. social relations). Finally, macroeconomic policies and the external environment have also been important influences in performance, making attribution difficult.

A second reason for the difficulty in establishing quantitative micro-macro links relates to the state of the art of economic analysis applied to broader issues of structural adjustment. While, for example, applied general equilibrium modelling is well developed and sheds light on the economy-wide consequences of many microeconomic policies, the micro-macro linkages will always remain a matter of controversy, not to mention the empirical foundation of the models themselves. But the real deficiency with this type of analysis is that it is concerned only with equilibrium and hence does not concern itself with dynamic market processes. Yet it is exactly this question (i.e. the efficient functioning of market mechanisms) which lies at the centre of many structural reforms dealt with in this volume. Analytical tools do of course exist, but they are rather underdeveloped in the area of micro-macro linkage.

As regards possible improvements to the process of micro-economic policy formulation and implementation, several approaches appear promising. One would be to improve coherence across micro-policy reforms and sectors, which appears to be rather underdeveloped as yet. This would allow priorities to be established more clearly, as well as help identify how policy measures interact with each other while affecting different sectors. Such inter-connections may cut both ways in that they also point to the possibility of governments acting in politically less-sensitive areas in order to step up pressures to ease rigidities in sectors where direct policy action might be difficult. Hence, in designing micro-economic policy changes, increased attention should be given to indirect effects and long-term dynamic consequences; side-effects on other policies or sectors may militate against the favourable impact expected from certain reform efforts, when important inter-linkages exist that have not explicitly been recognised and taken account of.

With respect to the coordination of different micro-policy actions, the experience of *New Zealand* provides an interesting example. The fundamental policy shift that began in 1984 was based on the belief that, together with the redirection of macro-economic policies, a profound change was necessary in the nature and philosophy of government intervention in the economy. An appreciation that improved market "contestability" can enhance efficiency is central to the reappraisal of public regulation. Markets are made more "contestable" by establishing the possibility of bringing competitive pressures effectively into markets where barriers to entry and exit are high, irrespective of the number of firms that exist at a given point in time. This idea can help even in areas where government intervention could be fully justified on traditional public policy grounds, because many of the rigidities introduced by regulation and intervention can be avoided. Overall, such an approach may prove to hold potential for other countries as well, in serving as a unifying theme to define a programme for structural reform. For a more extensive analysis of coherence – inter-temporal and otherwise – the assessment would also need to cover two other aspects of the process of structural reform, namely the sequencing of reforms and the appropriate speed of implementation.

Given the difficulty in implementing many theoretical relationships, the range of micro-structural indicators clearly needs to be broadened. This should naturally be accompanied by efforts to investigate the analytical underpinnings of the structural measures while paying attention to their empirical verification within and across countries. Experience from the country structural analysis, however, suggests that governments' choice of a set of such indicators – apart from analytical robustness – would be motivated by political considerations as well. In the light of the marked differences observed in the OECD countries' microeconomic conditions, it may prove difficult to have a limited number of structural indicators adopted that would also be valid across countries. A case in point may be the range of conventional indicators pertaining to labour markets and wage formation used in Chapter 2 where it is obvious that a narrower approach would imply a loss of empirical richness and analytical depth. Moreover, governments may differ in their policy judgement in respect of the interpretation to be put on specific indicators.

Note

1. The links between high, and often extremely arbitrary, tax rates and economic performance have been covered at some length in various OECD publications in addition to the Country Reviews, most recently in *Structural Adjustment and Economic Performance* (1987), and have also been the subject of several articles published in *OECD Economic Studies*, including "The Role of the Public Sector" (1985). Deficit finance and government indebtedness have also been the subject of extensive OECD analysis, e.g. Chouraqui and Price (1984); Price and Muller (1984); Chouraqui, Jones and Montador (1986).

Chapter 2

GREATER FLEXIBILITY
IN THE LABOUR MARKET

Introduction

The problem of structural adjustment in OECD countries has perhaps its most visible manifestation in labour markets. By the mid-1980s, unemployment in the OECD area had risen above 8 per cent, compared with around 3 to 3½ per cent in the 1960s and early 1970s. The origins of high unemployment in the mid-1980s go back many years. Tight labour markets in the 1960, and increased industrial conflict, culminating in the wave of strikes and disputes which hit many European countries during the period 1968-71, created a difficult legacy. Perhaps largely because of concern about the wider social and political repercussions of industrial conflict, macroeconomic policy in many countries failed to resist, and in some cases actually worsened, serious inflationary pressures[1]. At the same time, microeconomic policies increased structural rigidities in the labour market. The overall result was that in the late 1960s and early 1970s real wage costs grew faster than productivity[2]. Problems were, then, beginning to emerge well before the commodity price explosion and the first oil shock; and they were primarily domestic in origin.

The major deterioration in the international environment that occurred in the early 1970s made matters worse. Higher oil prices, more intense international competition, rapid structural change and often depressed world markets strained even smoothly functioning labour markets. As a recent OECD report has noted, government policy signals were ambiguous at least until 1979 as policy alternated between a primary concern with inflation and fears about unemployment[3]. As wage growth started to accelerate once again in the late 1970s (the exact timing differed from country to country, see Diagram 2.1), macroeconomic policy had to aim above all at reducing inflation and to pay more attention to real wages as a factor determining employment[4]. Unemployment rose, and wage inflation fell steadily

DIAGRAM 2.1

WAGES, PRICES AND UNEMPLOYMENT

········· Private consumption deflator per cent change *(left scale)*
——— Total compensation per employee per cent change *(left scale)*
▨ Unemployment rate *(right scale)*

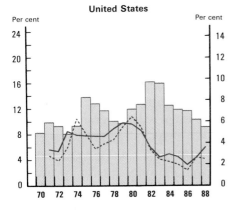

United States

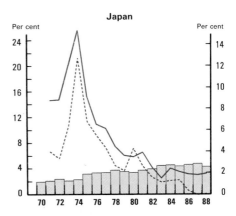

Japan

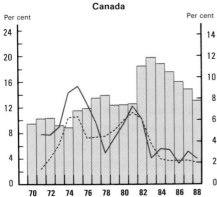

Canada

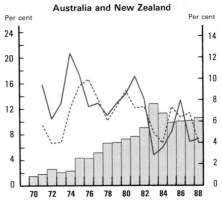

Australia and New Zealand

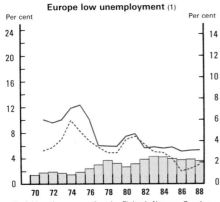

Europe low unemployment (1)

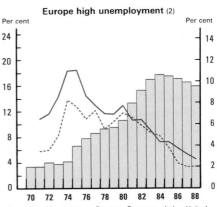

Europe high unemployment (2)

1. *Arithmetic average:* Austria, Finland, Norway, Sweden, Switzerland.

2. *Arithmetic average:* France, Germany, Italy, United Kingdom, Ireland, Netherlands, Portugal, Spain, Belgium, Denmark.
Source: OECD Secretariat.

reaching, by 1987, its lowest rate for almost twenty years. At the same time, many governments began to take measures to reduce restrictive practices in labour markets.

The special labour market chapters in the country surveys were written against this background. Seventeen special chapters were published in all, the first in December 1984 and the most recent in February 1988[5]. These chapters contain detailed accounts of how the principle institutions in various countries' labour markets worked. While these details can hardly be summarised here, these reviews did suggest that labour markets in countries with very different systems can function equally well. No industrial relations system can be regarded as optimal on *a priori* grounds. Nonetheless, some common themes and issues did emerge in these special chapters, and these provide the main focus of this chapter. The following sections review these issues, indicating how thinking about labour market problems has evolved over the last fifteen years or so, and drawing also on work done elsewhere.

The first section of this chapter reviews the experience of unemployment across OECD countries, highlighting where experience has differed from country to country. In the early 1970s, a significant part of these differences could be attributed to the evolution of real wages which, in some countries, were too high or were too unresponsive to economic shocks. The second section explores this question, using the concept of "real labour cost gaps" (explained below), and discusses how behaviour changed from the first to the second oil shock and then the 1980s. The following section reviews the evidence that the "natural" rate of unemployment (in the sense defined below) may have drifted higher in many countries during the last decade or so. Next, the main structural features of labour market performance are reviewed. Many countries have sought to improve performance: the measures taken are examined in these sections. Conclusions are presented in a final section.

The experience of unemployment

During the decade from 1973 to 1983, the unemployment rate in the OECD area rose in every year but two (in 1978 and 1979 when it was flat): from an average of 3½ per cent in 1973, it reached a peak of almost 9 per cent in 1983. Since then, it has fallen slowly each year, to about 7½ per cent by 1988 (Table 2.1). High levels of unemployment have thus persisted during most of the 1980s. But behind this overall performance lie sharp differences in individual country experiences. While such diverse experience reflects many factors, this chapter examines primarily how far labour-market functioning can explain the important differences between countries. Countries can be divided into two broad groups:

- In the first group unemployment rates have been brought down almost to their pre-OPEC I levels: the *United States, Canada, Japan* and some European countries (*Austria, Finland, Norway, Sweden* and *Switzerland*) are all in this category. In this group as a whole, the unemployment rate had, by 1988, fallen to 4.6 per cent, only a little higher than in 1973 (shown in the final line of Table 2.1). But within this group, two quite different categories can be distinguished. The first category includes *Japan* and those *European countries* where unemployment has traditionally been low and stable. Indeed institutional arrangements in these countries have often contributed to apparently inflexible employment practices. But this has often been offset by flexible wage determination – an important issue reviewed more fully below. The steep fall in the unemployment rate in *North America* after OPEC II, which reflects both stronger demand and a greater readiness to hire new employees than in other countries, is particularly remarkable;

- In a second group unemployment was, by 1988, still close to its peak rate. This includes most *European countries* (the *major four* plus *Belgium, Denmark, Ireland, the Netherlands, Portugal* and *Spain*). The average unemployment rate rose sharply from 1973 to 1983, and has fallen only a little since then. By 1988, the average unemployment rate was more than twice as high as in the first group;

- *Australia* and *New Zealand* are in a third group: unemployment has remained much higher than at the beginning of the 1970s, but not as high as the second group of European countries. And in recent years *Australia* – where employment adjusts quickly to market conditions as in North America – has seen a significant fall in the unemployment rate.

Uneven rates of unemployment across countries reflect, in part, different growth of output. Economic growth has been faster, on average, in low-unemployment countries than in medium- and high-unemployment countries. In the low-unemployment group, average GDP growth accelerated from a little over 2 per cent over the period 1973-83 to about 4 per cent after 1983 (see Table 2.1). In the high-unemployment group, growth picked up to only around 2¾ per cent. The contrast thus became sharper after 1983.

The largest increases in employment from 1983 to 1988 occurred in the *United States, Canada* and *Australia* – all countries where annual growth in GDP was

Table 2.1. **Growth and labour market performance**

Average annual growth rates

	GDP		Employment		Labour force		Change in participation rates		Unemployment rate		
	1973-83	1983-88	1973-83	1983-88	1973-83	1983-88	1973-83	1983-86	1973	1983	1988
United States	1.8	4.0	1.7	2.7	2.2	1.8	0.7	0.8	4.9	9.6	5.5
Canada	3.0	4.5	2.1	2.9	2.8	2.0	0.9	1.0	5.5	11.9	7.8
Japan	3.6	4.5	0.9	1.0	1.0	0.9	0.2	−0.3	1.3	2.7	2.5
France	2.3	2.2	0.1	−0.1	0.8	0.3	−0.2	−0.3	2.7	8.4	10.3
Germany	1.6	2.6	−0.6	0.6	0.1	0.6	−0.6	0.2	1.0	8.2	7.9
Italy	2.2	3.2	0.7	0.6	1.1	1.1	0.2	0.2	5.9	9.2	11.1
United Kingdom	1.0	3.5	−0.5	1.7	0.4	1.1	−0.1	1.0	2.1	11.2	8.5
Austria	2.4	2.0	0.1	0.5	0.4	0.5	−0.3	−0.1	0.9	3.7	3.7
Belgium	1.8	2.1	−0.4	0.6	0.7	0	0.1	−0.3	2.3	12.9	10.5
Denmark	1.5	2.1	0.1	1.6	1.1	1.2	0.7	0.6	1.0	10.4	8.5
Finland	2.8	3.4	0.5	0.4	0.9	0.2	0.8	0.1	2.5	5.4	4.7
Ireland	2.5	1.4	0.5	−0.7	1.5	−0.1	−0.1	−0.7	5.7	14.0	16.6
Netherlands	1.9	2.3	−0.4	1.1	1.0	0.5	0.3	−0.5	3.1	15.0	12.5
Norway	3.9	3.3	1.6	1.7	1.8	1.6	1.2	1.2	1.6	3.4	3.1
Portugal	2.6	2.9	2.1	0.8	2.7	0.5	1.0	−1.8	2.2	7.9	6.5
Spain	1.9	3.6	−1.4	1.1	0.4	1.4	−0.8	−0.2	2.2	18.2	19.5
Sweden	1.5	2.4	0.8	0.7	0.9	0.4	0.7	0	2.0	2.9	1.7
Switzerland	0.3	2.7	−0.4	0.9	−0.3	0.9	−0.8	−0.1	0	0.8	0.7
Australia	2.1	4.2	0.8	3.1	1.6	2.5	0	0.8	2.3	9.9	7.4
New Zealand	0.9	1.8	1.1	0.8	1.6	0.8	0.1	4.8	0.2	5.4	5.3
Total OECD	2.1	4.2	0.7	1.6	1.3	1.2	0.2	0.4	3.5	8.9	7.4
OECD Europe[1]	1.8	4.2	0	0.9	0.8	0.8	−0.1	0.1	3.5	10.4	10.3
Of which:											
Low unemployment countries[2]	2.1	2.8	0.4	0.8	0.6	0.7	0.2	0.1	1.3	3.1	2.6
High unemployment countries[3]	1.7	2.8	−0.2	0.8	0.7	0.8	−0.2	0.1	2.7	10.6	10.6
Low unemployment countries[4]	2.2	4.1	1.4	2.0	1.8	1.4	0.5	0.5	3.4	7.2	4.6

Note: Percentage changes (or rates) for groups of countries are the percentage changes (or the ratios) of the aggregate series for the group. GDP aggregates are expressed in US dollars at constant exchange rates.
1. Excluding Greece, Turkey, Yugoslavia.
2. Austria, Finland, Norway, Sweden, Switzerland.
3. Germany, France, United Kingdom, Italy, Belgium, Denmark, Netherlands, Portugal, Spain.
4. Countries listed in (2) above plus United States, Japan and Canada.
Sources: OECD, *Economic Outlook, Historical Statistics, 1960-1987.* Estimates for 1988 are from *Economic Outlook* 44 (December 1988).

around 4 per cent or more (Table 2.1). Only in *Japan* was growth as strong. Among the major European countries, the *United Kingdom* grew fastest, and this was reflected in both a significant fall in the unemployment rate and higher labour force participation. By 1988, the unemployment rate in the *United Kingdom* had fallen to around 8½ per cent[6].

The labour-intensity of growth also differed considerably among countries. Expansion appears to have been most labour-intensive in North America. In the *United States* average annual rise in GDP of almost 4 per cent over the period 1983-88 was associated with annual employment growth of 2¾ per cent. A broadly similar expansion of employment took place in *Canada*, although GDP grew faster (Table 2.1). *Australia* also experienced higher-than-average employment growth, coupled with a sustained rise in output. European countries in general experienced much lower employment growth than non-European countries. Output grew rather more slowly in *low-unemployment European* countries than in North America, but employment expanded more slowly still (at about ½ per cent a year). For most of the countries in the *high-unemployment European* group, employment in 1988 was still below the level last attained in 1973: the notable exceptions were *Italy* and *Portugal*.

Countries with the strongest employment growth have also experienced the fastest increase in the supply of labour in the last fifteen years. The labour force in the *United States*, *Canada* and *Norway* grew by close to 2 per cent annually, reflecting strong natural growth of the working-age population as well as a considerable rise in participation rates, of adult women in particular[7]. In *Australia*, continued immigration as well as demographic factors explain the strong labour force growth. In Europe, by contrast, the labour force grew by about ¾ per cent annually and participation rates barely changed (Table 2.1). Even modest labour force growth did not prevent rising unemployment rates, except in *Austria*, *Sweden* and *Switzerland*.

A number of country surveys have examined the role of international labour mobility in changes in the supply of labour – as barriers to movement among many European countries are reduced, this is likely to become more important in the operation of labour markets. In *Switzerland*, the supply of immigrant labour is indeed rather flexible and this has been an important element of labour market adjustment – a feature which was discussed in detail in the 1985 Survey. *Switzerland* is the only OECD country where the labour force actually fell (by almost 3 per cent) over the period 1973-83, following the same trend as employment. The exceptional degree of flexibility of labour supply is due to the regulation of migratory movements for workers with short-duration permits and the high sensitivity of participation rates to cyclical variations in labour demand. Migration has also been an important counter-cyclical adjustment mechanism in *New Zealand*. A resumption of large-scale emigration from *Ireland* explains the virtual stagnation in labour force growth from 1983: without emigration, unemployment would have been still higher. But emigration was often not the best solution to poor job prospects at home: indeed there is evidence that emigration was not an option for the long-term unemployed who were frequently older and more tied by family obligations[8]. In the case of *Portugal*, moreover, migration aggravated rather than alleviated cyclical unemployment. The massive return of Portuguese from former colonies after 1974 coincided with the international recession; and difficult labour market conditions in other European countries where Portuguese worked led many to return home[9].

High unemployment has brought down wage inflation in almost every country to, in many cases, rates lower than seen before the early 1970s (Table 2.2). For the OECD area as a whole (unweighted average basis), the rise in average earnings has, in the last couple of years, fallen a little below 4 per cent (Diagram 2.2).

Table 2.2. **Wages, prices and unemployment**

| | Per cent change | | | | | | Unemployment rate | | |
| | Wages[1] | | | Prices[2] | | | | | |
	1970	1980	1988	1970	1980	1988	1970	1980	1988
United States	5.2	9.6	6.0	4.5	10.8	4.2	5.0	7.2	5.5
Canada	3.2	9.5	4.0	3.6	10.0	3.4	5.7	7.5	7.8
Japan	16.7	5.8	3.2	7.2	7.1	0	1.2	2.0	2.5
France	10.2	15.2	4.5	5.0	13.3	2.6	2.5	6.4	10.3
Germany	16.6	7.0	3.7	3.6	5.8	1.3	0.6	3.3	7.9
Italy	17.6	21.4	6.6	5.0	20.3	4.9	5.0	7.1	11.1
United Kingdom	12.5	18.9	7.8	5.8	16.2	4.6	2.4	6.1	8.5
Austria	8.0	7.6	2.7	4.5	6.4	2.0	1.1	1.5	3.7
Belgium	11.8	9.8	3.2	2.6	6.2	1.2	1.9	7.7	10.5
Denmark	10.4	11.1	1.1	6.6	10.7	4.8	1.3	7.0	8.5
Finland	15.3	13.4	11.9	1.7	11.6	5.2	2.0	4.7	4.7
Ireland	..	21.3	4.0	8.1	18.6	2.2	5.8	7.3	16.6
Netherlands	13.3	6.0	1.6	4.4	6.9	0.7	1.7	6.3	12.5
Norway	..	10.1	6.2	9.8	10.0	5.8	1.4	1.7	3.1
Portugal	10.5	22.3	10.5	3.4	21.4	9.0	3.8	8.0	6.5
Spain	11.5	16.8	6.2	5.9	16.5	4.8	0.9	11.5	19.5
Sweden	9.4	11.0	8.0	6.1	12.4	6.0	1.2	1.7	1.7
Switzerland	11.1	5.4	3.9	4.0	4.5	2.0	0	0.2	0.7
Australia	8.4	10.7	7.0	4.9	10.5	6.8	1.6	6.0	7.4
New Zealand	12.3	17.8	7.6	5.2	19.1	6.4	0.1	2.7	5.3

1. Total compensation per employee.
2. Private consumption deflator.
Sources: OECD, *National Accounts, Labour Force Statistics.* Estimates for 1988 are from *Economic Outlook* 44 (December 1988).

DIAGRAM 2.2

WAGES, PRICES AND UNEMPLOYMENT
IN THE OECD

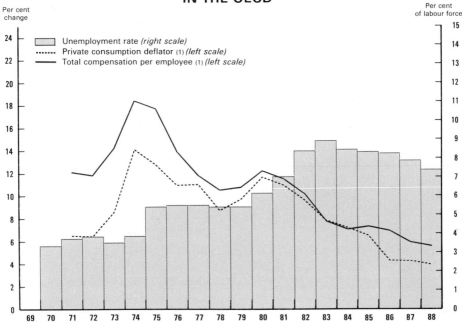

Per cent
change

Per cent
of labour force

☐ Unemployment rate *(right scale)*
•••••• Private consumption deflator (1) *(left scale)*
—— Total compensation per employee (1) *(left scale)*

1. Simple arithmetic average of all countries except Greece, Iceland,
Ireland and Turkey.
Source: OECD Secretariat.

Incidence of unemployment

The distribution of unemployment among different groups of the labour force is shown in Table 2.3. From the early 1970s to 1983, *youth unemployment* rates rose steeply in all countries, reaching, for the OECD area as a whole, about 18 per cent. Thereafter, youth unemployment rates declined in several countries (*United States, Canada, Germany, United Kingdom, Finland, Netherlands, Norway, Sweden* and *Australia*). The positive correlation between the excess of youth over total unemployment rates and the level of unemployment suggests that the burden of unemployment has been disproportionately heavy on the young. This correlation suggests the importance of structural factors in explaining unemployment: differences in aggregate demand *considered by themselves* would presumably affect all

Table 2.3. **Characteristics of unemployment**

	Unemployment rates								Share of total unemployment			
	Youths[1]				Female				Long-duration[2]			
	1973	1979	1983	1987	1973	1979	1983	1987	1973	1979	1983	1986
United States	9.9	11.3	16.4	11.7	6.0	6.8	9.1	6.2	3.3	4.2	13.3	8.7
Canada	10.1	12.9	20.0	13.7	5.1	8.7	11.6	9.3	..	3.5	9.8	10.9
Japan	2.3	3.4	4.5	5.2	1.2	1.9	2.6	2.8	..	16.5	15.5	17.2
France	4.0	13.3	19.7	23.0	3.1	7.9	10.6	13.4	21.6	30.3	42.2	47.8
Germany	0.9	3.4	10.7	7.9	1.1	4.1	9.3	9.3	8.5	19.9	28.5	32.0
Italy	12.6	25.6	30.5	35.5	4.7	13.3	15.4	18.6	..	35.8	41.9	56.4[4]
United Kingdom	3.1	10.3	23.4	17.4	0.9	3.9	8.9	8.1	26.9	24.8	36.5	41.1
Austria	..	..	..	..	1.7	3.1	5.1	3.1[6]	7.4	8.6	9.0	12.6
Belgium	..	..	..	..	3.3	12.5	17.9	16.5[6]	51.0	58.0	62.8	68.9
Finland	4.5	10.8	10.5	9.0	2.4	5.5	5.3	4.4	..	19.3	22.3	21.1[5]
Netherlands	2.8	8.1	24.9	18.9	1.6	4.9	12.9	12.5	12.8	27.1	43.7	56.3
Norway	5.6	6.6	9.4	5.3	2.4	2.4	3.7	2.5	..	3.8	6.7	6.7
Spain	4.8	21.1	38.7	38.9	2.2	10.7	21.3	27.9	..	27.5	53.6	56.6
Sweden	5.2	5.0	8.0	4.2	2.8	2.3	3.6	1.9	..	6.8	10.3	8.0
Australia	3.3	12.2	17.9	14.6	2.7	7.7	9.9	8.3	..	18.1	27.5	27.5
Total OECD[3]	5.3	11.1	18.0	15.8	2.8	6.2	9.6	9.6	18.8	20.3	28.2	30.3
OECD Europe[3]	4.8	11.6	19.5	17.8	2.4	6.1	10.1	11.0	21.4	23.8	32.5	36.7

1. Youths refer to the 15 or 16 to 24 year-old age group.
2. 12 months and over.
3. Above countries only.
4. 1984.
5. 1985.
6. 1986.
Sources: OECD, *Employment Outlook; Economic Outlook*.

groups of workers equally, implying no correlation. In low-unemployment countries where data are available (*Japan, Norway* and *Sweden*) youth unemployment rates vary between 5 and 7 per cent, whereas in high-unemployment countries they reach about 40 per cent (*Italy, Spain*). In many countries, however, the ratio of youth to adult unemployment rates has been falling since OPEC II. This may be explained partly by the recovery, and partly by the maturing of the baby-boom generation and a wide variety of employment and training measures which many countries have put in place to help the young unemployed.

Another disturbing trend in many countries is that an increasing proportion of those unemployed has been out of work for more than one year. Indeed, the share of *long-term unemployment* (one year and over) appears positively correlated with unemployment. In *Italy, Belgium, the Netherlands* and *Spain*, for example, more than half of all unemployed persons have been without a job for more than one year, whereas in *Japan, Norway, Sweden, Austria* (but also in *North America*), the share of long-duration unemployment is around 10 to 20 per cent.

In countries where unemployment is comparatively low, women do not suffer from higher unemployment than men. In contrast, in some high-unemployment countries the female unemployment rate exceeds that of men by a wide margin (*France, Italy, Belgium, Portugal* and *Spain*).

Why did unemployment rise so far in the early 1970s and why has it stayed so high in many countries? There is no one simple explanation. Some early answers to this question put particular stress on the deficiency in aggregate demand. After the first oil shock, the transfer of spending power to OPEC countries with only limited absorptive capacity was widely regarded as deflationary. On this view unemployment was mainly *Keynesian*. But as unemployment persisted – and as wages in many countries showed no sign of moderation – attention shifted to other explanations. The simplest alternative explanation was that wages were too high. The absence of profitable opportunities at prevailing cost/price ratios discouraged both investment and employment – in other words unemployment was thought to be largely *classical*. Attempts in a number of country surveys (and indeed in other OECD reports) to analyse the "appropriate" level of real wages made extensive use of the concept of real labour cost "gaps".

Measuring real labour cost gaps

In principle, the *real labour cost gap* measures the difference between actual real labour costs and the level consistent with full employment. In practice, of course, the concept of full-employment real labour costs is unobservable, and some operational proxy has to be used. Under certain simplifying assumptions, in particular if the economy's aggregate production function is assumed to be Cobb-Douglas, the labour cost gap can be identified with movements in the share of wages in value added, adjusted for the change in the terms of trade. To keep labour's share of national income constant, real labour cost growth should equal the sum of the nation's terms-of-trade gain and productivity growth[10]. If the rate of growth in labour costs exceeds that warranted by the rate of productivity growth plus terms-of-trade effects (so-called "warranted real labour costs"), classical unemployment emerges.

The concept of real labour cost gaps has many shortcomings – it is based on some arbitrary base period and on extremely simplified assumptions about the economy. Also, excessive real wages will drive the least profitable domestic industries out of

33

business, create unemployment and thus inflate measured average productivity. This will reduce the labour cost gap – but cannot be interpreted as good performance. But in suggesting the magnitude of the real wage adjustment made necessary by a major terms-of-trade change and a marked productivity slowdown, the concept was illuminating – if somewhat elusive. Also, in a number of countries, heavier employers' social security contributions inflated labour costs. Table 2.4 summarises the main elements in labour cost gap calculations for 1973-75 (the first oil shock), 1979-82 (the second oil shock) and finally for 1975-87 (the whole period since the first oil shock).

The first oil shock implied a major terms-of-trade loss for most OECD countries. At the same time, in many countries, productivity growth decelerated. In the *United Kingdom*, for instance, "warranted" real labour costs declined by 2.1 per cent – 1.3 per cent due to the decline in productivity and 0.8 per cent due to the worsening terms-of-trade (see Table 2.4). Because real wages continued to grow, most OECD countries experienced a widening of the real labour cost gap after OPEC I , see Table 2.4, panel A[11]. Despite a movement in the opposite direction after 1975 or 1976, the adjustment was often incomplete and, at the time of the second oil shock, the gap had not returned to its 1973 level in many countries. The main exceptions to this were the *United States, Norway, Finland* and, to some extent, *Germany*: indeed the greater flexibility of real wages in the *United States* was frequently cited as an important reason for that country's adjustment after the first oil shock: note that real wages actually fell from 1973 to 1975, while they rose everywhere else[12]. Even in *Japan*, a substantial labour cost gap emerged after 1973, as nominal wage growth was fuelled by excess demand[13].

While real labour cost gaps appeared to have provided a good – if only partial – explanation of the onset of high unemployment in the mid-1970s and the persistence of high unemployment during the second half of the 1970s, the steep rise in the 1980s is harder to explain. Indeed, after OPEC II, nominal and real wage growth was in general more moderate than after the first oil shock: from 1979 to 1982, real wages actually fell in about half of the countries shown in Table 2.4, panel B. As a result the real wage gap declined appreciably in most countries despite a significant rise in social security charges in some countries[14]. The main exceptions to this were *Italy* and, to a lesser extent, *France*.

Over the period 1975 to 1987 as a whole, the labour cost gap was reduced in *all* the countries shown in Table 2.4. The two main elements behind the lower labour cost gap were:

Table 2.4. **Real wages, productivity and the terms of trade**

	Productivity	Terms-of-trade gain (+)/ loss (−)	Warranted real labour costs [= (a) + (b)]	Real wages	Non-wage costs	Actual real labour costs [= (d) + (e)]	Change in labour costs gap [= (f) − (c)]
	(a)	(b)	(c)	(d)	(e)	(f)	
A. 1973-1975							
United States	− 1.3	− 0.6	− 1.9	− 2.2	0.8	− 1.4	0.5
Canada	0.5	0.5	1.0	3.1	0.4	3.5	2.5
Japan	1.0	− 1.7	− 0.7	3.7	0.5	4.2	4.9
France	1.5	− 1.2	0.3	3.9	0.7	4.6	4.3
Germany	1.5	− 0.6	0.9	1.9	0.7	2.6	1.7
Italy	− 0.7	− 0.7	− 1.4	0.3	1.2	1.5	2.9
United Kingdom	− 1.3	− 0.8	− 2.1	3.0	1.0	4.0	6.1
Finland	1.0	0.4	1.4	3.4	0.3	3.7	2.3
Netherlands	3.8	− 2.1	1.7	4.0	0.2	4.2	2.5
Norway	3.1	− 1.4	1.7	3.8	0	3.8	2.1
Spain	2.9	− 0.8	2.1	2.8	0.9	3.7	1.6
Sweden	0.9	0	0.9	0.9	3.0	3.9	3.0
B. 1979-1982							
United States	− 0.5	− 0.2	− 0.7	− 0.4	0.3	− 0.1	0.6
Canada	− 0.2	0.5	0.3	0	0.2	0.2	− 0.1
Japan	2.7	− 1.0	1.7	0.2	0.6	0.8	− 0.9
France	1.8	− 0.9	0.9	1.4	0.3	1.7	0.8
Germany	0.6	− 0.9	− 0.3	− 0.3	0.2	− 0.1	0.2
Italy	1.1	− 0.5	0.6	1.9	0.1	2.0	1.4
United Kingdom	1.5	0.5	2.0	1.5	0.3	1.8	− 0.2
Finland	1.7	− 0.9	0.8	1.1	− 0.1	1.0	0.1
Netherlands	0.8	0	0.8	− 1.4	0.2	− 1.2	− 2.0
Norway	0.5	1.7	2.2	− 0.6	0.1	− 0.5	− 2.7
Spain	2.9	− 1.2	1.7	− 0.1	0.5	0.4	− 1.3
Sweden	0.5	− 0.6	− 0.1	− 2.9	0.6	− 2.3	− 2.2
C. 1975-1987							
United States	0.7	− 0.1	0.6	0.3	0.2	0.5	− 0.1
Canada	1.2	0	1.2	0.1	0.2	0.3	− 0.9
Japan	3.2	− 0.1	3.1	1.2	0.5	1.7	− 1.4
France	2.2	0	2.2	1.3	0.4	1.7	− 0.5
Germany	2.2	0.1	2.3	1.4	0.2	1.6	− 0.7
Italy	2.1	0.2	2.3	2.3	− 0.1	2.2	− 0.1
United Kingdom	2.2	0.2	2.4	1.5	0	1.5	− 0.9
Finland	2.6	− 0.2	2.4	1.5	0.1	1.6	− 0.8
Nertherlands	1.8	− 0.1	1.7	0.4	0	0.4	− 1.3
Norway	2.0	− 0.8	1.2	0.3	0	0.3	− 0.9
Spain	2.9	0.2	3.1	1.3	0.4	1.7	− 1.4
Sweden	1.2	− 0.2	1.0	− 0.3	0.8	0.5	− 0.5

Definitions of variables:
Wages = compensation per employee;
Non-wage costs = employers' social security contributions;
Terms of trade = measured by changes in deflators for exports and imports of goods and services as a per cent of current GDP;
Productivity = real GDP/total employment.
Source: OECD Secretariat.

- Relatively low increases in real wages. Only in one country – *Italy* – did real wages grow more than 1½ per cent annually;
- Rather resilient growth in productivity – the *United States, Canada* and *Sweden* being the main exceptions.

The narrowing of the labour cost gap prevented unemployment rising still further in the face of prolonged weakness of demand.

The, albeit modest, recovery of labour *productivity* in many countries is an interesting feature of the adjustment process since 1975. It is revealing that performance in the more open sector of the economy (manufacturing) was often much better: see Table 2.5 (discussed more fully below). *Japan* is perhaps the most striking case in point: even those industries hard-hit by rising energy costs and competition from the Asian NICs (particularly the heavy industries – chemicals, basic metals, iron and steel and non-ferrous metals) managed to adjust by boosting productivity. But *Japan* was not alone. Productivity growth in *manufacturing* accelerated in many countries (cf. productivity in the period 1979-87 with that of 1973-79 in Table 2.5) and remained quite strong relative to overall productivity growth. However in *France, Germany* and a number of smaller European countries, productivity growth decelerated. In sum, the tendency towards lower real labour cost gap in the 1980s in many European countries owed much to brisk productivity growth of the open sector of the economy, largely reflecting labour-shedding, as real wage costs remained high (see Table 2.5).

Part of this labour shedding was induced by a rise in the price of labour relative to capital, shown in Diagram 2.3. The most striking feature is the contrast between the *United States* and the other major countries. The price of labour relative to capital remained broadly constant in the *United States* over the period to the mid-1980s whereas the relative price of labour rose everywhere else. A second feature is that most of the rise took place before 1980: since then, the relative cost of labour, although remaining rather high, has in most countries stabilized or fallen. The two main exceptions to this are *Japan* and *Italy*. In *Japan* much of the rise in the relative price of labour reflected substantial declines in capital goods prices – one element in the user cost of capital calculation – due to rapid technical progress. Related to these trends, the decline in the non-wage share of national income has, in most countries, been reversed (Diagram 2.4).

One consequence of the higher relative price of labour was that the substitution of capital for labour "explained" much more of the growth in labour productivity in the OECD area after 1973 than before. Up to 1973, annual labour productivity

36

Table 2.5. **Labour productivity and factor substitution**[1]

	Pre-1973		1973-1979		1979-1987		Memorandum: Labour productivity in manufacturing	
	Total	Accounted for by factor substitution	Total	Accounted for by factor substitution	Total	Accounted for by factor substitution	1973-1979	1979-1987
United States	2.2	0.7	0.3	0.4	0.5	0.5	0.9	3.3
Canada	3.0	0.7	2.0	0.9	1.0	1.2	1.0	1.3
Japan	8.8	2.5	3.2	1.4	3.0	1.1	5.0	5.1
France	5.9	1.6	3.5	1.4	2.4	1.1	3.9	2.9
Germany	4.7	2.1	3.4	1.5	2.0	1.1	3.1	1.8
Italy	6.6	1.8	2.6	0.9	1.9	0.7	3.0	3.7
United Kingdom	3.3	1.3	1.3	1.0	1.7	0.7	0.6	4.2
Austria	5.3	2.5	3.9	2.1	2.1	1.3	3.5	3.3
Belgium	4.8	1.1	2.8	1.3	2.2	1.0	5.0	4.8[3]
Denmark	3.5	1.8	1.8	1.7	1.5	1.0	3.1	1.6
Finland	4.8	1.6	3.1	1.5	3.0	0.7	2.5	4.8
Ireland	5.0	0.7	4.8	0.7	0.7	0.9	4.9	4.1[4]
Netherlands	5.1	1.8	2.8	1.6	1.6	1.2	3.9	1.0
Norway	3.1	1.0	4.3	1.3	2.1	0.6	0.5	2.8
Spain	5.8	2.5	4.2	2.8	2.3	1.7	2.6	4.0
Sweden	3.4	1.6	2.2	1.4	1.7	1.0	1.2	2.8
Switzerland	3.4	1.7	0.7	1.5	1.5	0.8	2.9	0.2
Australia	2.9	1.2	1.8	1.3	1.1	0.6	2.5	1.8
New Zealand	1.8	1.2	− 1.0	1.5	1.3	1.1	..	..
Total OECD	4.2	1.4	1.8	1.0	1.4	0.8	2.4	3.5[3]
OECD Europe[2]	5.1	1.8	2.9	1.4	2.0	1.0	2.6	2.9[3]

1. Factor substitution is equal to growth in K/L ratio multiplied by the 1985 capital share.
2. Including countries listed above; weighted by 1982 GDP at 1982 prices and exchange rates.
3. 1979-1986.
4. Industrial production index/employment in manufacturing.
Sources: OECD, *Economic Outlook* 42 (December 1987), pp. 39-48; *Historical Statistics*, 1960-1986; *Main Economic Indicators*.

growth was 4.2 per cent, and only about 1.4 percentage points of this measured growth could be attributed to factor substitution (Table 2.5). After 1973, labour productivity slumped to below 2 per cent, with more than half of this reflecting greater capital intensity. The emphasis on capital-deepening was particularly marked in *Europe*, and comparatively little substitution took place in the *United States*. A simple measure of the degree of capital-deepening is shown in the factor substitution column in Table 2.5, giving over 1 per cent annually for *Europe*, and less than ½ per cent for the *United States*. In this sense, growth in the *United States* tended to favour employment. In many European countries sluggish capital accumulation in the 1980s mainly aimed at rationalisation rather than the expansion of capacity[15].

37

DIAGRAM 2.3

RELATIVE PRICE OF LABOUR
IN SEVEN MAJOR OECD COUNTRIES (1)

1973 = 100

1973 = 100

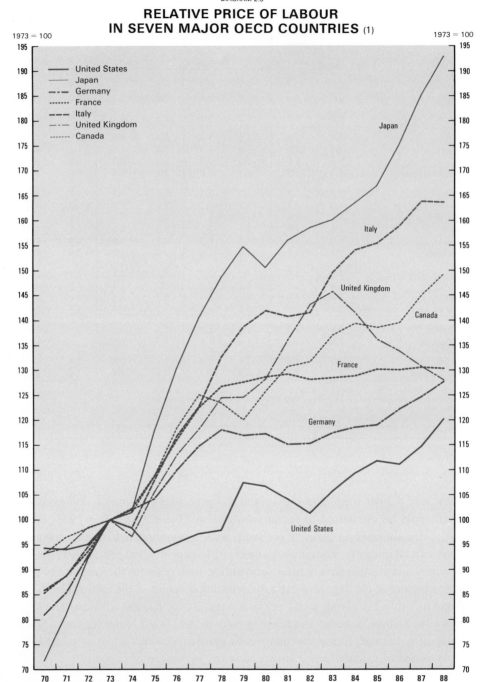

1. Index of compensation of employees in the private sector divided by
the index of user cost of capital.
Source: OECD Secretariat.

DIAGRAM 2.4

PROFITABILITY

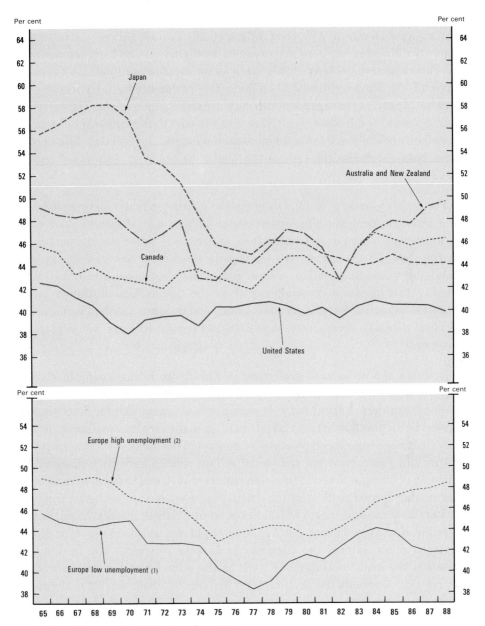

1. *Arithmetic average:* Austria, Finland, Norway, Switzerland.
2. *Arithmetic average:* France, Germany, Italy, United Kingdom, Ireland, Netherlands, Portugal, Spain, Belgium, Denmark.
Source: OECD Secretariat.

To illustrate the consequences of the slower expansion of capacity, a number of surveys constructed Okun curves, charting the unemployment rate (as a measure of the "intensity" of labour use) against capacity utilisation ("intensity" of capital use). The Okun curve for *Europe* traces a clearer upward zigzag than for either the *United States* or *Japan*. (Diagram 2.5). Over the last twenty years in *Europe*, a given degree of capacity utilisation has been accompanied by higher-and-higher unemployment rates. This suggests a growing imbalance in factor supplies in Europe, as a result of perhaps inadequate investment and an increasing preference for labour-saving and capital-deepening, at the expense of capacity-expanding, investment. The surveys of *France, Belgium,* and *Ireland* all attributed this in part to the significant changes in relative factor prices which favoured more capital intensive production. This appears to have been much less the case in the *United States* or in *Japan* – at least in the 1980s.

The striking pattern of Okun curves for *Europe* suggests the possibility of *capital-shortage* unemployment, a point stressed in a number of surveys. As demand rises, available capacity may become fully utilised well before unemployment has been absorbed. To the extent that inadequate investment has its roots in weak demand, this would be essentially a short-run problem, as higher investment would eventually ease capacity constraints and as the possibilities of capital/labour substitution increased. But if inadequate investment is due to distorted factor prices, investment would be permanently depressed and capital-shortage would persist in the long run[16].

However, the widespread preference in *Europe* for labour-saving investment during years of high and rising unemployment can only partly be attributed to relative factor prices. Labour markets were not functioning well for other reasons: overprotective legislation in many countries often made employers reluctant to hire; unduly rigid wage negotiation processes often limited flexibility in the determination of wages; and government tax and social welfare policies have often distorted the functioning of labour markets. These elements were reviewed in depth in most of the labour market special sections of the country surveys. A key conclusion from this work was that those countries in which the operation of labour markets faced the kind of impediments outlined above also had rather rigid real wages (in the sense defined below) and often suffered the steepest rise in unemployment. The next section summarises the main conclusions of work on the wage formation process and the following section reviews the key structural features of labour market performance and considers how the microeconomic functioning of labour markets may have improved in recent years.

DIAGRAM 2.5

UNEMPLOYMENT RATES AND CAPACITY USE (a)

(Okun Curves)

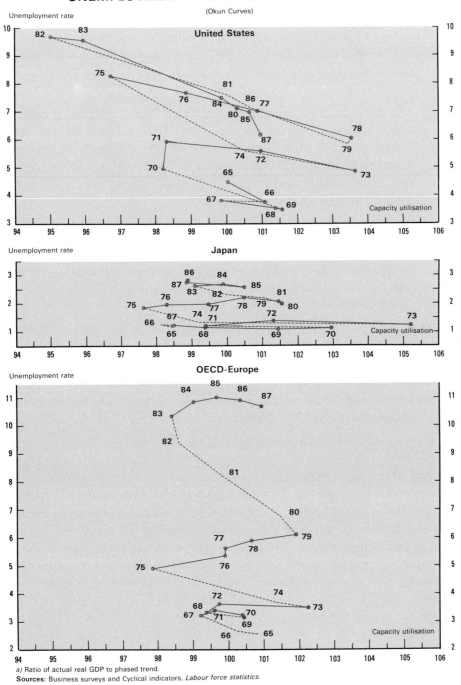

a) Ratio of actual real GDP to phased trend.

Sources: Business surveys and Cyclical indicators, *Labour force statistics.*

The wage formation process

Attempts to analyse the wage formation process in many country surveys started from estimates of expectations-augmented Phillips curves. Such estimates are reported in Coe (1985), Chan-Lee *et al* (1987), and Klau and Mittelstadt (1986). A recent re-estimation of the wage equations originally reported in Coe (1985) yielded the following results:

–   The short-run responsiveness of wages with respect to prices is higher in *Europe* and in *Japan* than in the *United States* and *Canada*. As wages eventually follow prices fully in the long run, the short-run real wage flexibility of the United States means a slower, rather than incomplete, adjustment. This limits the squeeze on profits after a price shock and so reduces the need for labour shedding;

–   Estimates of the sensitivity of wages to the unemployment rate show the greatest wage responsiveness to labour demand for *Japan* and *Austria*, a slightly lower one for the *United States, Canada* and *Finland*, and lower still for the other countries. The *United Kingdom* stands out as being the least responsive of countries surveyed (perhaps because of "hysteresis" – discussed below).

A synthetic indicator based on these two elasticities reveals a high degree of short-run real wage flexibility for the *United States, Canada* and *Japan* but much less flexibility for most European countries. For some countries (the *United States, Japan, Germany* among the major seven), cyclical productivity growth is estimated to have a significant impact on wage increases, and, if incorporated into the calculation, increase the degree of measured flexibility[17].

The country surveys also pointed out that countries with greater aggregate real wage flexibility also have wider wage differentials between sectors. There is of course no simple or one-way relationship between the size of wage differentials and the efficiency of the labour market. If labour is highly mobile, for instance, only relatively small wage differentials would in practice emerge as workers move readily from low to high-productivity occupations. But wage differentials appear to be smaller in some countries where labour mobility also appears to be low. In such cases, the coexistence of smaller differentials *and* lower mobility may suggest some labour force misfunction. This may be particularly true in *Europe* where labour mobility – both geographic and by occupation – is lower than in *Japan* or in *North America*[18]. In a number of countries, the wage determination process does not take adequate account of regional differences in labour demand. Sometimes national wage negotiation procedures are responsible. Also, corporate "culture" in major companies often militates against regional differences in basic pay. Such equalising forces on pay can be particularly strong in the public sector. It is, however, unclear how far the decline in labour mobility can be attributed to inadequate wage differentials, as weaker demand for labour itself discourages labour mobility[19]. In this case lower mobility may be as much the result, rather than the cause, of poor employment performance.

To the extent wage differentials reflect differences in marginal products of various types of workers, wider differentials provide greater incentives for a more efficient allocation of the workforce across sectors and hence result in greater labour demand. International comparisons of the coefficient of variation of the inter-industry wage differentials (Table 2.6) suggest that wage differentials in the *United States, Canada* and *Japan* are generally far greater than in most European countries. However, this result does not unambiguously translate to relative wage flexibility since the limited degree of disaggregation may conceal more fundamental differentials depending on profession, age, sex, tenure and/or size of firms. Indeed, the coefficient of variation for labour costs (compensation of employees) across the broad sectors in the economy (agriculture, mining, manufacturing and so on) reverses this ranking[20]. But on both measures, wage differentials are smaller in *Germany* than in any other major OECD country.

There is evidence that greater flexibility in differentials *by age* improves employment prospects. The wave of "baby boomers" into the *United States* labour market reduced the real average earnings of young men by about one quarter, and this induced employers to accept a higher share of young workers[21]. In much of *Europe*, by contrast, the relative wages of youths were more inflexible, and in some countries actually increased. There is evidence that countries where the relative earnings of younger workers declined had less youth unemployment than other countries[22].

There is some evidence that those countries with relatively rigid real wages also suffered the steepest rise in unemployment between 1973 and 1987: see Diagram 2.6, panel B. Adequate real wage flexibility obviously facilitated adjustment to the "stagflationary" oil price shocks in the 1970s. But the situation in the 1980s was rather different: oil and other commodity prices fell, and in this case a quick response in nominal wages (high short-run elasticity to prices) would be needed to moderate real wage growth given continued high unemployment. On this question, recent estimates prepared in the OECD suggest that the price coefficients in standard wage equations for both *France* and *Germany* have fallen in the period 1984-87. This

Table 2.6. **Measuring wage flexibility**

	Average unemployment rate used in computation	Elasticity of nominal wages with respect to[1]		Short-run real wage flexibility			Memorandum: Coefficients of variation of	
		Prices short-run	Unemployment rate	Productivity	Without productivity impact	With productivity impact	Inter-industry wages[4]	Inter-sectoral labour costs[5]
United States	Linear	0.14	−0.61	0.18	—	0.18	24.7	32.9
Canada	Linear	0.18	−0.51	—	0.35	—	23.6	23.2
Japan	1.9	0.66	−1.87	0.40	0.27	0.29	26.0	25.5
France	Linear	0.50	−0.29	—	1.52	—	15.1	53.8
Germany	3.6	0.75	−0.11	0.30	—	1.80	14.2	20.6
Italy	7.2	0.6	−0.39	1.54	1.00	—	16.4	44.2
United Kingdom	Linear	0.33	−0.15	—	2.01	—	16.5	43.7
United Kingdom[2]	Linear	0.33	−0.44	—	—	—	—	—
Austria	1.9	0.27	−0.87	—	0.50	—	—	—
Belgium	Linear	0.25	−0.25	0.04	—	0.86	18.7	—
Denmark	5.6	0.25	−0.10	0.12	—	1.13	—	20.9
Finland	Linear	0.33	−0.54	0.44	—	0.34	—	12.8
Netherlands	6.5	0.50	−0.27	—	1.85	—	—	—
Spain	7.6	0.25	−0.20	0.26	—	0.54	—	—
Sweden	1.9	0.25	−2.17	—	0.12	—	12.3	17.7
Switzerland[3]	Linear	0.50	−0.28	0.26	—	0.92	16.1	—
Australia	Linear	0.50	−0.39	—	1.28	—	—	—

1. The elasticities are from the recent reestimation of the wage equations originally reported in Coe (1985). The short-run price elasticity refers to the impact in the first half year. The unemployment semi-elasticity refers to the negative impact on wage growth (expressed at a semi-annual rate) of a 1 percentage point increase in the unemployment rate. For some countries, the Phillips curve is non-linear so that the elasticity with respect to unemployment rate depends on the initial level of unemployment. Where the Phillips curve is linear, this is indicated in the first column. For these countries, the semi-elasticity is calculated from the average unemployment rate in the estimation period (the first column). If the unemployment rate used was for a more recent period (hence higher), the elasticity would be smaller, implying lower flexibility.
2. Coefficients based on the equation which incorporates the hypothesis of hysteresis in the unemployment rate.
3. An employment rate was used instead of the unemployment rate as an indicator of labour market disequilibrium. See *Economic Survey of Switzerland,* December 1985, Annex I.
4. The calculations are based on hourly wage earnings over the period 1965-1985 in manufacturing, except for Japan where only total labour costs are available. For France and the Netherlands data were available from 1967 and from 1972. For Belgium and Switzerland only from 1975.
5. The broad economic sectors used were:
   Agriculture, Mining, Manufacturing, Electricity and Gas, Construction, Trade and Hotels, Transport and Communication, Business Services and Real Estate, Other non-government services, Government Services and Other producers (i.e. domestic servants and private non-profit institutions).
Sources: Swedish Employers' Confederation; OECD, *National Accounts*; Klau and Mittelstadt (1986); OECD Secretariat.

appears to suggest that wages respond less to flat or falling prices than to price increases.

Another indication of flexibility is the speed with which employment adjusts to output changes – employment adaptability[23], a measure used in the *Survey of Austria* (April 1987). For a given degree of real wage flexibility, countries with highly

DIAGRAM 2.6

REAL WAGE RIGIDITY

A. Real wage rigidity (1) and the degree of corporatism (2)

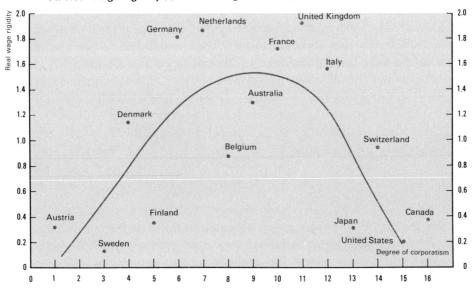

B. Real wage rigidity (1) and unemployment

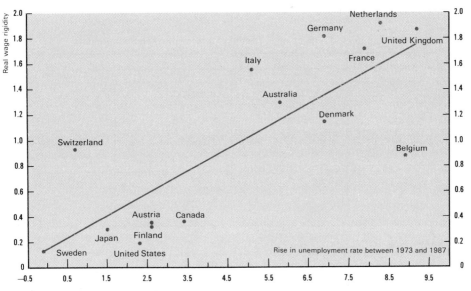

1. Real wage rigidity is measured by the short-run rigidity indicator reported in Table 2.6. It is calculated *with* a productivity impact for the following countries: United States, Japan, Germany, Belgium, Denmark, Sweden and Switzerland, which increases measured flexibility. For the United Kingdom, real wage rigidity is calculated from the specification excluding the hypothesis of hysteresis; hysteresis itself is an indication of low flexibility.

2. Countries are ranked from the most centralised (close to the origin) to the least centralised. The ranking is that used in Calmfors, Lars and John Drifill (1988), "Centralisation of wage bargaining and Macroeconomic performance", *Economic Policy*, April. Also see OECD, *Economic Outlook 43*, June 1988. **Source:** OECD Secretariat.

adaptable employment would experience a quicker and greater rise in unemployment after a negative supply shock. This would in turn induce a stronger nominal wage response. The adjustment would be damped in a country where employment is more rigid. In a sense, economies characterised by high real wage flexibility can afford some rigidity in employment adjustment: output can remain profitable (and thus viable) as flexible wages allow employment to be maintained. *Japan* and *Austria* would be the most striking examples in this category[24] (see Diagram 2.7). In the *United States* and *Canada*, where employment is highly adaptable, a pronounced rise in unemployment would exert a relatively strong moderating influence even though the elasticity of wages to unemployment is average. The worst of both worlds is one where real wages are inflexible and employment not very adaptable: *France, Belgium, the Netherlands* and *the United Kingdom* appear to be in this category. If neither wages nor employment can adjust readily to changed conditions, the viability of enterprises risks being compromised, creating the danger of large-scale redundancies associated with bankruptcies.

Estimates of Phillips curves were also used to calculate the rate of unemployment consistent with stable inflation. Two closely related concepts have been exploited in the country surveys. The first was the *non-accelerating inflation rate of unemployment* (or NAIRU). The second was the rate of unemployment consistent with real wages growing in line with productivity, the so-called *non-accelerating wage*

Diagram 2.7. **Real wage flexibility and employment adaptability**

Long-run real wage flexibility[1]	Employment adaptability[2]		
	Low	Intermediate	High
High	Japan Austria Sweden	Finland	
Intermediate	Italy	Germany	United States Canada
Low		France Belgium Netherlands United Kingdom	Australia

1. Long-run real wage flexibility is measured by the elasticity of nominal wage changes with respect to the rate of unemployment. See Table 2.6 for details.
2. Employment adaptability is measured by the output coefficient b in the equation:

$$(q-l) = a + bq_t + cq_{t-1}$$

where q is output growth, and l is employment growth.
The observation period is 1960-86. Employment is highly adaptable, if the b coefficient is low, and vice versa.
Sources: OECD, *Economic Survey on Austria* (February 1988); and OECD Secretariat.

rate of unemployment (the NAWRU): this has been regarded by some as the "natural" rate of unemployment[25]. In equilibrium, and in the absence of shocks, the two concepts become identical. Both concepts are discussed more fully below.

An important general conclusion from the econometric results described below is that the level of unemployment "needed" to contain inflation has risen over the past couple of decades: there was an apparent shift in the Phillips curve. With the exception of the *United States*, it is a near-universal finding of recent studies that NAIRUs and NAWRUs are now much higher than before the shocks of the 1970s (see Table 2.7). This finding is usually attributed to a slowdown in the trend of productivity growth, sizeable external price shocks and to a deterioration in the

Table 2.7. **Estimates of NAIRUs**

	Time period	NAIRU estimates	Changes in the NAIRU due to:[a]		
			q	pm	w
United States	1967-1970	3			
	1971-1975	6	½	2	0
	1976-1980	6	0	0	0
	1981-1983	6½	1	0	0
Canada	1968-1970	4			
	1971-1975	7	−½	2½	−1
	1976-1980	8½	1	0	0
	1981-1983	7½	½	−1	−½
Japan	1971-1975	1			
	1976-1980	1½	0	½	0
	1981-1983	2	0	0	0
France	1967-1970	2½			
	1971-1975	3½	0	5	−3
	1976-1980	3	1	−1	−1
	1981-1983	8	½	4½	0
Germany	1967-1970	1			
	1971-1975	1½	−½	2	−1
	1976-1980	3	0	0	1½
	1981-1983	8	0	3½	1½
United Kingdom	1967-1970	1			
	1971-1975	7½	−½	8½	−2
	1976-1980	7½	4	−3½	−½
	1981-1983	6	1	−2½	1
Italy	1967-1970	4½			
	1971-1975	7	1	4	−2½
	1976-1980	6½	1½	−1	−1
	1981-1983	6½	0	½	0

a)   q is trend productivity growth, pm is the rate of change of import prices and w is the growth of wages.
Source: Coe (1985).

flexibility of labour markets. It is notable that natural rates appear to have risen most in those countries in which actual unemployment has also increased the most.

This observation raises an important problem with the whole concept of a "natural" rate of unemployment. It suggests that the downward pressure that high rates of unemployment exert on wages tends to decline over time: in other words, the "natural" rate of unemployment gravitates towards the prevailing rate of unemployment. This indeed is the so-called "hysteresis" hypothesis, that the level of unemployment, once it has risen (because of some "shock"), has only a very weak tendency to fall back to earlier levels. The term "fragile equilibrium" has been coined by some analysts to describe this situation where outcomes are very sensitive to shocks, and may be history dependent[26].

The notion of human capital investment provides one possible rationalisation of hysteresis: those who are unemployed for long periods of time lose their skills and so tend to effectively withdraw from the labour market. A second possible rationalisation given much importance in recent literature relates to the distinction between "insiders" and "outsiders". According to this view, those regularly or normally employed ("insiders") dominate wage developments: in this case, larger numbers of long-term unemployed ("outsiders") exercise little influence on wage developments. A third possible rationalisation is that potential employers may tend to regard the unemployed as unemployable. To the extent that employers do use the length of unemployment as a "screening device", the "natural" rate of unemployment will tend to rise with the *actual* unemployment rate.

A second problem is that such econometric estimates rarely – if ever – take explicit account of structural aspects of the labour market. While it is possible to test for shifts, it is difficult to quantify structural determinants which may change only slowly[27]. It is therefore difficult to say which structural reform would reduce the "natural" rate. These considerations call into question the usefulness of the concept of a natural rate of unemployment. Indeed, the issue is sufficiently controversial (some of the estimates are discussed below) to warrant considerable caution in the use of the natural rate as a guide to policy[28].

The NAIRU

The "non-accelerating inflation unemployment rate" (or NAIRU) depends in part on non-wage pressures on prices. For instance, if import prices are rising sharply, unemployment will have to increase to produce an offsetting decline in wage growth needed to maintain price stability. Hence the faster import prices rise, the higher will be the NAIRU. Equally, faster productivity growth will tend to reduce the NAIRU[29].

Estimates of the NAIRU for the major seven OECD countries in different periods and the major elements are shown in Table 2.7. Virtually everywhere, the NAIRU rose substantially up to 1983. An important reason for the increase in the NAIRU in the early 1970s was the rise in import prices; in general, the impact of slower productivity was more marked after the mid-1970s. After 1983, import prices rose little or even fell. As a result the estimated NAIRUs dropped sharply. Largely because of import price developments, the NAIRUs estimated for the period 1983 to 1987 dropped to 2.7 per cent for the *United States*, 0.5 per cent for *Japan*, 3.7 per cent for *Germany*, with similar declines in other countries.

Perhaps the principal lesson from these calculations of the NAIRU was that, without more flexible labour markets, substantially higher unemployment was needed to offset the terms-of-trade and productivity shocks of the 1970s. Indeed, the experience of the last fifteen years has borne out this rather pessimistic conclusion.

The NAWRU

The second concept is less sensitive to import price developments. Although not yet reported in many country surveys, recent OECD work has emphasized the NAWRU, derived also from estimated wage equations but without incorporating "shocks" which affect import prices. At this rate of unemployment, real wages grow in line with trend productivity[30]. OECD estimates suggest that the NAWRU has increased in every major OECD country except the *United States* (Table 2.8)[31]. A major reason for this has been the decline in trend productivity growth which has been particularly marked in European countries. A second reason explored in a number of surveys was the uneven geographic incidence of unemployment. Although national unemployment rates rose, many regions enjoyed much more prosperous labour markets and this may have exerted greater upward pressure on wages than national unemployment rates would have suggested. South-east *England*, northern *Italy*, central *Canada* were all areas enjoying stronger economic growth than other parts of these countries[32].

By 1988, unemployment rates were still above the estimated NAWRU everywhere except in the *United States*. The gap between actual unemployment and the NAWRU was particularly large in continental *Europe*. In *France*, the actual unemployment rate in 1987 was 10.6 per cent, more than twice the NAWRU of 5 per cent. Similar discrepancies can be noted for *Germany* and *Italy*. The size of these gaps might appear to support the conclusion that considerable downward pressure on wage increases remains in most continental European countries – *if* estimates of natural rates can be taken at face value.

Table 2.8. **Estimates of the NAWRU**

	Time period	Average unemployment rate	Estimates of the NAWRU	Average trend productivity growth
United States	1965-1972	4.5	6.3	0.5
	1973-1979	6.5	6.6	0.3
	1980-1983	8.5	6.7	0.2
	1984-1987	7.0	6.5	0.3
	1987	6.2	6.0	0.4
Canada	1966-1972	4.8	6.8	1.3
	1973-1979	7.0	6.6	1.4
	1980-1983	9.5	8.5	0.5
	1984-1987	10.1	8.1	0.6
	1987	8.9	7.5	0.9
Japan	1965-1972	1.2	1.5	4.8
	1973-1979	1.8	1.8	2.6
	1980-1983	2.3	2.0	1.8
	1984-1987	2.7	2.0	1.5
	1987	2.8	2.0	1.4
Germany[1]	1965-1972	0.9	2.9	2.4
	1973-1979	3.1	3.0	2.1
	1980-1983	5.7	3.5	1.2
	1984-1987	8.1	3.7	1.1
	1987	7.9	4.0	1.1
France	1965-1972	2.1	Negligible	3.1
	1973-1979	4.4	0.9	2.4
	1980-1983	7.6	3.9	1.5
	1984-1987	10.3	4.7	1.2
	1987	10.6	5.0	1.2
Italy	1965-1972	5.3	4.0	3.1
	1973-1979	6.2	5.3	2.0
	1980-1983	8.2	6.7	1.2
	1984-1987	10.1	7.7	0.8
	1987	11.0	7.8	0.8
United Kingdom[2]	Pre 1973	2.2	..	1.7
	1973-1979	3.9	..	1.5
	1980-1983	9.2	..	0.6
	1984-1987	11.3	..	1.1
	1987	10.4	..	1.4

Note: These estimates are derived from estimated wage equations.
1. The NAWRU estimated for Germany appeared to be unreasonably low. The estimates reported in the table therefore have been adjusted upward by 2 standard errors.
2. The wage equation used to estimate the NAWRU incorporates hysteresis effects. In this case, these is no long-run relationship between the level of unemployment and nominal wage growth. Hence it is impossible to calculate the NAWRU.
Source: OECD Secretariat.

Does hysteresis exist ?

But there are good reasons for scepticism about whether NAIRUs or NAWRUs provide good guides to inflationary pressure. One study suggested that periods when the unemployment rate was below the NAIRU have almost always been periods of accelerating inflation. But the converse was not generally true[33]. One possible explanation for this is the hysteresis phenomenon cited above. It is conceivable that as high unemployment persisted, its inflation-reducing impact has diminished and may even have disappeared. Because the period of high unemployment is rather short for very precise statistical tests, any conclusion must necessarily be tentative.

The "human-capital", "insider/outsider" and "screening device" explanations of hysteresis cited above would all suggest distinguishing between those unemployed for a short time and those unemployed for a long time. Examination of wage equations along these lines revealed some evidence of hysteresis[34]. In some European countries (and particularly the *United Kingdom*), the *long-term* unemployed appeared to have affected aggregate wage growth less than did *short-term* unemployed[35]. The survey of the *United Kingdom* (January 1986) also found that the wage restraining influence of unemployment tended to disappear as the duration of unemployment grew. The main implication of this is that lower unemployment in the *United Kingdom* may carry greater risks of renewed wage pressure than elsewhere.

A second test for hysteresis examined whether the natural rate could be defined simply as a lagged moving average of the *actual* unemployment rate. The strongest evidence of hysteresis was found for the *United Kingdom*, and perhaps for *Germany*, *Australia, Finland,* and *Spain*[36]. In a related test, the survey of the *United Kingdom* (July 1987) found that the *rate of change* of employment – reflecting the position of "insiders" – was a more important influence on the wage bargaining process than the *actual* rate of unemployment which does not discriminate between "insiders" and "outsiders".

Terms of trade and real-wage targets

Finally several country surveys have pointed out a number of significant modifications to the expectation-augmented Phillips curve approach to wage determination. The survey of *Japan* suggested that wages reacted to changes in the terms of trade, and not simply to past rises in consumer prices. When a rise in consumer prices was due to a deterioration in the terms of trade, wages tended to rise much less than consumer prices, adding an important stabilization mechanism to "shocks" from abroad. Subsequent research identified large and significant terms-of-trade effects in the case of *Germany* and of the *United Kingdom.*

There is also evidence that wage-earners seek to attain a certain "target" of real earnings. Wage pressures tend to ease as this target is achieved. Hence a higher level of *real* earnings tends to moderate wage increases in subsequent periods[37]. This finding may suggest that slower real wage growth in the 1980s may have been partly responsible for the apparent shift in the Phillips curve during this period. The argument is that people tended to continue to expect the same real wage increases in the 1980s as they had received during much of the 1970s – a force that may have kept up nominal wage increases even in the face of weak labour markets. In this case, higher unemployment may reduce "target earnings" (or slow the speed with which workers seek to adjust actual to "target" wages), but this process may take time.

Structural aspects of labour market performance

The macroeconomic evidence that labour markets did not work effectively during the 1970s (particularly in Europe) led a number of country surveys to examine why. The rather diverse factors reviewed in the country surveys can be grouped under three broad headings: wage bargaining institutions; tax and social spending policies; and over-protective legislation. Many country surveys reviewed in some detail the link between these microeconomic elements and macroeconomic performance. In recent years, a number of countries have taken measures to improve the microeconomic functioning of labour markets. The following paragraphs review these issues, considering in particular structural reform.

The institutional wage bargaining process

The first major element in the way labour markets work is the institutional wage-bargaining process. As with any other market, labour markets need to cope with changes in supply and demand if scarce human resources are to be used as efficiently as possible. If institutional arrangements impede such flexibility, then real incomes can suffer. In particular, higher wages where labour is more productively employed can encourage a more efficient allocation of labour. At the same time, institutional arrangements that limit inflationary wage-price spirals can help macroeconomic stability.

Either centralised or decentralised wage negotiation mechanisms can possess such useful properties. Indeed, analysis in the country surveys established that neither centralisation nor decentralisation guaranteed superior performance. While centralised wage-bargaining processes were blamed in several surveys for eroding productivity-related differentials in pay, "corporatism" in the organisation of wage negotiations was given credit for helping to reduce labour market disequilibria in the *Nordic* countries and *Austria*.

More recent OECD work has examined the relationship between collective bargaining structures and macroeconomic performance in periods of inflation and disinflation[38]. For this exercise, countries were grouped into three main categories according to the degree of centralisation of collective bargaining. The centralised group consisted of *Austria, Norway, Sweden, Denmark* and *Finland.* The decentralised group consisted of the *United States, Canada, Japan, France, the United Kingdom, Italy* and *Switzerland. Germany, the Netherlands, Belgium, New Zealand* and *Australia* made up the intermediate group. (However, this classification is inevitably somewhat arbitrary because the degree of centralisation cannot be defined unambiguously – see below.) Macroeconomic performance was measured with reference to unemployment and inflation rates. Although there was no consistent relationship over time between bargaining structure and macroeconomic performance, centralised bargaining systems appeared to have performed slightly better on average.

Perhaps the main conclusion from this approach was that the smallest increases in unemployment rates occurred in the most, as well as the least, centralised groups. By contrast, unemployment increased most in the intermediate group, where industry-wide bargaining was common. By this measure, then, performance was better with the *most* and with the *least* centralised bargaining structures. The most centralised countries, however, had a lower level of unemployment than the other two categories.

The second conclusion was that inflation appeared to be more volatile – perhaps more responsive to demand pressures? – in those countries with centralised or decentralised bargaining systems. In these countries, price inflation increased more in the 1970s (when demand pressures were stronger). This was especially true in those countries with very decentralised bargaining structures. Equally inflation rates decelerated more in these two categories when demand weakened in the first half of the 1980s.

Closely related analysis used in some country surveys ranked countries according to the degree of centralisation. One such ranking – based on Calmfors and

Drifill (1988) – is shown in Diagram 2.6, panel A. According to this scheme, *Austria* has the most centralised system (ranked 1, closest to the origin in the diagram) and *Canada* the least centralised system. This diagram suggests that bargaining structures appeared to be related to the flexibility of labour markets, as measured by the indicator of the short-term real wage rigidity discussed above. The most flexible labour markets (according to this very partial indicator) were those with the most and the least centralised systems, yielding a bell-shaped curve (Diagram 2.6, panel A)[39].

Nevertheless, it should be noted that significant ambiguities arise in defining the degree of centralisation in collective bargaining. For instance, judged by the limited extent of nationwide collective agreements, industrial relations in *Switzerland* are highly decentralised. In 1985, less than 10 per cent of collective agreements in force had a nationwide coverage. And many national agreements contain only general rules for negotiation procedures and do not include wage settlements which are covered by local or firm-specific agreements. On the other hand, there is a broad social consensus normally associated with centralised systems: indeed most collective agreements explicitly forbid strikes, lockouts and boycotts. It is this combination of centralised and decentralised features that facilitates the high sectoral wage flexibility in *Switzerland*[40].

The *United States* has one of the most decentralised and flexible labour markets in the OECD. It has also shown the highest degree of wage flexibility. But, as pointed out in the country survey of the *United States*, "... such flexibility derives in part from the system of three-year contracts. This means a slow rather than incomplete adjustment of wages to inflation."[41]. A decline in union membership, and in the "union premium" over non-union wages, has gone hand-in-hand with the emergence of a more competitive labour market. Over the 1979-1982 period, more than two and a half million workers covered by collective agreements had to make wage and benefit concessions, although most of these concessions took the more gradual form of foregoing wage and/or cost-of-living increases rather than outright wage cuts (only 440 000 people suffered actual cuts). In addition, many more employees had to accept sometimes significant cuts in non-wage benefits.

In *Japan*, unionisation is more extensive, but decentralised: the enterprise-based system ensures that maintaining the viability and prosperity of the employee's own company is central in the wage formation process. With a more difficult economic climate emerging after 1973, individual company performance began to dominate wage negotiations and the weight attached to comparability and cost of living – paramount criteria before – declined considerably[42].

Some countries have sought to reform certain elements of the bargaining process. Curbing the power of trade unions has been an aim of policy in the *United Kingdom*: various measures were taken to reduce the legal protection enjoyed by trade unions in organising strikes and to make unions more responsive to their members[43]. There is some evidence that these changes lowered real wages in some sectors. In a number of other countries, the authorities have sought to use taxation and public expenditure to influence centralised wage negotiations, and so moderate wage growth without having to suffer the very heavy unemployment that might otherwise have been required. A tradition of such intervention is rather strong in the *Nordic countries* and in *Austria*: at the same time employment was relatively stable (Diagram 2.7). In *Australia* a consensus between social partners and government may on occasions have helped to achieve nominal wage moderation; but – in contrast to the pattern in European countries – employment adaptability (the speed of employment adjustment to output changes) is as high as in North America.

Reforming indexation mechanisms

The spread of indexation to compensate for price increases created problems in many countries. But in recent years a number of countries have sought to remedy this and enhance real wage flexibility by partially de-indexing wages. In *Italy* and *Belgium*, where the wage indexation tradition had been strong, reforms were introduced in 1982/83. These aimed at reducing the degree of indexation and the backward-looking character of these schemes. In 1984 the mechanism provided for a freeze of real wages in *Italy* and further measures considerably reduced the scope and degree of indexation. However, full indexation was re-established in *Belgium* as from 1984. From 1986, wage negotiations in *Portugal* were also conducted in terms of prospective, rather than past, price increases: in this way, external disinflation was exploited to secure a simultaneous deceleration of nominal wage increases.

The degree of indexation has also declined in countries with only informal mechanisms. In *North America*, the cost-of-living adjustment clauses resulting from direct bargaining between unions and employers have gradually become less important since the late seventies, with an actual reversal in terms of nominal wage concessions during 1982-84. *Germany* and *France* have traditionally not applied explicit indexation clauses. Contractual indexation is illegal in *Germany*. Informal backward-looking indexation was very widespread in *France* up to 1983: in recent years, however, the degree of indexation has been reduced and the orientation has become more forward-looking. In the *United Kingdom*, where informal indexation was an important feature of wage bargaining in the past, a shift in policy from 1979 led to growing decentralisation in wage bargaining. In *Germany*, *France* and the *United Kingdom* the practice of payment-by-results has been extended, and productivity clauses, bonuses and profit-sharing schemes have become more common. Among the Nordic countries, *Denmark* suspended indexation in 1983, and *Sweden* and *Finland*, having allowed the temporary use of indexation clauses, have adjusted them to the anticipated inflation rate. If inflation turns out to be higher, compensation is granted only for the excess of inflation over the target rate. In *Finland*, furthermore, the inflation-rate adjustment has occasionally been corrected for terms-of-trade changes.

Tax and welfare payments

The second major influence on the functioning of labour markets was tax and social transfer payments. During recent years there has been increasing awareness of the way in which tax and welfare policies may have exacerbated the unemployment problem. The distortions that arise fall under three main headings:

- The extent to which unemployment benefits that replace a high proportion of income subsidise leisure and/or longer job search, implying a higher reservation wage (the lowest wage at which an individual is willing to accept a job offer);

- Higher payroll taxes (usually social security contributions paid by the employer) have, in some countries, driven a wedge between labour costs and gross wages. The larger this is, the lower the level of employment associated with a given level of wages. In addition, heavier income taxation and high employee social security contributions further reduce take-home pay thus distorting labour supply;

- Tax concessions and subsidies to capital investment lower the cost of capital relative to labour and make investment unduly labour saving thus discouraging employment.

These elements are considered in turn.

i) High unemployment benefits

During the 1970s, unemployment benefit replacement ratios tended to rise, sometimes rather steeply; since 1980, however, this trend has generally been reversed. Some – necessarily highly approximate – aggregate estimates are shown in

56

Table 2.9; an attempt is also made to calculate some *hypothetical* replacement ratios for the first full year of unemployment. Legal provisions vary considerably, and many country surveys have attempted to estimate hypothetical replacement ratios for particular earners, taking account of income tax treatment and of family status. In *Austria*, replacement ratios thus computed have fallen from about 40-42 per cent of after-tax income to around 25-30 per cent from the mid-1960s to 1970s. Replacement ratios have also been reduced in *Ireland*[44].

Table 2.9.   **Unemployment benefit replacement ratios**

Per cent

	Aggregate ratios[1]			*Memorandum item:* Hypothetical rate[2]
	1965-1970	1971-1979	1980-1985	
United States	11	13	10	48
Canada[3]	43	57	46	70
Japan	35	31	24	. .
France	28	25	37	72-71
Germany	59	52	36	70-72
Italy	6	8	10	90-80
United Kingdom	29	29	23	74-76
Austria	32	42	37	. .
Belgium[4]	40	50	45	80-82
Denmark	47	65	56	97-93
Finland[5, 6]	15	14	13	. .
Ireland[7]	. .	28	28	90-80
Netherlands[5]	56	41	37	88-82
Norway[8]	. .	53	79	. .
Portugal[9]	. .	4	5	. .
Spain[6]	12	17	19	. .
Sweden[5]	23	26	39	92-40
Switzerland	62	55	58	. .
Australia	4	17	23	55
New Zealand	17	39	25	. .

1. Ratio of unemployment benefits per unemployed person, *divided* by compensation per employee.
2. Numerator is unemployment benefits plus social transfers, net of tax; denominator is after tax income for a married unemployed person on average earnings, with two children, non working spouse, first full year of unemployment. Figures refer to 1982-1983, but to 1981 for the U.S., Canada and Australia, and 1980 for Sweden. When there is a range, the first rate is after 1 month of unemployment, the second after 13 months. For Sweden, they refer to two different insurance schemes.
3. From 1966.
4. From 1970 to 1982.
5. The first column refers to the year 1970.
6. Last figure available is 1984.
7. From 1978.
8. From 1973.
9. From 1977.
Sources: OECD, *National Accounts,* and Table 2 in Chan-Lee et al (1987).

However, effective disincentive effects of unemployment benefits are often made worse because social welfare and tax systems are not harmonized:

- While earned income is taxed, short-term welfare payments are often tax-free;
- Welfare payments increase with the number of children, but there are no tax allowances for dependent children in many countries. This means that replacement ratios rise with the number of children;
- The right to welfare payments depends on weekly or monthly income while tax allowances depend on income earned *per year*. This means that periods of unemployment can give rise to tax rebates.

Even after recent reforms, replacement ratios, in certain cases, remain very high. Also the larger number of households with multiple earners means that more families may effectively enjoy very high replacement ratios once lower income tax payments by the spouse are taken into account[45]. A final problem is that the conditions of entitlement can discourage job search. In *Canada*, for instance, those who are unemployed in high unemployment areas receive more generous benefits and this may discourage people from moving to areas where jobs are available.

None the less, there has been a general tendency to reduce replacement ratios as part of the policy of budgetary restraint pursued for much of the 1980s. This is true notably for the *United States* and the *United Kingdom*. Indeed, the short duration of unemployment benefits in the *United States* (up to twenty-six weeks) acts as a strong incentive for employment. In *France* and *Germany* the duration of benefits has been increased in recent years (though in *France* both coverage and average benefits have been reduced). Generous unemployment provisions have been characteristic of *Sweden* and *Denmark*. But in *Denmark* unemployment benefits were frozen in nominal terms from 1983 to 1986. The *Netherlands* have also reduced real benefits; they remain among the most generous, however, in terms of duration and eligibility. Replacement ratios for young unemployed were also high in *Australia*, although these have been reduced recently. While unemployment compensation was traditionally very low in *Italy*, a system of almost total compensation for workers laid off in certain industries was developed. Under certain circumstances workers were entitled to up to 90 per cent of their previous wage for an indefinite period. This compensation scheme is now undergoing substantial changes. Unemployment benefits have been substantially reduced in *Belgium* for those unemployed who are not household heads.

Secondly, the reduction in benefits has been supported in many countries by efforts to link entitlement to benefits more closely with willingness to work. In a number of countries, persistent refusal to accept a job can now lead to the suspension of unemployment benefits. And often registration in training programmes for young workers is a precondition for the receipt of any benefits.

ii)   The tax "wedge": high non-wage labour costs

The cost of labour to a potential employer includes social insurance and pension charges he may be obliged to contribute; the wage received is subject to income tax and social security contributions. In many countries, the rising burden of taxation has driven a wedge between the cost of labour and the real after-tax wage, and this may have reduced the supply of labour. An employer will be prepared to hire as long as the cost of labour equals or is less than the expected productivity of the new worker. But the worker's decision will be based on his after-tax wage. By creating a gap between the cost of labour and after-tax wages, the tax system thus discourages potentially productive employment[46]. Secondly, reductions in after-tax income may encourage higher wage claims to offset the earnings loss[47]. A number of country surveys have analysed the overall impact of the main taxes in creating such a wedge. Perhaps the widest wedge occurred in *Ireland*: although real wage costs rose by 15 per cent between 1979 and 1984, real after-tax income fell by more than 15 per cent[48].

Perhaps most emphasis has been placed on non-wage labour costs – employers' contributions for social security and pensions. Such charges often introduce additional distortions by including significant fixed elements, being levied per employee rather than proportionately with income. Because the cost per employee is increased relative to hourly wage costs, employers have an incentive to use fewer workers, and rely more heavily on overtime[49]. Some international comparisons of non-wage labour costs are shown in Table 2.10. These charges can be significant: in *France*, *Italy* and *Sweden* they exceed 30 per cent of total wages, and tended to rise steeply during the 1970s. Although a number of countries have sought to brake the rise of non-wage labour costs, the results achieved to date have been rather disappointing.

iii)   Cheapening capital

The perception that creating more jobs required higher investment led a number of countries to resort to a mixture of grants and tax relief designed to stimulate investment. In some cases, particularly small countries, the authorities have sought to encourage foreign investment as a means of creating jobs. The danger with such policies is that the relative price of labour and capital is distorted, and this may

Table 2.10. **Non-wage labour costs**

As a percentage of wages and salaries

	1960	1970	1980	1985	1986
United States	8.7	12.1	19.8	20.5	20.3
Canada	4.6	6.8	9.3	10.8	11.0
Japan	..	9.0	12.4	15.5	15.5[1]
France	26.8	31.9	37.2	40.3	40.7[1]
Germany	15.9	17.1	22.4	24.1	24.1
Italy	35.2	38.5	35.3	37.8	38.3[1]
United Kingdom	7.4	10.1	15.2	15.0	14.8[1]
Austria	..	16.8	20.3	22.6	22.3
Belgium	..	15.3	16.0	15.8[1]	..
Finland	11.1	16.1	22.7	22.6	22.8
Netherlands	..	24.6	30.2	30.5	29.7
Norway	..	..	17.2	16.7	16.7
Portugal	9.1	12.3	16.8	20.8	..
Spain	..	..	29.3	32.4	..
Sweden	..	15.1	37.2	37.3	37.3
Switzerland	11.5	12.2	14.7	15.0	15.0
Australia	..	3.5	5.8	8.0	8.0

1. Estimates.
Source: OECD, *National Accounts.*

actually discourage employment. Industrial policy in *Ireland*, for example, may well have had this effect. Greater realisation of the possibility of such perverse effects has prompted a reorientation of policy aimed at fostering more labour-intensive activities.

Labour legislation

In many countries legislation has traditionally been intended to protect employees: hiring and dismissal procedures are often regulated, and minimum wages are fixed by law in many countries[50]. Moreover, many countries extended the scope of measures designed to give greater security of employment during the 1960s and 1970s. As it became more difficult to dismiss workers, one consequence of such measures was that firms became more reluctant to employ them, particularly given the greater uncertainties after 1973. There is indeed evidence that much of the increase in unemployment in *Europe* can be explained by greater employer reluctance to hire new employees. In *North America, Japan* and *Australia* the trend rise in unemployment resulted largely from an increase in the *inflows* to unemployment. But in *France, Germany* and the *United Kingdom* there was little secular rise in inflows into unemployment. Instead there was a large drop in *outflows* from unemployment[51]. A second consequence was that, in some cases, employment has diverted away from firms subject to legislation – typically large firms – to other firms – small firms or even the underground economy.

Realisation that measures designed to promote job security could have such unintended effects prompted a number of reforms in several countries. Such reforms have sometimes included the easing of hiring and firing practices, reducing the cost of dismissals, and the shortening of fixed-term and the easing of regulations governing temporary contracts. Recently, the administrative procedures required by the State before dismissals or redundancies could be enacted were significantly eased in *France*. In particular, the need for firms to seek official permission for any dismissal (the *autorisation administrative de licenciement*) was dropped in 1986. To some extent, labour market practices have slowly moved in the direction of customs prevailing in the *United States*, where restrictions are few and dismissal procedures are not a practical obstacle to quick employment adjustment. However, some observers have noted the beginnings of a change in *United States* labour markets as court decisions have increased *employees' property rights in their jobs*, but it is too early to assess the long-run implications of this[52]. Recent legislation has also imposed a 60-day notice period for dismissals. In *Germany*, legislation passed in 1985 increased the possibilities for concluding employment contracts of limited duration and improved employment opportunities for persons seeking part-time jobs.

Minimum wage legislation has also been reformed during the 1980s. A number of countries had established minimum wages, in some cases high enough to compress wage scales. Minimum wages exist in the *United States, Canada* and *France*. In the first two countries (and especially in *Canada*) their real value has declined steeply over time: there are indications in both cases that this increased employment. In *France*, revision of the statutory minimum wage was the main instrument for indexing the whole wage structure, provoking inordinately large wage increases in 1974-75 and again in 1981 and 1982. Since then, increases in minimum wages have declined broadly in line with the lower trend of consumer prices. *Belgium, the Netherlands* and *Spain* also have a minimum wage system, with reduced benefits for youth. In the *United Kingdom*, wage councils establish minimum wages for certain groups of workers, but coverage is confined to just over 10 per cent of the labour force, and young workers have recently been excluded.

Belgium has recently relaxed its minimum income rules. *Portugal* instituted minimum wages after the 1974 revolution, although their real value declined sharply in the subsequent inflationary period. However, there was a catch-up from 1985 when minimum wages were increased substantially; in 1987, its coverage was extended to 18 to 20 year olds. In *New Zealand*, minimum wages doubled from 1984 to 1987, while the average wage rose by 40 per cent: as a result, the minimum wage rose to around 50 per cent of average wages, a ratio that is very high by international standards.

Many governments have combined reform of labour legislation with more vigorous efforts to provide adequate retraining of displaced workers. One example is the *Canadian* policy, introduced in 1985, of providing work experience and training and so improve labour supply. The package included skill investment for workers whose jobs are threatened; easier job entry for youth; job development for the long-term unemployed; a programme to reduce specific skill shortages and incentives to innovate, new ideas, experimentation and pilot projects. Such work experience programmes can also help the employer not mainly by providing cheaper labour but rather by allowing him to learn first-hand about the abilities of new employees. By thus removing uncertainty about how well new workers perform, hiring can be encouraged.

In many other countries, traditional labour market mechanisms fulfil this training role. The lifetime-employment system in *Japan* has probably encouraged an emphasis on training: because it is almost impossible to transfer, in mid-career, from one large enterprise to another, the costs of retraining can easily be recouped by the company making the investment. The existence of giant companies with interests in many different sectors made it easier to retrain and transfer workers from declining to expanding areas. Traditionally, many European countries have had extensive apprenticeship programmes – these programmes are particularly successful in *Switzerland*. More recently, steps have been taken in a number of countries to improve training. The youth training scheme and industrial training in the *United Kingdom*, training schemes in *Germany*, vocational training schemes, employment training and apprenticeship contracts, and "sandwich" courses in *France*, are examples of efforts to improve the quality of labour supply in Europe.

Do governments devote enough resources to training and to other "active" labour-market measures? A recent OECD review of public spending in this area found that in only four OECD countries (*Sweden, Norway, Greece* and *Portugal*, expenditure in the latter two countries being influenced by programmes financed out of the European Social Fund) did spending on "active" measures exceed income maintenance (for those unemployed)[53]. Although there is *a priori* reason for spending more on "active" measures, there does appear to be a case for better co-ordination between "active" and income-supporting policies. Unemployment benefits inevitably reduce job search to some extent: by combining such benefits with in-depth counselling, placement efforts and follow-up measures, this disincentive can be reduced. An efficient combination of policies should offer each jobless person the least costly kind of support required to get him back to work.

Other measures affecting unemployment

The previous section outlined how a number of governments have sought to improve the functioning of labour markets by reducing or reforming government intervention, whether through regulations or through the tax system. But some other measures taken by governments have been more interventionist.

First, a number of countries have had recourse to traditional policies to create employment – public employment programmes and employment subsidies have been tried in the *Nordic* countries, *France, Belgium* and *Spain*. Community work schemes in *Sweden, Finland* and *France* and the employment promotion programme and INEM contracts of *Spain* (employment contracts between national institutions of employment and public agencies) are examples of recent general government job creation activities.

Secondly, governments have also provided financial incentives for firms to hire the unemployed (*France, Finland*). Several countries (including *Belgium, France, Ireland* and *the United Kingdom*) have introduced schemes which permit the "capitalisation" of unemployment insurance benefits thus helping the unemployed to set up their own firms. In some countries funds have been created to finance special employment measures. The use of employment funds has increased in *Japan*, and in *Belgium* firms reducing their workforce must make additional contributions to the fund. In *Sweden* and *Finland* regional investment funds are used to alleviate financing problems encountered by new firms established in the high unemployment areas.

Thirdly, a number of policies have – often indirectly – had the effect of reducing the labour supply, and this has exerted downward pressure on measured unemployment rates. *Elderly workers* have been perhaps most affected. The retirement age was lowered, or the early retirement schemes reformed in *France, Germany, Austria, Switzerland, the Netherlands* and *Finland*. Wider pension coverage was introduced in *Spain*. The development of pensions in *Japan* and private pension schemes in the *United States* have tended to reduce the labour force participation of those over 65[54].

Secondly, some countries have taken measures to *extend the schooling age (Finland, Portugal, Spain* and *Sweden)* or lengthen probation periods (*Belgium*). Training programmes have also served to temporarily depress the unemployment rate. Finally, there have been efforts to encourage *work-sharing* – measures aimed at increasing part-time work have been taken[55].

Conclusions

In many OECD countries, persistently high unemployment constitutes one of the most difficult challenges to economic policy. The uneven incidence of unemployment remains a matter of some concern. Youth unemployment is particularly high in those countries with the highest unemployment; and much the same applies to the long-term unemployed.

The analysis of labour markets in the country surveys suggests that no particular industrial relations system can be expected to provide a panacea. For instance, both centralised and decentralised labour markets can, according to the country, function well. But the surveys do point out many cases where regulations, tax and other policies, restrictive practices and so on impede labour market functioning. It is now widely recognised that the resulting rigidities often actually reduce employment and make it harder to cut inflation. It is not a coincidence that countries with relatively rigid employment practices suffered the steepest rise in unemployment between 1973 and 1987. Conversely, *Canada* and *the United States* – with traditionally highly flexible labour markets – have seen the steepest declines in unemployment since 1983.

There is general agreement that labour markets have become more responsive to economic conditions in recent years in almost all OECD countries. While it is impossible to quantify the degree of change, the overview in Table 2.11 suggests the qualitative importance of these changes.

Any overall assessment is perhaps premature as many of the reforms are too recent to permit any very strong conclusions to be drawn about how far the workings of labour markets have been improved. It took major external shocks in the early 1970s before the consequences of the deterioration in labour market functioning during the 1960s were to become fully evident. Recent reforms have not been tested by any major shock – indeed recent international conditions have been peculiarly favourable for industrial countries, with growth strong and international commodity prices broadly stable.

The labour market situation has improved and unemployment rates have been falling in the OECD area for the last five years with particularly steep declines in unemployment in the *United States, Canada, Australia*, and (more recently) *the United Kingdom* and a number of smaller European countries. Nevertheless, it took more than a decade of high unemployment to bring wage inflation closer to acceptable levels. Had labour markets been more flexible, this disinflationary process could have been much shorter. It is true that there have been some signs that wage growth in the first half of the 1980s declined more rapidly than earlier experience would have suggested. But formal econometric tests of the stability of wage equations provide no statistical evidence of a particularly unusual degree of nominal wage moderation in most OECD countries in the first half of the 1980s. While wage increases up to 1985 were, in some countries, somewhat below what equations based on earlier periods would have suggested, the discrepancy was usually within the bounds of statistical error[56].

But since 1986, wage increases have, in many countries, been higher than the *level* of unemployment would have suggested in the past. In many cases, the steep drop in oil prices did not lead to a commensurate fall in nominal wage growth. More recently, there have been signs of renewed wage pressures as employment growth has resumed, even in countries where unemployment remains high. This development is a warning about the future difficulty of unwinding the rise in unemployment without reviving inflation. Despite major progress, significant rigidities still exist in labour markets. In many cases, policies to inject greater flexibility into the working of labour markets have not gone far enough. In a number of areas impediments continue to hamper the efficient working of the labour market and so limit the expansion of real incomes and of employment. Not all of these impediments are created by government: many reflect deeply engrained habits or procedures in the private sector. In many – if not most – OECD countries, there are few grounds for relaxing efforts to make labour markets more flexible and responsive.

Reforms in other markets are also needed to support more flexible labour markets, a theme pursued in a number of country surveys and summarised in the following chapters. The country surveys have also underlined the importance of appropriate macroeconomic policies in assuring a durable reduction in unemployment. International competitiveness is also important, especially for small open economies. Equally, macroeconomic policies work much better when labour markets are flexible and wage pressure moderate.

Table 2.11. Change

	United States	Japan	Germany	France	United Kingdom	Italy
1. Short-run real wage rigidity[a]	Low	Low	Intermediate	High	High	Intermed
2. Intersectoral labour cost differentials[b]	Average	Average	Low	High	Low	High
3. Change in (2)	Rising	Stable	Rising	Falling	Falling	Fallin
4. Inter-industry wage differentials[c]	High	High	Low	Low	Low	Avera
5. Change in (4)	Rising	Rising	Rising	Falling	Falling	Fallin
6. Change in dispersion of intersectoral productivity differentials[d]	Falling	Stable	Rising	Rising	—	Fallin
7. Change in ratio of female to male wages[e]	—	Falling	Rising	Stable	Rising	Risin
8. Change in ratio of female to male unemployment rate	Falling	Rising	Rising	Falling	Rising	Fallin
9. Change in ratio of youth to adult wages	Falling	Stable	—	Stable	Rising	—
10. Change in ratio of youth to adult unemployment rates	Falling	Falling	Rising	Rising	Rising	—
11. Minimum wages[f]	Low falling	Not relevant	No legal minimum	High stable	Not relevant	No leg minimu
12. Unemployment replacement rates[g]	Low	Low	High	High	Low	Avera
13. Change in part-time employment relative to full-time employment	Small increase	Small increase	Strong rise	Strong rise	Small absolute	Avera rising
14. Change in annual hours worked per employed person	Small fall	Small rise	Average fall	Strong decline	Strong decline	Smal declin
15. Earnings exempt from employers' social security contributions	Zero	Intermed.	Intermed.	Zero	High	High
16. Rise in unemployment relative to high capacity use (shift in "Okun curve")	Small	Small	Moderate	Strong	Strong	Stron

a) Short-run price coefficients divided by cyclical coefficient (money wage equations for private non-farm business sector).
b) Coefficient of variation of sectoral labour cost differentials (compensation per employed person).
c) Coefficient of variation of inter-industry hourly wage differentials (pay for time worked).
d) Coefficient of variation of sectoral output per employed person.

anada	Belgium	Finland	Ireland	Netherlands	New Zealand	Portugal	Spain	Sweden	
Low	High	Low	Intermediate	High	High	Low	Intermediate	Low	1.
Low	—	Low	Low	—	Low	Low	—	Low	2.
ising	—	Falling	Stable	—	—	—	—	Falling	3.
High	Low	Low	Average	—	Low	—	—	Low	4.
table	Falling	Rising	—	—	—	—	—	Falling	5.
—	—	—	—	—	—	—	—	Rising	6.
—	Stable	Rising	Rising	Rising	Rising	Rising	—	Rising	7.
alling	Rising	Stable	Stable	Rising	Stable	Stable	Rising	Falling	8.
alling	—	Stable	—	—	—	Stable	—	Rising	9.
alling	—	Falling	—	—	—	Stable	Falling	Rising	10.
Low alling	Lower rate for youth	—	Not relevant	High falling	Not relevant	Low stable	Average falling	No legal minimum	11.
erage	High	High	High	—	Average	Low	Low	High	12.
mall rise	Strong rise	—	—	Strong rise	Average rise	—	—	Strong rise	13.
erage fall	—	Average fall	—	Average fall	Average fall	—	—	Average fall	14.
Low	—	—	—	—	—	—	—	—	15.
derate	Strong	Small	Strong	Strong	Small	Small	Strong	Small	16.

ourly adult wages.
elative to the wage of average productive workers.
nemployment benefits per unemployed person as a percentage of net income of average production worker.
es: F. Klau and A. Mittelstadt (1986); J. Chan-Lee, D. Coe and M. Prywes (1987); and subsequent updating.

Notes

1. The *McCracken Report* noted (p.52) that policy making in the period 1969 to 1971 was, in some countries, over-influenced by "a sense of unease to which the discord in labour markets – and in the streets – had given rise". See also OECD (1988b).

2. See Andersen (1984) for an estimate of the effect of this on unemployment.

3. See OECD (1987b), p.120.

4. For a discussion of the main features of key policy changes in a number of countries during this period, see OECD (1988b).

5. The following *OECD Economic Surveys* have reviewed labour market developments:

Belgium	December 1984
Luxemburg	December 1984
Netherlands	February 1985
Germany	June 1985
France	July 1985
Canada	October 1985
Switzerland	December 1985
United Kingdom	January 1986
Spain	April 1986
Portugal	May 1986
Finland	June 1986
Italy	July 1986
Japan	November 1986
United States	November 1986
New Zealand	May 1987
Ireland	December 1987
Austria	February 1988

Unless otherwise indicated, all references to country surveys in this chapter refer to the above surveys.

6. How far the correlation between strong growth and lower unemployment is evidence of the relative importance of demand as opposed to structural factors is moot. One important consideration is that structural policies themselves can make higher growth possible. Part of the academic literature has focused on a somewhat narrower question, the relative importance of demand and of real wages in explaining unemployment. A

recent study by Coen and Hickman (1987) found that the sharp rise of unemployment in all the countries studied during the 1980s was induced primarily by deficient demand, although exacerbated by large wage gaps in the United Kingdom and the United States. McCallum's (1986) cross-country examination of the unemployment performance of fourteen OECD countries led him to conclude that differences in unemployment have been largely due to fiscal and monetary policy, with real wages playing a minor role. Andersen (1984) found that large wage gaps were responsible for the rise in unemployment up to 1984 but not thereafter. See also Gordon (1987).

7. Over the last twenty years or so, participation rates have increased much more in North America than in Europe or Japan. See Chart 2.4, p.55, *OECD Employment Outlook* (September 1987).

8. See the statistical analysis in the *Economic Survey of Ireland* (December 1987) particularly pp.38-40 and the results presented in Table 15.

9. These movements are discussed in the *Economic Survey of Portugal* (May 1986) pp.36-37.

10. This is, of course, only true given certain strong assumptions. One simplified version would be as follows. Starting with the definition of labour's share of national income,

(1) $\dfrac{w.L}{PY.Y}$

where w = average wages
       L = total employment
       PY = GNP deflator
       Y = real GNP

Incorporating terms-of-trade effects in the simplest way, consumer prices (PC) can be defined by:

(2) $PC = PY^{1-a}PM^a$

where PM = import prices
       a = share of imports in private consumption

Using (2) to rewrite (1) and then differentiating, using a "hat" to denote proportional rates of change, it follows that:

$$\left[\frac{w\hat{L}}{PY.Y}\right] = \left[\frac{\hat{w}}{PC}\right] - a\left[\frac{P\hat{Y}}{PM}\right] - \left[\frac{\hat{Y}}{L}\right]$$

To hold labour's share constant (i.e. left hand side of above equation is zero), it follows that:

$$\left[\frac{\hat{w}}{PC}\right] = a\left[\frac{P\hat{Y}}{PM}\right] + \left[\frac{\hat{Y}}{L}\right]$$

11. These developments were summarised in the OECD *Economic Outlook* of July 1977 (see particularly pp.62-63) and underlined in many subsequent country surveys. Sachs (1979) also provided an early analysis of these issues.

12. The *Economic Survey of the United States* (November 1986) noted that, in contrast to Europe, there was little tendency for a gap to open up between real wages and productivity. See also Bruno and Sachs (1985). The Bruno (1986) update of the earlier work concluded that, among the eight countries studied, the wage gap played an important role [in the rise in unemployment] mainly in the mid-1970s and primarily for the United Kingdom, Belgium and Denmark. Coen and Hickman (1987) reviewed four major countries and found that classical unemployment has never been a dominant factor in Germany.

13. There are, however, statistical and other reasons why the labour cost gap was a rather unreliable indicator in the case of Japan. The original OECD calculations took 1970 as a base year and this overstated the labour cost gap. This was because capital's share in national income peaked in 1970 in Japan in the wake of extremely rapid, and investment-intensive, growth in the late 1960s.

14. In addition, other taxes rose, leading in some cases to large tax wedges: this is discussed in chapter 5 of this book. The tax wedge effect was particularly strong in Italy once direct taxes on labour are also considered; for details see *Economic Survey of Italy*, July 1986.

15. By no means all of the weak growth in investment in the first half of the 1980s can be attributed to the high relative price of labour. For example, Andersen (1987) suggests that the main cause of weak investment growth was below-trend growth of demand.

16. For analyses of this issue, see Burda (1988) and Kohli and Ryan (1986).

17. The synthetic indicator is very sensitive to specification. However the relatively favourable situation of the United States and Japan *vis-à-vis* European countries appears to be a rather robust conclusion. Moreover, for some other countries, the terms of trade (or profitability) was found to be a significant explanatory variable: this further increases flexibility.

18. For a discussion of labour mobility and wage differentials, see OECD (1987), pp.134-138.

19. As labour demand declines, the expected gain from moving or changing jobs is likely to be reduced thereby tending to lower labour mobility.

20. For international comparisons of wage differentials, see Klau and Mittelstadt (1986): see also Diagram 10 in the *Economic Survey of Germany* (June 1985) showing the relationship between real wage rigidity and wage differentials.

21. Between 1970 and 1985, the prime-age-male premium (i.e. those 25 and older) over youth (16 to 24-year-olds) rose from 43 to 90 per cent in the United States. See Freeman (1988).

22. See regressions of youth unemployment rates on adult unemployment rates and the ratio of youth to adult pay in pooled time series cross section of OECD countries in Bloom and Freeman (1986) and OECD (1986b).

23. This concept was developed in Newell and Symons (1985).

24. The apparent correlation must be interpreted with caution as unemployment is itself one of the explanatory variables in the wage equations used to compute the index of real wage rigidity.

25. Use of the term "natural" rate of unemployment in this context is controversial because it is not related to market-clearing conditions in labour markets. Also the fact that *any* rate of wage increase will be consistent with a given NAWRU causes some unease with the concept.

26. Blanchard and Summers (1988) use an illuminating analogy to expound their notion of "fragile equilibrium": "Consider a ball on a hilly surface. If the surface is bowl-shaped, there will be a uniquely determined equilibrium position for the ball – at the bottom of the bowl. This is the view implicit in the natural rate hypothesis. But the European experience suggests other possibilities. If the surface contains two pronounced valleys, or is extremely flat, or contains many mild depressions, the ball's position will depend sensitively on just how the ball is shocked. We use the term "fragile equilibria" to refer to situations of this type."

27. For one attempt to relate the natural rate to structural aspects of the labour market (based on job search) see Darby *et al* (1985).

28. See Coe (1985). For further elaboration of these points, see Cornwall (1988).

29. The simplest way to see these points is to consider, for example, a simple linear wage-price "block":

   i) $\quad W = a_0 + a_1 P_{-1} - a_2 u + a_3 G$

   ii) $\quad P = b_0 + b_1 W - b_2 G + b_3 PM$

   where

   W   = rate of growth of money wages
   G   = rate of growth of labour productivity
   u   = rate of unemployment
   P   = rate of change of prices
   PM = rate of change of import prices

   Solving for the rate of unemployment yielding *stable* price inflation (viz $P = P_{-1} = P$) yields

   $$u_N = \left\{ b_0 + a_0 b_1 + (b_1 a_3 - b_2)G + b_3 PM - (1 - b_1 a_1)P \right\} / b_1 a_2$$

   The results cited in the text follow from this.

30. The NAWRU is derived from the wage equation only. Using equation *(i)* in footnote 29, and using a "bar" to denote trend, and the condition that real wages rise in line with trend productivity (i.e. $\overline{W} - \overline{P} = \overline{G}$), the natural rate is:

   $$U = [a_0 + (a_1 - 1)\overline{P} + (a_3 - 1)\overline{G}]/a_2$$

   If $a_1 = 1$ (absence of money illusion in the wage equation), then

   $$U = [a_0 + (a_1 - 1)\overline{G}]/a_2$$

   See the *Economic Surveys of Finland* (June 1986) and *Denmark* (July 1987) for detailed applications of the NAWRU.

71

31. The slight decline in the United States NAWRU reflects an increase in the proportion of the labour force in the 30 to 40 age group (which has the highest propensity to be employed) as the "baby-boomers" mature. See *Economic Survey of the United States* (May 1988), p.65.

32. For an examination of this issue in the Canadian context see Grignon and Moray (1988). They suggest that better balance in the regional pattern of growth would significantly reduce the estimated NAIRU.

33. Cornwall (1988) tested the NAIRU hypothesis by using data for various sub-periods between 1961 and 1983 for nine OECD countries. His findings may be summarised as follows, where each sub-period/country is taken as an observation, yielding a total of 65 cases in all:

	U > NAIRU	U < NAIRU	Total
Inflation accelerating	26	22*	48
Inflation decelerating	14*	3	17
Total	40	25	65

* = cases predicted by the hypothesis.

34. See Coe (1988).

35. Layard and Nickell (1985) reached much the same conclusion.

36. See Coe (1988).

37. Preliminary work in the OECD suggests the existence of such effects in all the major seven OECD countries except the United States. Earlier research by Andersen (1984) and Sachs (1983) reached a similar conclusion. Andersen suggests that at least part of the apparent shifts in Phillips curves in many countries (implying higher NAIRUs) can be attributed to the omission of real earnings from the estimated equations for wages.

38. This is reported in "The structure of collective bargaining, unemployment and inflation", *OECD Economic Outlook 43*, May 1988.

39. Other studies have also suggested that more "corporatist" structures can reduce inflationary pressure – but have also pointed to some significant nuances. Bruno and Sachs (1985) introduced an index of corporatism in their estimates of the Phillips curve and conclude that highly corporatist economies have a significantly lower NAIRU *ceteris paribus*. Similarly, Bean, Layard and Nickell (1986) concluded that corporatist arrangements have helped employers and employees to agree on curtailing wage increases to the level that is justified by the country's economic performance in Austria, Germany, the Netherlands and the Scandinavian countries. However, Calmfors and Driffill (1988) found a non-linear relationship between measures of "centralisation" and success in macroeconomic adjustment, and argued that industry-wide wage settlements are the least conducive to real wage restraint because interest groups may be most harmful when they are strong enough to cause major disruption but not sufficiently encompassing to bear any significant fraction of the costs to society of pursuit of their own self-interest.

40. See *Economic Survey of Switzerland* (December 1985), pp.49-51 and Danthine and Lambelet (1987).

41. The three-year contract became the norm in the United States only in the 1960s and 1970s. In the mid-1950s only one-fifth of major contracts lasted three years or more; by the mid-1970s, this had risen to three-quarters. By the mid-1980s, less than half such contracts lasted as long.

42. See *Economic Survey of Japan* (November 1986) p.71.

43. The main measures were the removal of legal immunities for picketing, other than by employees at their place of work and for secondary industrial action; the institution of secret ballots to approve closed shop arrangements; and the removal of legal immunities from civil actions in any industrial action not agreed in advance by a secret ballot of the membership. Carruth and Oswald's assessment of these measures (1987) concluded that in 1980-82 "real wages did not crash, but they trembled".

44. See *Economic Survey of Austria* (February 1988) p.51 and *Economic Survey of Ireland* (December 1987) pp.48-50. See also the hypothetical calculations reported in Chan-Lee *et al* (1987), Table 2, p.127.

45. One study of the total labour supply effects of major income transfer programmes in the United States concluded that such programmes reduced labour supply by around 5 per cent (see *Economic Survey of the United States* (November 1987), p.71).

46. This assumes that labour supply is positively related to after-tax wages. Because income effects are important, the reverse could be true (backward-sloping supply curve): lower after-tax income reduces the demand for leisure and so can increase the supply of labour. In practice, however, distortions often take the form of substituting non-taxable (underground economy) for taxable work, not conducive to the most efficient use of labour.

47. For a discussion of such tax-push effects, see chapter 5, "The Public Sector: Restoring the Balance" in this book. For other evidence of tax-push effects see Sachs (1983) and Andersen (1984).

48. See *Economic Survey of Ireland* (December 1987) particularly Diagram 7, p.47.

49. For a number of countries, there is evidence that the relationship between overtime and unemployment shifted with a given rate of unemployment being associated with a much more intensive use of overtime. Flanagan (1988) noted that this shift was particularly dramatic in Italy and the United Kingdom, where a *positive* relationship between overtime and unemployment has emerged since the early 1980s.

50. For a summary of legislation for employment protection in different countries, see Table III-1 (pp.95-105) in OECD *Flexibility in the labour market: the current debate* (1986). See also Emerson (1987) where regulations in different countries governing individual dismissals (annex 1), collective redundancies (annex 2) and arbitration mechanisms (annex 3) are summarised. In some countries, strict regulations also apply to hiring. The survey of *Italy* discussed the legal obligation on large firms to select job applicants in numerical order from waiting lists of job seekers at public employment offices. These waiting lists ("collocamento") are drawn up on the basis of a system that

ranks job-seekers according to the time they have been unemployed, age and family situation. The system severely penalises young people entering the labour market for the first time.

51. See Flanagan (1988). He also points out that if rising unemployment reflected greater reluctance to hire, one would expect to see unemployment concentrated increasingly among "outsiders". As the right to unemployment insurance payments typically depends on having work experience, he used the "uninsured unemployed" as a proxy for unemployed "outsiders". For most European countries, he found that uninsured unemployment grew much more rapidly than insured unemployment.

52. See, for example, *The Economist*, 23rd January 1988. For a discussion about the possible consequences of unpredictable, but large, court awards in the United States, see Flanagan (1986). See also Mendelsohn (1988).

53. See OECD (1988c).

54. In the United States public pension provision has improved, although the 1983 Act discourages early retirement. Still, the earnings test acts as a strong disincentive against full-time employment of older workers. In most private corporate pension schemes, maximum pension entitlement has been reached by the age of 60, and this may discourage continued employment beyond this age.

55. The sectoral agreements and work-sharing programmes introduced in Belgium, and the reforms in part-time working conditions and limited duration employment contracts in Spain are examples beyond the almost universal trend towards cutting working hours. Italy has also embarked upon a series of important reforms of labour legislation concerning part-time work.

56. See Chan-Lee *et al* (1987). However, Gordon (1988) found evidence of a "new regime" in wage formation: almost all of his equations showed a marked tendency to overpredict wage change for 1981-87 on the basis of coefficients estimated for 1954-80.

References

Andersen, P.S. (1984), "Real wages, inflation and unemployment", *BIS Working Paper* no.9 (July).

Andersen, P.S. (1987), "Profit shares, investment and output capacity", *BIS Working Paper* no.12 (July).

Bean, C.R., P.R.G. Layard and S.J. Nickell (1986), "The Rise of unemployment: a multicountry Study", *Economica 53* (Supplement).

Blanchard, O.J. and L.H. Summers (1988), "Beyond the natural rate hypothesis", *American Economic Review*, Papers and proceedings (May).

Bloom, D. and R. Freeman (1986), "The Youth Problem: age or generational crowding", NBER Working Paper, no.1878.

Bruno, M. (1986), "Aggregate supply and demand factors in OECD unemployment: an update", *Economica 53* (Supplement).

Bruno, M. and J.D. Sachs (1985), *Economics of Worldwide Stagflation*, Basil Blackwell, Oxford.

Burda, M.C. (1988), "Is there a capital shortage in Europe?", *Weltwirtschaftliches Archiv*, (March).

Calmfors, Lars and John Driffill (1988), "Centralization of wage bargaining and macroeconomic performance", *Economic Policy*, April.

Chan-Lee, James H., David T. Coe and Menahem Prywes (1987), "Microeconomic Changes and Macroeconomic Wage Disinflation in the 1980s" *OECD Economic Studies*, no.8 (Spring).

Carruth, A. and A. Oswald (1987), "Wage Inflexibility in Britain", *Oxford Bulletin of Economics and Statistics*, February 1987.

Coe, D.T. (1985), "Nominal wages, the NAIRU and wage flexibility", *OECD Economic Studies* no.5, Autumn.

Coe, D.T. (1988), "Tests for hysteresis in aggregate wage equations" in Rod Cross (Ed.) *Unemployment, Hysteresis and the Natural Rate Hypothesis*, (Blackwell, 1988).

Coen, Robert M. and Bert G. Hickman (1987), "Keynesian and Classical unemployment in four countries", *Brookings Papers on Economic Activity* 1:1987.

Cornwall, John L. (1988), "A reappraisal of Phillips curve analysis", Department of Economics, Dalhousie University, (mimeo). Forthcoming, Oxford: Basil Blackwell.

Danthine, Jean-Pierre and Jean-Christian Lambelet (1987), "The Swiss recipe: Conservative policies aren't enough!", *Economic Policy*, 5.

Darby, M.R., J. Haltiwanger, and M. Plant (1985), "Unemployment rate dynamics and persistent unemployment under rational expectations", *American Economic Review* 75 (September).

Emerson, M. (1988) "Regulation or deregulation of the labour market: Policy regimes for recruitment and dismissal of employees in the industrialised countries", *European Economic Review* (April).

Englander, S. and A. Mittelstadt (1988), "Total factor productivity: macroeconomic and structural aspects of the slowdown", *OECD Economic Studies* no. 10 (Spring).

Flanagan, R.J. (1986), "Labour market barriers to economic growth", Mimeo.

Flanagan, R.J. (1988), "Unemployment as a hiring problem", *OECD Economic Studies*, no.11 (Autumn).

Freeman, R. (1988), "Evaluating the European view that the United States has no unemployment problem", *American Economic Review*, Papers and proceedings (1988).

Gordon, R.J. (1987), "Productivity, wages and prices inside and outside manufacturing in the United States, Japan and Europe", *European Economic Review* (April).

Gordon, R.J. (1988), "The role of wages in the inflation process", *American Economic Review*, Papers and proceedings (May).

Grignon, L. and K. Moray (1988), "Geographic labour mobility in Canada", Department of Finance (Canada), Working Paper no.88-1

Klau, F. and A. Mittelstadt (1986), "Labour market flexibility", *OECD Economic Studies*, no.6 (Spring).

Kohli, U. and C. Ryan (1986), "Australian business investment: a new look at the neoclassical approach", *Economic Record* (September).

Layard, P.R.G. and S.J. Nickell (1986), "Unemployment in Britain", *Economica* 53 (Supplement).

McCallum, J. (1986), "Unemployment in OECD countries in the 1980s", *Economic Journal* (December).

McCracken, P. *et al, Towards full employment and price stability* (OECD, Paris, 1977).

Mendelsohn, S. (1988), "The status of wrongful termination litigation in the United States and its effect on the employment relationship", OECD, Department of Manpower and Social Affairs (mimeo).

Newell, Andrew and James Symons (1987), "Corporatism, laissez-faire and the rise in unemployment", *European Economic Review*.

OECD (1977), *Economic Outlook*, Paris.

OECD (1986a), *Flexibility in the labour market: the current debate*, Paris.

OECD (1986b), *Employment Outlook*, Paris.

OECD (1987), *Employment Outlook*, Paris.

OECD (1987b), *Structural adjustment and economic performance*, Paris.

OECD (1988a), *Economic Outlook 43*, (June), Paris.

OECD (1988b), *Why economic policies change course*, Paris.

OECD (1988c), *Employment Outlook*, Paris.

Sachs, J.D. (1979), "Wages, profits and macroeconomic adjustment: a comparative study", *Brookings Papers on Economic Activity*, vol.9.

Sachs, J.D. (1983), "Real wages and unemployment in OECD countries", *Brookings Papers on Economic Activity*, vol.13.

Chapter 3

FINANCIAL MARKETS:
THE CHALLENGES OF MODERNISATION

Introduction

Since the late-1970s OECD financial markets have been undergoing what is perhaps an unprecedented degree of structural transformation. The scale of financial operations has expanded, sometimes dramatically, with new markets and instruments emerging. What distinguishes these developments from earlier innovation and change are the extent of their geographic coverage and the broad similarity of direction (convergence) taken by policy reforms in this area. At the same time, however, individual country experience has been extraordinarily varied, reflecting diversity in initial conditions, in the strategies adopted by local financial institutions and in the role played by government policy. While these developments should be viewed in the context of the broader trend toward a less interventionist approach to economic management, whereby greater scope is being accorded market forces in decision making, the pervasiveness of financial market reform has been striking.

The repercussions of these profound modifications in the structure and functioning of financial markets have been wide-ranging. Their implications for macroeconomic performance are difficult to quantify, but by according an enhanced role to market forces, they should contribute to more efficient resource allocation and a higher level of income. However, the conduct of monetary policy has at times been made more difficult and the degree of systemic risk may have increased. This latter aspect, which reflects a conflict between the efficiency and stability objectives facing regulatory reform, has highlighted the need for adaptation, and greater international coordination, of prudential supervision.

The present Chapter covers the main findings of Country Surveys which have analysed financial-market developments between mid-1984 and the beginning of

1988 (that is, 18 of the 24 OECD Member countries plus *Yugoslavia*)[1]. It follows the pattern of these Surveys, appraising in turn:

i) The *structural factors* (whether internal to the financial sector or of external origin) which have exerted pressures on the financial markets, thereby leading to reform and change;

ii) The *salient features* of developments, including regulatory and policy reform, and the functioning of financial markets;

iii) Some *implications for economic performance* in respect to the efficiency of intermediation, the operation of monetary policy, and the supervisory problems posed by deregulation and the associated proliferation of financial innovations, before drawing together some concluding observations in the final section.

Pressures for change

Three broad forces have been generally identified in Country Surveys as importantly conditioning to varying degree the process of change in financial markets:

i) Shifts in *sectoral financial balances* – including the increased financing needs of governments and, during the 1980s, the strengthening of corporate-sector finances – have implied a redirection of net credit flows among sectors and shifts in relative supplies of assets;

ii) The interaction between an *uncertain economic environment* – characterised by high and variable inflation as well as interest- and exchange-rate volatility – and advances in communications *technology* have provided a powerful stimulus to financial-market integration and competition, and led to the spawning of new financial instruments;

iii) The progressive *globalisation of financial activities,* leading to stiffer competition among financial centres and greater asset substitutability across frontiers.

Shifting patterns of financial balances

Shifts in the size and pattern of *sectoral financial balances* imply pressures on the structure of financial intermediaries to the extent that established financial asset and liability balance sheets differ between sectors. Two broad trends have been observed in a number of countries (Diagram 3.1). First, the public sector has increased its demands on the financial system reflecting a redirection of savings flows. With few exceptions (notably *Switzerland*, where government borrowing requirements have been relatively stable and of limited size), financing needs increased substantially during the 1970s (*Italy, Canada, Sweden, Denmark* and *the United Kingdom*). In several cases, these requirements persisted or even increased in the early 1980s (*United States* and *Portugal*). Chapter 5 discusses these developments in more detail. Second, a number of countries have witnessed a sustained reduction in non-financial corporations' net demand for outside funds during the 1980s. While recourse to external borrowing reflects *inter alia* traditional attitudes and the depth of capital markets (Table 3.1), companies' reduced demands have resulted from both the recovery of profits and the high levels of real interest rates. The latter has both discouraged investment in physical assets and provided strong incentives for strengthening balance sheets by substituting equity for debt. This turnaround in the non-financial corporate sector's financial situation has been marked in *Canada*, where profits recovered sharply after a wave of take-overs and the 1981-82 recession, as well as in the *Netherlands* and, to a lesser extent, *Italy*, countries with a traditionally high degree of dependence on external funding of investment. In the *United Kingdom* – where exploitation of North Sea oil has also been an important factor – the enterprise sector became a net supplier of savings early in the 1980s.

The changing sectoral financial balances had a differential impact across countries. Where money and capital markets were relatively under-developed at the beginning of the 1970s (e.g. *Italy* and *Sweden*), monetisation of public-sector deficits proved an obstacle to the effective use of monetary policy. This circumstance provided strong incentives for governments to make good the deficiency by fostering the development of active capital markets (OECD, forthcoming). Attractive rates of return on government debt have found public favour and led to substantial modifications in the banking sector's role (see Committee of the Italian Treasury Ministry, 1987). *Spain* and *Portugal* experienced a similar development at the beginning of the 1980s.

Where capital markets were already well-developed and efficient, financing of the public debt has had less effect on intermediaries' activities. In *Canada*, for instance, the public did not have an equivalent pent-up demand for portfolio diversification, and the role of intermediaries has even been strengthened. The latter have been able to absorb the securities issued by the public sector, while offering assets compatible with the ultimate lenders' preferences (see Department of Finance Canada (1985)). In the *United States*, the supply of government debt has, to a certain extent, been the counterpart to the financing of the external deficit by foreigners.

DIAGRAM 3.1

SECTOR FINANCIAL BALANCES
Per cent of GDP

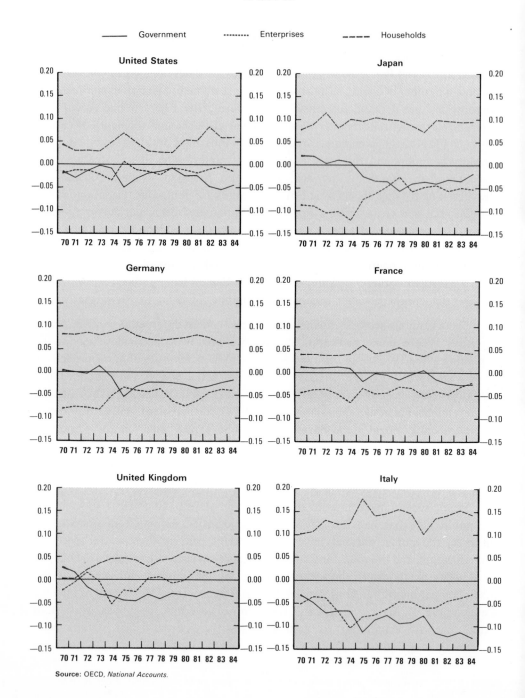

Source: OECD, *National Accounts*.

DIAGRAM 3.1 (continued)

SECTOR FINANCIAL BALANCES
Per cent of GDP

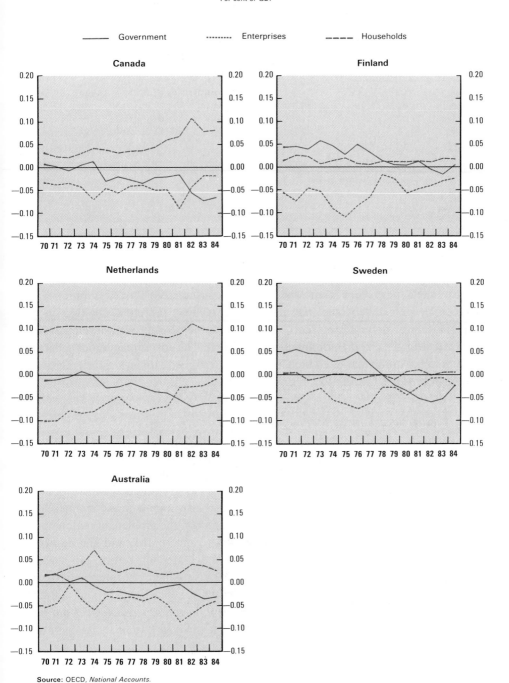

——— Government   ·········· Enterprises   - - - - Households

Source: OECD, *National Accounts.*

Table 3.1. **Corporate sector self-financing ratio**[1]

Per cent

	1970	1975	1980	1983	1984	1985	1986
United States[2]	79.2	111.1	82.1	104.0	90.7	103.7	103.6
Japan	81.2	40.9	57.3	74.4	67.6	58.0	..
France[3]	74.3	57.8	53.1	57.0	74.0	58.1	..
Italy	57.1	36.7	36.8	94.6	..	..	..
United Kingdom[4]	70.1	51.2	88.0	72.5	64.8	342.1	..
Canada	78.4	80.3	74.8	94.9	92.2	91.7	81.8
Finland	53.0	34.1	63.1	71.3	100.3	79.1	..
Netherlands[5]	..	..	64.9	116.6	112.3	107.3	..
Norway	..	33.3	66.4	100.9	90.1	101.2	..
Spain	..	..	..	31.1	44.2	61.7	..
Sweden	..	..	86.6	115.4	100.8	99.2	..

1. Retained income before depreciation and provisions as a share of investment in non-financial assets.
2. Includes also the net capital transfers received.
3. Industrial enterprises.
4. Large companies.
5. Manufacturing industries.
Source: OECD, *Non-financial Enterprises Financial Statements,* Paris, 1987.

While doubts have been expressed as to the sustainability of this process, the burgeoning public debt has not *per se* necessitated profound changes in the configuration of domestic markets. In *Denmark* the already well-developed bond market provided a channel for financing the deficit. The government quickly became a major issuer in the market, which in turn has expanded into one of the (relatively) largest in the OECD area.

A more uncertain economic environment

The more *uncertain economic environment* engendered by high and variable rates of inflation in the 1970s and early 1980s as well as the volatility of both interest and exchange rates (in comparison to the period prior to 1973) elicited demands on the part of economic agents for more flexible financial instruments to accommodate the attendant increase in risk (Diagram 3.2). For example, the problem of matching the maturity structures of assets and liabilities was exacerbated, and the degree of uncertainty surrounding expected (ex-post) real rates of return on financial investments increased. This supplemented demands on financial intermediaries for active cash management services by increasingly sophisticated (and affluent) household and corporate clients. In related developments, *technological advances* resulting from the application of new computer technologies to financial operations

DIAGRAM 3.2

INFLATION, INTEREST AND EXCHANGE RATES

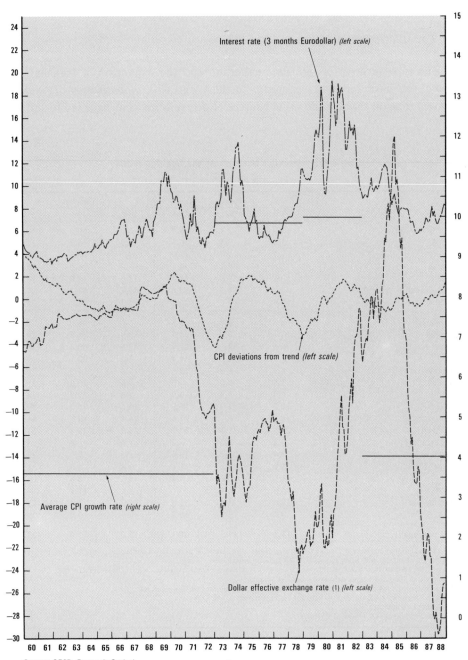

Source: OECD, *Economic Outlook*.
1. Deviation from 1970: Q1.

(Revell, 1983) allowed the introduction of new instruments and facilities together with the creation of new markets. This gave further impetus to change in the patterns of intermediation and the role of financial intermediaries[2].

The internationalisation of markets

The rapid growth of international trade and the expansion of transnational corporations have acted as a stimulus to the progressive *globalisation of financial markets*[3]. The oil shocks, and other sources of disequilibria that have led to shifts in

Table 3.2.   **Foreign business of the banking sector**[1]

Per cent of balance sheet

	Assets			Liabilities		
	1970	1980	1986	1970	1980	1986
United States A[2]	2.9	12.1	8.4	6.2	10.2	8.2
Japan A	3.7	3.5	6.6	3.1	6.5	11.3
Germany G	8.7	9.7	13.0	5.6	8.7	·8.0
France A	15.8	30.1	34.1	17.0	26.0	33.1
Italy D	12.6	9.6	11.9	12.6	13.0	17.0
United Kingdom A[3]	46.1	64.6	64.6	49.7	67.3	77.4
Canada C	19.8	19.6	20.2	14.3	22.4	28.4
Australia B[4]	0.6	0.4	3.5	—	1.0	7.6
Austria A	10.7	23.0	28.7	9.9	26.5	29.6
Belgium A	36.6	52.7	61.9	42.6	60.4	76.3
Denmark A	6.7	24.5	39.4	7.0	22.1	39.3
Finland A	4.3	8.9	19.5	5.6	14.2	28.8
Greece D	3.5	6.2	8.0	4.6	20.2	25.0
Iceland E	1.0	2.9	3.5	2.6	14.5	24.3
Ireland A[5]	35.7	42.7	16.0	30.1	45.2	30.7
Luxembourg G	84.5	96.7	97.6	74.4	89.3	86.1
Netherlands A	27.0	35.1	35.7	25.9	35.8	31.9
New Zealand F	7.2	7.2	6.2	1.0	2.5	5.5
Norway A	7.4	2.1	10.9	5.5	7.3	23.7
Portugal E	5.6	9.2	11.7	0.8	3.0	1.2
Spain A	3.5	7.2	9.4	4.2	12.8	9.8
Sweden A	4.9	8.8	—	3.8	15.9	—
Switzerland A	37.6	35.5	33.5	32.2	23.9	23.4
Turkey A	0.7	2.3	10.2	0.9	0.7	19.1
OECD average[6]	13.1	18.2	21.3	13.0	20.0	25.4

1.   A = Deposit money banks; B = Trading and savings banks; C = Chartered banks; D = Commercial banks; E = Commercial banks and Savings banks; F = Trading banks; G = All banking institutions.
2.   From 1984, certain commercial bank foreign assets and liabilities previously reported on gross basis are now net.
3.   From March 1983, forty-three new banks included in data.
4.   From December 1984, exclude Australian dollar denominated position with non-residents.
5.   Prior to December 1982, the data include non-resident offices of the banks.
6.   Excluding Luxembourg.
Source: IMF, *International Financial Statistics.*

the pattern and magnitude of current-account deficits, reinforced the demand for intermediation and a range of other financial services. However, with the widespread liberalisation of international capital movements, the growth of financial markets has far outstripped that of international trade. Over the period 1973-1985, foreign and international bond issues rose from the equivalent of 1.6 to 9.4 per cent of world exports, while total medium- and long-term funds raised in the international markets grew from 5.5 to 16.0 per cent[4]. Participation in the globalisation process has been more recent in countries which earlier had enforced strict exchange controls. In Europe, the EC objective for unification of capital markets by 1992 is providing fresh impetus.

The globalisation process is reflected in the structure of banks' balance sheets. In the great majority of countries the relative importance of foreign assets and liabilities has grown. They have long represented a sizable part of banks' balance sheets in *Belgium, Luxembourg* and the *United Kingdom* as well as, though to a somewhat lesser extent, in *Ireland,* the *Netherlands* and *Switzerland* (Table 3.2). *United States* banks' foreign assets and liabilities experienced a remarkable expansion during the 1970s and early 1980s. However, after reaching the highest absolute value in the OECD area, they declined in both absolute and relative (to total balance sheet) terms, with the emergence of the LDC debt crisis and increased emphasis on off-balance-sheet activities. Substantial increases in foreign activity have been registered in *Australia, Denmark, Finland, France, Japan, Norway* and *Turkey*, whereas in *Italy, Sweden* and *Canada* foreign assets' share in total banking business has remained broadly stable.

General overview of change in financial markets[5]

Within the context of a widespread reappraisal by governments of interventionist approaches to economic policy management, the structural pressures outlined above have led to the liberalisation of regulatory systems and to important changes in some countries' methods of monetary policy implementation. Generally, official attitudes have been sympathetic toward liberalisation, given increased awareness of the costs attaching to established regulatory systems and of the need to ensure the international competitiveness of domestic financial institutions and markets. The most notable features of reform, which has been far-reaching virtually throughout the OECD, include:)i progressive abolition of constraints on the operation of market forces in interest-rate determination, with decreased reliance being made on administrative controls and portfolio constraints; *ii)* a shift towards market-based monetary-policy implementation; *iii)* liberalisation of entry constraints, including erosion of barriers between intermediaries (desegmentation), with an ensuing increase in competition. At the same time, more specific measures have been taken in a number of countries to promote the development of capital markets. A major underlying objective of reform has been to foster competition and raise efficiency.

The nature and extent of structural change has been importantly conditioned by individual countries' "starting points". Particularly where relatively restrictive regulatory and/or policy regimes applied, the structure of markets has altered, sometimes radically and within a relatively short lapse of time (*Japan, Italy, France, New Zealand, Denmark* and *Sweden*). However, in some such countries (*Portugal, Spain* and *Turkey*) changes have been more marginal, though gaining momentum. Where financial markets were already operating virtually free of constraints in respect to both the quantity and pricing of credit flows (*Switzerland, Germany, Austria, Canada* and, in some respects, the *United Kingdom*), regulatory amendments have mainly aimed at strengthening domestic institutions in the face of growing international competition, and at adapting to ongoing financial innovation.

Improving policy neutrality and fostering competition

The Country Surveys note a decreasing reliance on direct controls over credit volume and interest-rates. This shift away from selective controls in favour of market-based modes of monetary-policy operation was inspired by a growing appreciation of the disadvantages associated with prolonged maintenance of such measures. Among these drawbacks are the high cost and administrative difficulties of enforcing credit or interest-rate controls which anyway have had only limited success in achieving desired ends, given their relative inefficiency as policy instruments. The fungibility of credit, the emergence of "grey" markets, and the exploitation of regulatory loopholes made effective control more and more cumbersome as well as precarious, necessitating ever-increasing degrees of administrative complexity (*Italy* and *Denmark*)[6].

In relatively few cases (*Iceland, Portugal, Yugoslavia,* and *Greece*) does the free play of market forces seem to remain seriously hampered by institutional constraints, though limited reforms have been introduced in some areas in these countries. In *Italy* the shift to indirect control of monetary aggregates began in 1982, following recognition of the drawbacks attaching to prolonged direct control over bank credit. Ceilings on the latter were discontinued in 1983, although they were briefly reintroduced at the end of 1985 and again more recently in response to exchange rate pressures. In *Denmark* and *Sweden* similar reforms were instituted during the early 1980s. In the first-mentioned country, the structure of quantitative controls had become increasingly complex in the course of the 1970s, with the perceived need successively to extend their ambit to an ever-wider array of intermediaries, as credit sources diversified in response to the authorities' actions and a "grey market" emerged. Accordingly, quantitative credit controls were abandoned over a five-year period, and replaced in 1985 by ceilings on deposit growth. In *Sweden*, the move away from quantitative controls was facilitated by the creation of a money market, providing the central bank with a tool to influence interest rates through open-market operations. In *France* the decision to phase out quantitative credit controls was taken in autumn 1986.

A prime objective of regulatory reform over the past ten years or so has been to foster *competition*, both by allowing domestic intermediaries to undertake new activities (de-specialisation) and by liberalising non-resident firms' access to home markets. Banks have moved, or have been authorised to do so, into areas from which they had traditionally been absent (for instance, into securities trading in the *United Kingdom* and *Canada*, and into medium-term lending and merchant banking in *Italy*), while other institutions, previously prevented from offering services related to the provision of means of payment, are now doing so (*Canada*). In countries where universal banking systems already prevailed (*Germany, Switzerland, Austria, France, Denmark* and *Sweden*), the role of capital markets has been reinforced[7]. Financial interpenetration has thus been a key feature of institutional change, although considerations have at times induced the authorities to adopt a cautious attitude. In the *United States*, within the limitations imposed by the Glass-Steagall Act concerning the separation of banking and securities trading in their domestic operations, banks have been able to engage in certain securities-related business via subsidiaries of bank holding companies. In *Japan* banks have been allowed since 1981 to sell central-government bonds and to deal more generally in public bonds. Within this context of rapid change, certain important issues remain open; for instance, in the *United States*, where numerous legislative constraints have been removed over the past few years, important questions concerning the structure of financial institutions and their permitted range of activities are under discussion.

Access to domestic markets by foreign financial institutions has been increased substantially in the past few years (Diagram 3.3), though rather unevenly, as national regulatory attitudes differ widely[8]. The process of European Community unification has entailed liberalisation of entry requirements in *Italy, Denmark* and *France*, while *Australia, Finland, New Zealand, Portugal, Sweden* and *Turkey* have

DIAGRAM 3.3

RELATIVE IMPORTANCE OF FOREIGN-OWNED FINANCIAL INSTITUTIONS

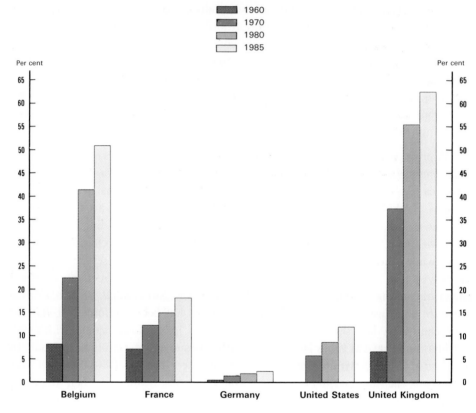

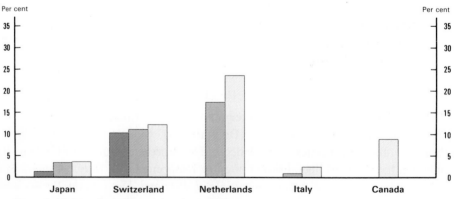

Source: Bank for international settlements, *Annual report*, 1987.

also liberalised the admission of foreign banks. After having maintained a total ban until 1980, *Canada* now admits new foreign bank subsidiaries – though subject to limitations on market share. Admission of foreign institutions is viewed as an important channel not only for enhancing contestability in a general sense, but also, and more specifically, for introducing modern financial techniques and instruments. Some countries require, however, reciprocity; that is, that their national institutions be accorded similar rights and privileges in foreign countries as these (and foreign institutions would) enjoy in the domestic market. Difficulties can arise where the restrictiveness of regulatory provisions (for example, in respect to bank branching and permitted range of operations) differs between two countries.

Financial market "deepening" and shifts in intermediation patterns

While the process of change within the OECD area has been far from uniform, financial "deepening" has been a common characteristic, as markets have expanded markedly faster than the stock of underlying real assets. This is reflected in the ratio of domestic financial assets to GDP which, even though it fails to capture off-balance-sheet activities, has reached new highs, exceeding six hundred per cent in the *United Kingdom* and *Japan*[9] (Table 3.3). While the ratio's absolute value reflects various country-specific factors (level of per-capita income, distribution of wealth, production structure, growth of government debt, etc.), it has tended to settle around broadly comparable values in countries with approximately similar characteristics. The tendency in *North America* for the ratio to decrease in the early 1970s, under conditions of generally negative real interest rates and increased inflation uncertainty, subsequently reversed.

Within the framework of overall financial deepening, patterns of intermediation have shifted. In many countries, inflation provoked a shift in both lenders' and borrowers' preferences towards shorter-term maturities, thereby exerting pressures on intermediaries – particularly those specialised in long-term fixed-interest assets (for instance, mortgage companies in *Canada* and Savings and Loans associations in the *United States*). On balance, the role of direct capital-market funding was boosted at the expense of traditional intermediaries' balance-sheet operations (Table 3.4). Thus, changes in intermediation patterns have been particularly marked in countries where capital markets were previously underdeveloped (e.g. *France* and *Italy*), or where rigid segmentation of financial intermediation had evolved as a result of regulation or custom. However, the share of investment outlays financed via bond and share issues has also increased in the *United States* and *Canada*, where capital markets were already well developed at the beginning of the 1970s (Table 3.5). The

Table 3.3. **Size of financial markets and degree of intermediation**[1]

Per cent

	1970	1975	1980	1983	1984	1985
United States						
TDFA/GDP	455.5	434.7	465.1	477.7	469.9	493.0
FAFI/TDFA	28.0	31.1	29.8	30.7	31.7	32.1
Japan						
TDFA/GDP	421.1	487.3	551.9	634.6	652.9	683.3
FAFI/TDFA	37.1	37.9	38.6	39.7	39.9	40.5
Germany						
TDFA/GDP	248.8	279.0	313.9	350.6	356.0	364.9
FAFI/TDFA	44.2	45.3	46.2	46.5	46.3	45.6
France						
TDFA/GDP	n.a.	355.7[2]	386.7	401.2	395.0	418.6
FAFI/TDFA	n.a.	41.5[2]	42.8	43.6	46.2	44.7
United Kingdom						
TDFA/GDP	n.a.	447.2	432.9	562.5	632.8	618.3
FAFI/TDFA	n.a.	33.4	34.0	35.9	36.5	38.3
Italy						
TDFA/GDP	281.1	340.4	359.9	316.0	334.0	381.8
FAFI/TDFA	35.6	39.3	31.6	35.8	32.7	29.0
Canada						
TDFA/GDP	404.2	385.3	437.3	439.1	433.9	443.8
FAFI/TDFA	33.3	36.0	39.0	39.5	39.1	39.2

1. TDFA = Total domestic financial assets.
   FAFI = Financial assets intermediated by financial institutions (excluding mutual funds, investment trusts, etc.). A value of FAFI/TDFA of 50 indicates that all financial transactions are intermediated by financial intermediaries.
2. 1976.

Sources: Canada: *The National Balance Sheet Accounts, 1961-1985,* Statistics Canada, Ottawa 1986; Italy: *Relazione del Governatore della Banca d'Italia,* Rome, various years; United States: *Flow of Funds Accounts - Financial Assets and Liabilities - Year-End, 1962-1985,* Board of Governors of the Federal Reserve System, Washington D.C. 1986; Germany: *Monthly Report of the Deutsche Bundesbank,* Frankfurt, various issues; United Kingdom: *Financial Statistics,* Central Statistical Office, various issues; France: Banque de France, *Statistiques financières annuelles. Séries rétrospectives* (1976 to 1986); Japan, *Annual Report on National Accounts.*

boom in stock markets until late-1987 is reflected in the sharp increase in the share of funds raised on capital markets in the 1980s. *Japan,* whose ratio has remained virtually stable since the late 1970s, emerges as a clear exception. On the other hand, Table 3.4 shows that the growth of intermediated transactions in *Germany* and *Italy* has been slightly slower than that of total domestic financial assets during the 1980s. The rise in the ratio between these two aggregates has broadly levelled off in *Canada,* but risen in *France, Japan,* the *United States* and particularly in the *United Kingdom.*

Table 3.4. **Issues of securities in domestic credit flows**[1]

Per cent

	1970/72	1973/75	1976/78	1979/81	1983/85
United States	40	36	37	33	50
Japan	23	26	38	39	38
Germany	21	23	27	24	36
France	24	22	21	25	41
Italy	30	27	35	18	51
United Kingdom	17	14	28	29	35
Canada	45	30	35	37	52

1. Value of net bond and share issues in per cent of total domestic credit.
Source: OECD (1987), *Financial Accounts of OECD Countries,* Paris.

Table 3.5. **Issues of securities as percentage of investment**[1]

Per cent

		1970	1975	1980	1983	1984	1985
United States	A	6.6	6.4	6.1	10.3	3.1	4.2
	B	25.4	23.1	14.3	14.8	14.2	20.3
Japan	A	6.4	4.8	3.2	3.4	2.4	3.8
	B	8.7	11.4	5.9	7.1	9.0	9.0
Germany	A	3.1	3.8	3.2	3.4	2.4	3.8
	B	4.7	3.0	3.6	3.4	3.2	6.3
France	A	5.7	4.5	4.2	9.4	9.6	12.5
	B		6.2[2]	6.9	13.7	13.8	16.8
United Kingdom	A	0.9	10.2	3.8	6.7	3.7	9.0
	B	5.2	11.5	4.6	7.9	4.6	11.3
Canada	A		3.6	8.7	15.6	9.8	13.0
	B		12.3	13.5	19.1	12.9	18.8

1. Percentage of private non-residential gross fixed investment financed by gross issues of: A. Shares, B. Shares and bonds.
2. 1976.
Sources: OECD, *National Account Statistics,* and *Financial Statistics,* Paris, 1986.

Initiatives have also been adopted – with more or less success – to promote markets for corporate securities. Measures to encourage investment in equities by individuals have been taken in the *United Kingdom* and *France*. Despite action taken in a number of countries to promote second-tier markets, small and medium-sized firms' access to capital-market financing remains generally limited in Europe. A possible exception is the development of the Unlisted Securities Market (USM) in the *United Kingdom* after 1980. Attitudes towards *venture capital* vary. In the *United Kingdom*, for instance, tax incentives have fostered the creation of a large number of venture capital firms, whereas in *Switzerland* no evidence of market failure has been found justifying public-policy intervention in this area.

The Country Surveys have pointed out that corporate financing strategies are importantly influenced by the depth of capital markets, traditional local attitudes towards widespread share ownership (stressed in the Swiss Survey) and by fiscal considerations. For example, countries with universal banking systems, or where for historical reasons domestic capital markets (in particular, stock exchanges) were not an important source of financing (*Germany, Switzerland* and *Japan*), are characterised by generally higher debt/equity ratios than countries with specialised financial markets (*United States, Canada* and the *United Kingdom*) (Table 3.6). However, the creation of new instruments and markets has supplemented the traditional menu of assets/liabilities, thus broadening corporations' scope for managing *inter alia* interest and exchange rate exposure and enhancing liquidity. Table 3.7 surveys the principal financial innovations and the main purposes which they serve. Futures, options, swaps, and floating-rate contracts have been devised to hedge against interest-rate fluctuations. Other innovations, for example, lock in high yields (warrant bonds carrying an option to acquire additional debt at fixed yields), take advantage of tax rules ("stripped" bonds which separate coupon and principal payments) or circumvent regulatory provisions (short-term annuities offered by insurance companies in *Canada*). Securitization of existing assets has expanded rapidly in some countries; the value of mortgage-backed securities in the United States now exceeds one-third of all outstanding mortgage loans[10].

Table 3.6. **Debt/equity ratios of the non-financial corporate sector**[1]

	1966-1973	1974-1979	1980	1981	1982	1983	1984	1985
Canada	0.99	1.22	1.14	1.27	1.34	1.14	1.12	1.08[2]
United States	0.54	0.96	0.77	0.92	0.87	0.78	0.90	0.83
Japan	3.08	3.31	3.14	2.91	2.92	2.68	2.11	1.82[2]
Germany[3]	2.38	3.36	3.85	4.13	4.11	3.48	3.42	2.39
France	1.17[4]	1.33	1.23	1.40	1.55	1.56	..	..
United Kingdom	0.67	1.38	1.13	1.23	1.03	1.87	0.74	0.70[2]

1. Gross liabilities excluding equity and trade credit as a proportion of equity at market prices, except for France and Canada where equity is at book values.
2. Estimated.
3. All enterprises excluding housing.
4. 1970-1973.
Sources: National balance-sheet data and OECD, *Financial Statistics,* Paris, 1987.

Table 3.7. **Nature and motives of financial innovation**[1]

Innovation:	A			B	C	D	E	F
	(a)	(b)	(c)					
A. On-balance-sheet								
1. Price-risk transfer:								
Adjustable rate mortgages				X				
Floating rate loans				X				
Back-to-back loans								X
2. Credit-risk transfer:								
Asset sales without recourse				X				
Loan swaps				X				
Securitized assets				X				X
Transferable loan contracts				X		X		
3. Liquidity enhancement:								
Sweep accounts and other money management techniques	X							
Negotiable money market instruments	X					X		
Money-market mutual funds	X				X			
4. Credit generation:								
Zero-coupon bonds	X		X	X				
"Junk" bonds								X
Equity participation financing						X		
5. Equity generation:								
Mandatory convertible debentures						X		
B. Off-balance-sheet								
Futures				X				
Options and loan caps					X			
Swaps						X		
Forward rate agreements				X				
Note issuance facilities				X				
Credit-enhancing guarantees on securities								X

1. The main motives for innovations are: A: Inflation-related: *(a)* Level of interest rates; *(b)* General price level; *(c)* Tax effects; B: Interest-rate volatility; C: Technological advances; D: Legislative initiative; E: Internationalization; F: Other (exchange rate variability).
Sources: Adapted from Bank for International Settlements (1986), *Recent Innovations in International Banking*, April; W.L. Silber (1983), "The process of financial innovation" in *American Economic Association Papers and Proceedings*, May.

Innovation and deregulation have allowed households to diversify portfolios and raise the level of returns – particularly where interest-rate ceilings had previously been imposed on deposits – to levels closer aligned to market rates. At times, substantial portfolio shifts out of money and deposits into short-term bills, bonds and shares have been recorded (for instance, in *Italy*), although a more pervasive trend has been the increased incidence in households' portfolios of claims on institutional

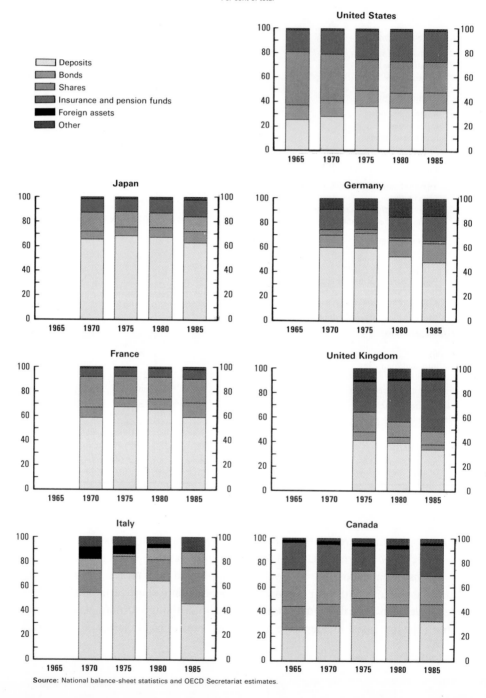

DIAGRAM 3.4

COMPOSITION OF HOUSEHOLDS ASSETS
Per cent of total

Deposits
Bonds
Shares
Insurance and pension funds
Foreign assets
Other

United States

Japan

Germany

France

United Kingdom

Italy

Canada

Source: National balance-sheet statistics and OECD Secretariat estimates.

investors (Diagram 3.4). For example, the introduction of mutual funds has led to important shifts in household portfolios in *Italy* and contributed to a surge in stock market activity there.

Growth of indebtedness

The accumulation of debt has given rise to concern in some countries (see Bank for International Settlements, 1987). Diagram 3.5 reveals a rather disparate picture

DIAGRAM 3.5

GROSS LIABILILTIES BY SECTOR
Ratio to GDP

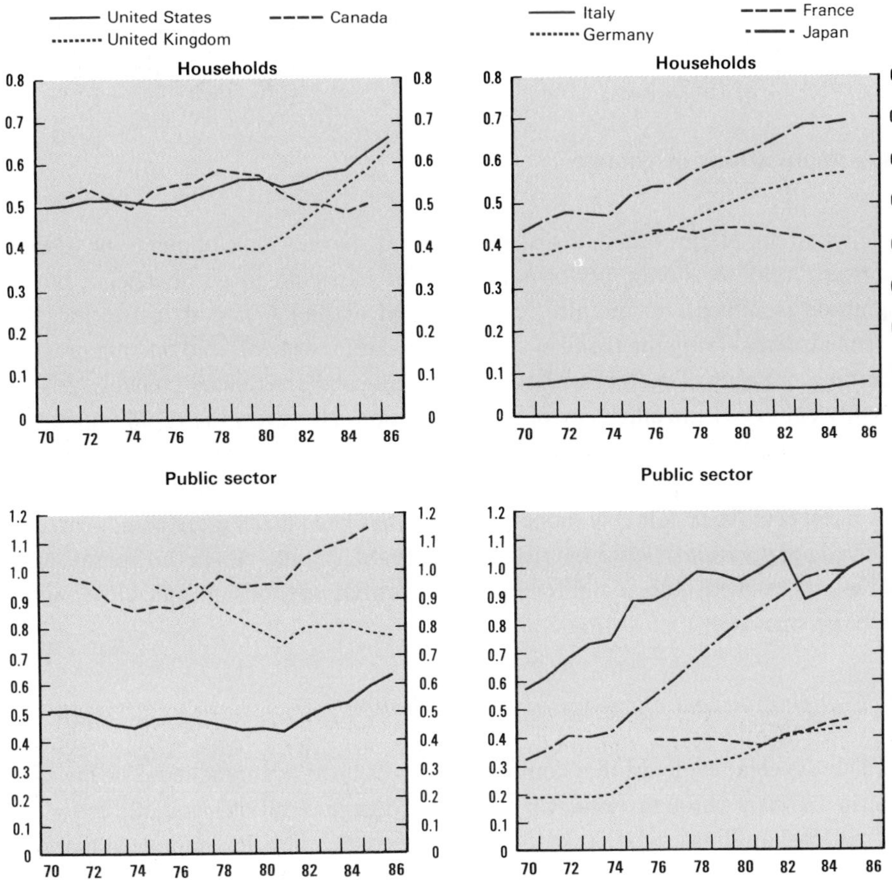

Source: See Table 3.6.

95

across the major OECD economies. Public-sector gross liabilities rose rapidly during the 1970s in *Italy* and *Japan*, and during the 1980s in the *United States* and *Canada*. On the other hand, the ratio of public liabilities to GDP in the *United Kingdom* has generally been declining since the mid-1970s. These patterns contrast strikingly with those observed for the household (personal) sector. In the *United Kingdom*, the household gross indebtedness ratio soared by 25 percentage points between 1980 and 1986 (helping fuel buoyant growth of private consumption), to reach a level close to that in the *United States*, where an upward movement has been evident since the mid-1970s. In *Germany* and, more particularly *Japan* which now has the highest level of household indebtedness (relative to GDP) among the major industrial countries, a clear rising trend is discernible throughout the 1970s and 1980s. The ratio has remained stable in *Italy*, where the level of indebtedness remains remarkably low by international standards, and in *France*. Finally, in *Canada*, households have generally reduced their debt ratio since the late 1970s, following several years of strong build-up.

Some implications of change

The effect of the broad thrust of financial market developments on OECD countries' "real" economic performance can be expected to be beneficial, but its magnitude is difficult to quantify. Competition among financial institutions has sharpened, diversifying the menu of services available to clients and putting pressure on earnings margins. Together with the dismantling of discretionary controls, this has probably enhanced the efficiency of intermediation. However, the rapid increase in the share of resources absorbed by the financial sector, to which the proliferation of new services and products has contributed, has drawn criticism. Furthermore, in certain respects the task facing monetary policy has been made more complicated. A perceived aggravation of systemic risks has spotlighted trade-offs in the liberalisation process and evoked both a tightening in prudential supervision and closer international cooperation.

Competition and efficiency of intermediation

There is clear evidence that competitive forces have strengthened. The lowering of entry barriers through regulatory reform (desegmentation) and reductions in information-handling costs thanks to technological advances has enhanced markets' contestability. The last-mentioned factor has facilitated direct dealing between borrowers and lenders and thereby favoured securitization, while eroding the traditional advantages enjoyed by established intermediaries. Banks are in many cases no longer the sole suppliers of certain financial services. In *Canada*, a number of financial intermediaries have penetrated the mortgage, insurance and deposit markets, which are now characterised by a high degree of competition. In *Switzerland* interest-rate cartels, though tolerated, have proved largely ineffective in arresting market trends, and the Competition Commission has found satisfactory levels of competition in individual markets.

The relatively high degree of concentration in the banking sector may be in part attributable to controls which have severely limited competition. A small number of institutions (usually around three to six) typically hold between one-third and one-half of total sector assets (Table 3.8). The most important exceptions are *Germany*, with its universal banking system covering a multitude of competing banking institutions, and the *United States*, where legislation originating in the 1930s has long prevented interstate branching, thereby reducing the scope for concentration. However, as there is some evidence that the provision of banking services may be

Table 3.8. **International comparison of bank concentration**

United States (1985)	Out of 13 739 commercial banks, the largest five control 12.8 per cent of total assets, the largest ten control 20.3 per cent, and the largest 100 control 57.5 per cent. Adding the assets of thrift institutions to those of the commercial banks reduces these percentages to 7.5 per cent, 11.8 per cent, and 33.5 per cent, respectively.
Japan (1986)	Out of 87 commercial banks, thirteen city banks control 56.7 per cent of total assets.
Germany (1987)	Out of 316 commercial banks, the six largest control 37.9 per cent of total assets. Adding the assets of 4 232 other banking institutions which provide a comparable range of services reduces this percentage to 8.8 per cent.
France (1986)	Out of 367 banks, three control 41.7 per cent of all assets. Excluding foreign-affiliated banks, this percentage increases to 62.2 per cent. Adding the assets of mutual and savings banks reduces these percentages to 29.5 and 44.0, respectively.
Italy (1984)	The five largest banks control 34.4 per cent, and the ten largest 52.3 per cent of total deposits (based on a sample of 200 banks representing over 80 per cent of total assets of the banking system).
United Kingdom (1986)	The five largest banks control 45.6 per cent of the total assets of the monetary sector.
Canada (1985)	The four largest banks control 51.2 per cent of all deposits, and seven banks account for over 80 per cent of all deposits.

Sources: "Interstate Banking Developments", *Federal Reserve Bulletin;* Federation of Bankers Associations of Japan, *Analysis of Financial Statements of All Banks* (1st April 1986 to 31st March 1987); Deutsche Bundesbank, *Monthly Report*, Vol. 39, No. 8, August 1987; Commission Bancaire, *Rapport 1985*, France; *Abstract of Banking Statistics*, Committee of London and Scottish Bankers, Vol. 3, May 1986; Economic Council of Canada, *Competition and Solvency* (1986); Barina-Carletti (1986), "Changes in the degree of concentration of the Italian Banking System: An international comparison", *Research papers* No. 5, Banca Nazionale del Lavoro, Rome, November.

characterised by economies of scale and of scope, there could well be a "natural" tendency toward concentration[11]. In *Italy*, such considerations have shaped official policy towards branch banking for a number of years. But the figures are difficult to interpret since many of the faster-growing financial services – which produce a fee/commission income rather than interest – are unrelated to asset/liability holdings (i.e. off balance sheet).

Efficiency in intermediation has two dimensions – "cost-efficiency" (markets' capacity to perform their intermediation function at minimum resource cost) and "allocational" (capacity to allocate scarce savings to investments yielding the highest social returns). The regulatory controls applied to both banking and non-banking activities repressed competition and thus probably boosted intermediation costs by creating conditions conducive to excess profits and/or overmanning, although these effects were partly offset in many countries by controls over institutions' profitability. Furthermore, interest and quantitative credit controls distorted rates of return on investments in different sectors thereby contributing to allocational inefficiency. Liberalisation has clearly spurred competition and can, accordingly, be expected to have boosted the overall efficiency of financial intermediation.

As regards cost-efficiency, the sector's contribution to GDP and its share of total employment provide measures of the resources devoted to producing financial services. However, institutions provide a range of services not directly linked to the redistribution of savings among deficit and surplus sectors – indeed, over the more recent period, these probably have constituted the fastest-growing elements of their activities – but the data do not generally distinguish intermediation. Diagram 3.6 shows the sector's growing contribution to GDP; value-added in the mid-1980s approached or surpassed 5 per cent of GDP in a number of countries, following substantial increases since the beginning of the 1970s (*Austria, Germany, Iceland,* the *Netherlands, Spain, Switzerland* and the *United States*). *Denmark* appears to be an exception, and while financial activities' share in GDP in *Finland* has been increasing rapidly, it remains relatively small. Where national accounts data do not differentiate between financial and real-estate related services, growth of the combined sectors' share could suggest that increasing resources are being devoted to the provision of financial services. Sector employment has been expanding very rapidly in *Switzerland* within a context of stagnant overall employment growth. Similarly, in the *United Kingdom*, financial-sector employment has increased by one-fifth since the late-1970s, while other sectors (notably manufacturing) have contracted sharply. In these two last-mentioned countries the surplus on external transactions attributable to financial activities is substantial and rising – being equivalent to about 3 and over 2 per cent of GDP in 1985 respectively.

DIAGRAM 3.6

SHARE OF FINANCIAL ACTIVITIES IN GDP

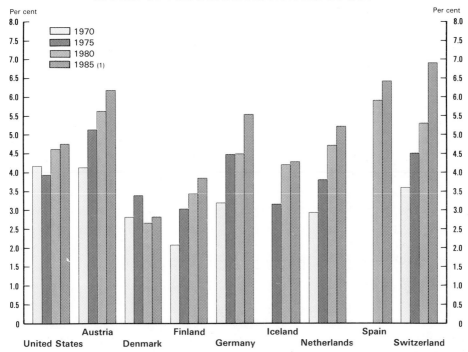

1. Excluding Netherlands and Switzerland, 1984.
Source: OECD, *National Accounts* and *Switzerland Survey.*

These macroeconomic data, together with "unreasonable" volatility of bond and stock prices, have been taken as evidence of "excessive" intermediation. According to this view, the spread of innovations and the growing number of financial markets (for example, options and futures) are absorbing real resources while contributing little to economic growth. By corollary, the imposition of a turnover tax on financial activities would reduce both "pointless intermediation" and the volatility of short-term capital flows (Tobin, 1984). However, both the premises and conclusions of this argument are disputed, and the OECD Country Surveys do not provide much support for it. It regards financial activities as essentially of a redistributive nature, and neglects the demand by both businesses and households for other financial services (for example, hedging facilities and international advisory services).

Focusing on banking, Country Surveys have made ample use of balance-sheet data, which are reasonably comparable across countries, to assess trends in costs and

Table 3.9. Income and cost margins in banking

Per cent of intermediated assets

Country	Interest margin[1]		Gross earnings[2]		Operating costs		Net earnings		Capital ratio	
	68/77	80/85	68/77	80/85	68/77	80/85	68/77	80/85	68/77	80/85
United States	2.20	3.21 +	3.52	4.27 +	2.29	2.90 +	1.23	1.36	6.04	5.97
Japan		1.45 −		1.72 −		1.22 −		0.50		2.36
Germany	1.97 +	2.35	2.26 +	3.25 +	1.57 +	2.10 +	0.69	1.13	3.42 −	4.02 +
France		2.68 −	3.53 −	3.17 −	2.68 −	2.16 −	0.86	1.01 +	2.57 −	2.54 −
Italy	2.71	3.21 −	3.50 +	4.43	2.25 +	2.89 +	1.25	1.53	2.16	3.82
United Kingdom		3.35 −		4.95		3.45 −		1.50		4.48
Canada		2.53	3.38	3.26	2.27	2.03 +	1.11 −	1.23	2.82 −	4.23 +
Austria	1.87 −	1.2	2.83 −	1.46 −	1.92 −	1.10 −	0.91 −	0.35	4.00 −	2.26
Belgium	1.00 −	1.72	3.63 −	2.18 −	2.89 +	1.82 −	0.74 −	0.36	3.83 −	2.50
Denmark	4.58	3.33	5.40	6.32	3.22 +	2.95 −	2.18	3.37	9.53 −	9.12
Greece		1.93 −		3.45 −		2.52		0.93 −		3.51
Norway	3.09 +	2.61	4.46 +	3.75	3.22 +	3.32	1.23	0.43 +	5.78 −	4.62
Portugal		2.31		3.43 −		2.09 +		1.34 −		5.91 −
Sweden	2.39	2.12	3.21	3.07	2.01	1.92	1.20	1.15	5.40 −	1.23
Switzerland	0.69	1.33 +	2.01 +	2.48 +	1.18 +	1.40	0.69	1.09 +	6.04 +	6.04
Average	1.84	2.34	3.43	3.31	2.18	2.37	1.08	1.05	4.50	4.37

1. Interest received *less* interest paid.
2. Interest margin *plus* fees and commissions.
Note: A plus or minus sign indicates a significant time trend within the subperiod. Data are not necessarily comparable across sub-periods or countries.
Sources: OECD (1987), *Bank Profitability*, and (1978) *Cost and Margins in Banking*, Paris; OECD estimates.

margins[12]. Table 3.9 reviews certain income measures as well as operating costs and capital in relation to banking-sector assets[13]. Although the picture is rather mixed, the data point to competitive pressures on earnings and costs during 1980-1985, a period of increasing financial liberalisation. As regards gross earning margins (GEM), which reflect the cost of all services supplied by the sector[14], more countries registered reductions in this period (*Austria, Belgium, France, Greece, Japan* and *Portugal*) than increases (*Switzerland, Germany,* and the *United States*). The decline in *Austria* was associated with the 1979 liberalisation of interest rate and branching regulations. While the *United States* data might reflect a pronounced shift towards off-balance sheet activities (particularly in response to pressures from the regulatory authorities to increase capital/assets ratios), the Swiss results seem to confirm an improvement in profitability since they are not accompanied by corresponding increases in the operating-cost ratio. Operating costs fell slightly in almost one-half of the countries listed (*Austria, Belgium, Denmark, France, Japan, Norway,* and the *United Kingdom*), but this was reflected in higher net earnings margins only in *France* and *Norway*; *Switzerland* also recorded improved earnings.

As regards trends in the cost effectiveness of direct capital-market financing, Table 3.10 shows that bond-issuing costs (relative to the value of funds raised) vary considerably across countries. Specialised financial systems tend to report lower costs than universal systems, possibly as a consequence of the thinness of capital markets in the latter. The fact that issuing costs in *Canada* do not compare favourably with those in the *United States* or even in *Australia* suggests the possible relative weakness of

Table 3.10. **Cost of bond issues in domestic markets**

1982-1983

Country	Maturity (years)	Total issue cost (as a percentage of the total issue)		
		Small	Medium	Large
United States	20	1.45	1.08	0.98
Japan	10	3.5 +	3.5 +	3.5 +
United Kingdom	20	1.83	1.15	1.08
Germany	10	3.6	3.6	3.6
Canada	10	2.5	2.1	1.75
Australia	5	1.57	1.61	1.60
France	10	3.3	3.2	3.2
Switzerland	10	2.85	3.0	3.0
Netherlands	10	2.7	2.5	2.4
Belgium	8	4.2	4.15	4.10

Note: A plus indicates a significant time trend within the period.
Source: J.R. Hakim, *Securities Markets,* IFC Occasional Papers, Capital Markets Series, Washington D.C. 1985.

competition in this area. Although Canadian capital markets are highly developed, important segments of the securities business were until recently isolated from international and domestic competition. Thus, the extensive deregulation and opening-up to competition which has taken place in this sector may have already altered the picture conveyed by Table 3.10.

Allocational efficiency and non-financial objectives

Detailed government regulation in the operation of financial markets was initially prompted by the large-scale banking failures of the 1920s and 1930s. Given the pervasive influence of financial markets on the "real" economy, the ambit of controls was subsequently expanded from ensuring the stability of the financial system to embracing macroeconomic policy objectives. Among these latter may be mentioned the reduction of regional disparities (e.g. *Italy*), encouragement of investment in areas of high social priority such as housing (e.g. *Australia, France, Iceland, Norway, Sweden,* and the *United States*) and agriculture (e.g. *France* and *Greece*), assisting industrial sectors in difficulty (e.g. *Italy, France* and *Greece*), favouring small- and medium-sized enterprises, and export aid (e.g. *Belgium* and *France*). Thus, regulation expanded from controlling financial market access/exit, delimiting institutions' permitted spheres of activity (segmentation) and establishing prudential standards, to steering savings towards perceived "priority" areas via a panoply of direct controls over the pricing, quantity and direction of credit flows (at times, rationalised as compensating for market failure). Discretionary action has included the imposition of interest-rate ceilings and the selective allocation of credit through portfolio constraints on intermediaries. The most favoured beneficiary has been the public sector which, through compulsory investment in government securities or use of the postal savings system, etc., has generally been able to obtain credit at below-market rates, implying a transfer of resources from savers to the public sector.

The Country Surveys cite numerous examples of the costs associated with using financial markets in pursuit of objectives external to the sector. For example, in *Spain* implicit subsidies due to mandatory banking-sector ratios – which could be taken as a measure of policy-induced distortions to resource allocation – were estimated at some 2.5 to 3 per cent of GDP in the late 1970s and early 1980s (Diagram 3.7). In *Greece*, subsidies to the agricultural sector through preferential interest rates alone have amounted at times to over 2 per cent of GDP. In some countries, influence over the direction of credit flows went hand-in-hand with credit ceilings as the main instruments of monetary policy. The allocative distortions generated by such

DIAGRAM 3.7

SPAIN: IMPLICIT SUBSIDIES THROUGH
COMPULSOR FINANCIAL RATIOS

Per cent of GDP

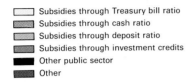

Subsidies through Treasury bill ratio
Subsidies through cash ratio
Subsidies through deposit ratio
Subsidies through investment credits
Other public sector
Other

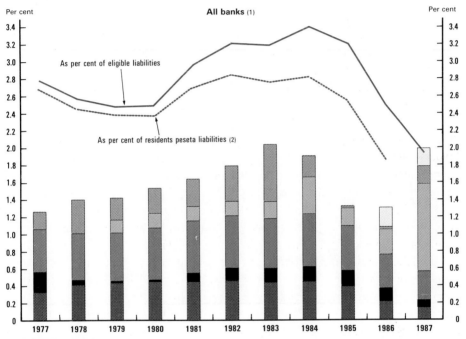

1. Excluding cooperatives.
2. Excluding interbank and Bank of Spain claims.
Sources: Bank of Spain, *Boletin Estadistico and Informe Annual,* Statistical Appendix data submitted by national authorities and OECD Secretariat estimates.

constraints are illustrated by Diagram 3.8 which shows that during periods of binding credit ceilings the regional dispersion of credit allocation in *Italy* has decreased (see Cottarelli *et. al.*, 1986). Another relevant example was noted for *Norway* where interest-rate controls had been deployed partly as a redistributive tool (i.e. housing subsidies). However, as a high net debt position was associated with high income, the low interest rate policy actually proved to be regressive. This was further compounded

DIAGRAM 3.8

CREDIT CONTROLS AND RESOURCE ALLOCATIONS
IN ITALY
Distortions by regions and by sectors

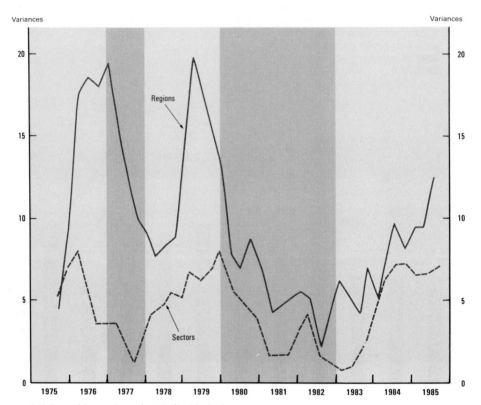

1. Variances of the annual rates of growth of bank lending by
sectors and by regions. Shaded are as indicate periods when
credit ceilings were binding.
Source: C. Cottarelli, G. Galli, P.M. Reedtz and G. Pittaluga
"Monetary policy through ceilings on bank lending", *Economic
Policy No. 3,* 1986.

by the practice of linking housing finance to the standard and size of dwelling rather than to the income levels of the borrower.

Fiscal structures also introduce distortions into the financial markets, resulting in widely differing effective after-tax financing costs and asset yields, through discriminating between domestic assets with similar characteristics (Fukao and

Hanazaki, 1987). Surveys have reported non-uniformities in tax provisions in most OECD countries (Table 3.11). Preferential treatment of savings deposits, accounts targeted to housing acquisition or retirement, and of public-debt instruments (*United States, Germany, Italy, France, Denmark*, etc.) affect rates of return and hence portfolio choice, without necessarily stimulating increased savings. Total or partial tax-deductibility of interest payments both provides incentives to reduce saving, lowers the real cost of borrowing and penalises equity funding (*Denmark, Sweden, United States*, etc.). Interest-expense deduction rules, investment allowances and the differential tax treatment of capital incomes depending on type of financial instrument often arbitrarily discriminate between different assets and liabilities and thereby influence the structure of corporate financing and households' portfolio composition. Similarly, international disparities in tax treatment impinge on cross-border portfolio movements (Table 3.12). For example, the differential treatment of interest payments provides an incentive to shift profits and debts, with possibly important implications for individual countries' revenue receipts. The booking of debt by multinational corporations was an important consideration in the recent tax reform in *Canada* and is of particular relevance for *EC* countries, in view of the 1992 objective of internal market unification. Tax considerations have been a major factor behind the growth of the Eurobond and Eurocurrency markets.

The abolition of quantitative credit and interest rate controls should contribute to a more rational allocation of resources and thereby raise allocative efficiency, which has great potential to affect overall macroeconomic performance. At the same time, one of the main features of financial-market developments noted earlier has been the progressive decline in importance of bank intermediation in favour of capital-market financing, a course of events which Country Surveys have generally welcomed. This trend cannot be evaluated simply by comparing the transactions costs of funding through intermediaries on the one hand and the securities markets on the other, but should take account of the broader implications for efficiency. Developed capital markets, besides offering firms a broader choice of liability structures, may better evaluate the relevant economic information regarding investment projects. However, following the work of Shiller (1981a, 1981b) and others, financial-market prices have been subject to extensive scrutiny to determine whether their variability is excessive, given the flow of underlying information which markets are deemed to consider relevant. Furthermore, some evidence suggests that close association with banks may lead to superior financial performance by non-financial firms (Cable, 1985). The debate is by no means settled[15], but caution is clearly called for in equating increased market-determination of financial-sector prices with increased efficiency in resource allocation.

Table 3.11. **Marginal tax rates on capital attributable to the corporate tax system (1983)**[1]

Per cent of pre-tax rate of return

| | Zero inflation | | | | | | Average inflation | | | | | |
| | Equipment | | | Structures | | | Equipment | | | Structures | | |
	Debt	New share issues	Retained earnings	Debt	New share issues	Retained earnings	Debt	New share issues	Retained earnings	Debt	New share issues	Retained earnings
United States	−91.4	3.3	34.9	−22.8	38.0	14.9	−137.8	21.0	−47.3	−72.3	54.1	1.3
Japan	−23.0	36.9	24.7	0.3	48.9	39.0	−66.5	52.5	28.2	−61.7	55.0	31.2
Germany	−39.2	−20.9	26.6	4.6	17.2	49.7	−76.8	−47.2	29.4	−49.0	−23.1	44.0
France	−38.1	−3.1	−0.1	−22.3	8.7	11.3	−105.6	−25.1	−18.1	−99.9	−20.8	−14.0
Italy	−22.1	−2.1	7.8	−3.0	13.9	22.2	−108.2	−48.2	−18.4	−110.8	−50.4	−20.4
United Kingdom	−108.3	−42.9	−19.5	−73.0	−18.7	2.5	−255.7	−101.2	−68.9	−208.6	−69.0	−37.5
Canada	−32.6	−6.9	7.6	−11.3	10.3	23.0	−74.7	−22.8	1.0	−69.9	−18.9	4.6
Australia	−76.4	4.8	−42.3	7.7	50.1	25.5	−127.9	28.9	−62.0	−63.1	63.9	−9.8
Austria	−77.0	−14.7	−24.1	−18.2	23.8	17.5	−96.7	−15.9	−30.4	−49.3	17.0	5.2
Belgium	−100.3	−42.1	−37.7	−42.7	−1.3	1.9	−146.6	−51.5	−44.2	−87.2	−9.4	−3.4
Denmark	−19.6	3.3	−75.4	−8.5	12.2	−59.2	−53.1	−6.0	−177.0	−51.6	−4.8	−174.8
Finland	−14.9	−61.2	−63.5	−6.7	−51.2	−53.7	−62.4	−134.3	−134.1	−57.5	−125.4	−129.1
Ireland	−245.6	−279.4	−405.6	−184.4	−212.3	−308.1	−262.7	−313.3	−527.6	−201.6	−246.2	−428.7
Netherlands	−76.4	−3.4	−124.5	−23.1	34.2	−56.7	−101.6	15.2	−174.6	−63.3	35.1	−125.9
New Zealand	−10.6	39.2	11.5	5.9	48.2	24.7	−61.7	67.3	−4.4	−77.5	58.6	−17.0
Norway	−22.8	25.7	2.5	−4.9	36.5	16.8	−79.5	28.9	−22.9	−72.6	33.0	−17.4
Spain	−80.6	−27.7	−41.1	−44.8	−2.4	−12.9	−132.5	−16.1	−47.8	−118.7	−6.3	−36.8
Sweden[2] HH	−67.9	−104.2	−72.8	−38.8	−71.5	−91.6	−100.1	−165.9	−141.2	−79.1	−135.0	−117.5
TE	—	−42.9		—	−20.0	—	—	−55.8	—	—	−34.1	—
Switzerland	−1.9	15.9	6.0	2.6	19.6	10.5	−7.3	19.1	0.8	−3.6	22.1	4.5

1. These rates apply to returns to both households and tax-exempt institutions except in Sweden, where the dividend tax credit of 30 per cent against personal income tax is available only to households.
2. HH: Households.
   TE: Tax-exempt institutions.
Source: McKee et al., "Marginal tax rates on the use of labour and capital in OECD countries", OECD Economic Studies, No. 7, Autumn 1986.

Table 3.12. **Main features of capital-income taxation**[1]

	Interest income	Capital gains	Dividends
Austria	Withholding tax	Not taxed below threshold	Double taxation; withholding tax of 20 per cent
Denmark	Taxed as income	Generally not taxed	Double taxation; withholding tax of 30 per cent
Finland	Taxed as income (except regulated rate income)	Long-term gains not taxed	Investment income not taxed below a threshold
France	Taxed as income	Not taxed below threshold	Not taxed below threshold
Germany	Taxed as income above threshold	Only short-term speculative gains on shares taxed as income	Taxed as income
Italy	Withholding tax	Not taxed	Tax credit in respect of taxes paid by companies
Norway	Taxed as income above threshold	Favourable	Exempt from local income tax
Sweden	Taxed as income	Long-term gains more favourable	Double taxation
United Kingdom	Taxed as income	Not taxed below threshold	Tax credit in respect of corporate taxes paid
United States	Taxed as income	40 per cent of long-term capital gains taxed at marginal rate; all short-term gains taxed at marginal rate	Double taxation; dividends not taxed below threshold

1. The table summarises the situation prevailing in the early 1980s.
Source: OECD, *Banking and Monetary Policy,* 1985.

The impact of higher financial-asset real yields on households' saving behaviour is a matter of controversy. The Surveys have not presented any evidence suggesting that earlier imperfections in capital markets had depressed household saving ratios *per se*, although the deductibility of interest payments may introduce a bias in favour of consumption (*Denmark, Norway* and *Sweden*). However, the wealth effects of the stock market boom in the 1980s may help explain the buoyancy of private consumption growth in some countries, relative to what could have been expected on the basis of past relationships. Stock-market reforms, to the extent they have contributed to the observed decline in corporate leverage (debt/equity ratios), should lower the short-run volatility of profits net of interest, and thereby dampen the pro-cyclical behaviour of domestic demand where cash-flow considerations influence the timing of investment[16].

A less stable policy environment

Concern over the adverse implications of financial-market developments for monetary-policy efficiency was raised in several Country Surveys. Three basic aspects of the interaction between financial markets and monetary policy were identified. First, in some countries, financial innovation as well as the resulting shifts in demand for financial assets and in the relationships between "money" and other economic variables have led to modifications in monetary policy's operating procedures, and sometimes to a change of its intermediate targets. Second, where the authorities have promoted financial liberalisation to facilitate the shift to a more market-based orientation of policy, significant changes in the transmission of monetary impulses to the real economy were found. In a third set of countries, overlapping with the previous two, the monetary authorities have been faced with a certain loss of autonomy owing to the growing international integration of capital markets.

Financial innovation was found to lie behind the increased instability of monetary aggregates targeted by the authorities in a number of countries. In some cases, this has led to a systematic review of intermediate targets. When quantitative credit controls in the *United Kingdom* were replaced after 1980 by a strategy of containing broad-money growth within gradually declining target limits, difficulties were encountered owing to instability of the aggregates stemming from financial innovation and liberalisation. Periodic redefinition, upward revision, and even suspension of the monetary targets eventually led to the adoption of a multiple-indicator approach. Similar problems caused the monetary authorities in *Canada* to suspend M1 targeting after 1982, and the effects of financial innovation led the authorities in *France* to modify the targeted monetary aggregate which had become unstable. On the other hand, relatively stable structural relationships have allowed the authorities to maintain monetary targeting in *Germany* (where major financial deregulation and liberalisation had been undertaken in the late 1960s) and in *Switzerland*. However, particular provisions of the Swiss prudential regulations have at times led to wide swings in the interbank overnight interest rate.

The possibility that reduced resort to quantitative controls may imply larger required interest rate movements to achieve a given macroeconomic objective has been at times perceived as a constraint, particularly in view of the possible aggravation of systemic risks (see below). Liberalisation of international capital movements and generalised floating have together increased the incidence of changes in monetary conditions impacting through exchange rates. The growing trans-border interdependence of monetary policies was a major focus of the Surveys of *Denmark* and *Sweden*. In the former it was noted that international capital mobility is severely limiting the scope for pursuing exchange- and interest-rate objectives in conflict with market expectations. While this lesson also applied to *Sweden*, it was remarked that that country's open discount-window policy, which allowed banks to counteract the central bank's liquidity management and thereby effectively to endogenise the money supply, had complicated the task of stabilising capital flows. In *Portugal*, where quantitative credit limits and interest-rate controls still apply, steps are being taken towards shifting to indirect control. There, the authorities are faced with the dual challenge of growing instability in the demand for money, resulting from financial market developments, and some prospective loss of control over domestic interest rates as a result of *EC* integration.

Some supervisory issues

Against the background of diminished autonomy faced by domestic policy, concern has grown that financial systems may have become intrinsically more vulnerable to abrupt increases in interest rates or downturns in economic activity (Corrigan, 1987). With global financial-market integration – thanks to advances in fund-transfer technologies and the trend towards around-the-clock trading – problems in one major institution could rapidly cascade, engulfing other institutions and markets. In particular, the limited experience with certain new financial instruments (for instance, swaps and options) has complicated assessment of risk exposure, including identification of ultimate risk-bearers. Instruments designed for hedging are also used for speculative purposes. That the new instruments tend to shift risk from intermediaries to ultimate borrowers has compounded concern over the build-up in private-sector debt. The novel features of some innovations have also raised questions as to the appropriate pricing of new financial instruments.

These considerations relate to the threat posed by excessive competition among financial institutions to the financial systems' integrity, which was a primary motive behind the initial introduction of regulatory controls. As indicated above, more vigorous competition probably helps explain the decline in banks' interest margins observed in recent years. Although the potential cost savings from compressing margins should not be underestimated (OECD area banking system assets are on average of an order of magnitude comparable to nominal GDP), seeking to reduce perceived "excessive" rates of return under oligopolistic conditions may give rise to problems of systemic soundness. The widespread reduction in bank capital/assets ratios observed during the 1970s caused concern among the regulatory authorities (subsequently reinforced by the LDC debt crisis) and provoked a progressive tightening of capital requirements. This action also led *ceteris paribus* to increases in required interest-rate margins. Aggregate evidence suggests in fact that the banking sector is not indifferent with respect to its liability structure. Increases in capital ratios tend to be associated with higher margins[17].

These regulatory challenges underscore the need for closer coordination among national supervisory authorities (Shafer, 1987). Indeed, they have long been recognised, and a strengthening of provisions has taken place at both the national and multilateral levels. The Basle Concordat of 1983 sets broad guidelines for cooperation and for the division of responsability in respect to supervising banks' foreign establishments. It, as well as the 1983 EC directive on supervision, also provides for bank supervision on the basis of worldwide consolidation of balance sheets. More recently, multilateral agreement has been reached under the aegis of the Bank for International Settlements on common standards for minimum capital requirements which take account of off-balance-sheet operations (swaps, interest-rate futures, options, guarantees, etc.). The stock market crisis has also stimulated a re-evaluation of mechanisms which might contribute to dampening price fluctuations in markets. While a consensus is far from established, measures have been taken in some countries (notably the *United States*) to limit the negative consequences of some potentially destabilising market practices (e.g. low margin requirements).

The blurring of demarcation lines with the growing interpenetration of financial sectors has spotlighted other regulatory issues. A broad consensus has emerged that supervision should be based on functional rather than institutional criteria, as the increasing number of financial activities being performed by individual institutions has exacerbated the difficulties inherent in harmonisation of treatment. However, in *Canada* (where additional complications result from the division of supervisory responsibilities between the federal and provincial governments) and *Denmark*, the function-based approach has been rejected in favour of streamlining and consolidating the separate regulatory bodies. The progressive break-down of barriers between intermediaries has also at times resulted in lack of uniformity in regulatory treatment (for instance, the application of reserve requirements to only part of deposit-taking institutions), or in duplication of tasks among different supervisory agencies. Harmonisation of regulations is called for to ensure competitive neutrality.

Conflict of interest questions have been taken up in several Surveys which examined supervisory issues of topical relevance in the respective countries[18]. The current reform of the regulatory system in *Canada* provides for strict curbs on the extension of commercial-financial linkages[19]. In *Italy*, where the Banking Law had long forbidden bank ownership of commercial interests, the increased profitability of large enterprises and sophistication of their financial management have led to concern about the possible acquisition of banks by industrial corporations. While the issue has not yet been resolved, the authorities have moved to regulate new institutions such as merchant banks, whose activities encroach on the traditional division between banking and commerce. Enhanced powers have been granted to the regulatory bodies in the field of securities trading, in order better to guarantee the soundness of operations. In the *United Kingdom*, it was recognised that the risk of malpractices had increased after abolition of the formal separation of stock-market broking and dealing functions. The regulatory system has thus been moving in two directions, emphasising at the same time both stricter self-governance and statutory control. In *Switzerland*, recent reforms have rendered insider dealing subject to criminal prosecution, thereby aligning local legislation to developing international standards.

Conclusions

Macroeconomic performance is importantly influenced by the behaviour of financial markets. The prices that are set there – interest and exchange rates as well as equity prices – exercise a pervasive influence over economic decision-making. In addition to assuring the means-of-payment function, financial markets allocate savings across economic sectors and countries and provide a means for evaluating the risks and returns on investment projects. Since their functioning is characterised by significant externalities – being based on trust that can easily evaporate in a crisis and thereby seriously affect other sectors – a case can be made for government regulation. However, controls were often extended to embrace objectives external to the financial sector itself. While the effectiveness of such measures in achieving their proximate targets is doubtful, to the extent they prove effective – e.g. in financing the public debt – they amount to a disguised form of taxation. The Country Surveys point to a number of instances where the unintended effects of regulation have contributed to resource misallocation or increased transactions and information costs by giving rise to "alternative" financial circuits. At the same time, many fiscal systems incorporate disincentives to saving (i.e. through tax deductibility of interest payments), while biasing the structure of corporate liabilities in favour of debt rather than equity and distorting investment patterns.

The material presented in Country Surveys documents a process of transformation in the financial markets which has been conditioned by, and interacting with, forces for change emanating from outside the sector. Financial markets have deepened and the range of products/services offered has diversified significantly as traditional barriers between intermediaries have been reduced or swept away. A striking feature of developments have been both their geographic extensiveness (change is evident to varying degree across the entire OECD area) and the broad similarity of direction taken by regulatory and policy reforms in this field, which have been oriented towards freeing markets of unnecesary controls and generally stimulating competition. Thus, the process of modernisation has been helped in most cases by official attitudes which have facilitated and, indeed at times promoted, change, with a view to buttressing the international competitiveness of domestic institutions. Substantial progress in a number of countries towards placing monetary policy on a more market-oriented footing will limit the negative side-effects of earlier policies based on quantitative controls.

Overall, these developments can be expected to lead to an improvement in the efficiency of markets which, while difficult to quantify, should impact favourably on economic performance generally and more particularly on sectors adversely affected by earlier distortions. The cost efficiency of intermediation has probably been improved; while the volume of resources devoted to financial activities has increased, competition has intensified and there are indications that intermediation costs have been compressed. Although it is generally agreed that financial innovation has not reduced aggregate business risk (see, for example, Leigh-Pemberton, 1986), on balance the new instruments and broader range of markets available to cover contingencies (particularly options and futures markets) have enhanced liquidity and should facilitate the appraisal and matching of risks, with beneficial effects for investment activity.

OECD countries have achieved a great deal in a relatively short space of time toward creating the conditions propitious for modern, flexible financial systems capable of responding to the exigencies of a more uncertain environment. However, much remains to be done, particularly in countries where reforms were inititated relatively late and/or policy and regulatory frameworks retain an important element of discretion. Governments have clearly indicated their intention to proceed further, and EC integration goals are providing an extra impetus to endeavours in this direction. Taxation reform, discussed more fully in Chapter 5, represents an area where policy action would help promote the efficiency of financial markets and affect their link with the "real" economy. Ensuring greater neutrality in respect to the choice between saving and consumption as well as among financial instruments would be clearly desirable from an economic efficiency viewpoint, constituting an encouragement to capital-market deepening. In this latter context, initiatives aimed at promoting the development and use of capital markets, particularly for small- and medium-sized enterprises, should be encouraged as well.

Experience gained so far has spotlighted certain of the difficulties engendered by liberalisation. National monetary authorities may have foregone a certain degree of policy autonomy. At the same time, globalisation of markets, increased private-sector indebtedness and uncertainties attaching to the risk implications of various financial innovations have heightened prudential concerns about systemic risk. Supervision has accordingly been strengthened and in particular international cooperation reinforced. The trade-off between liberalisation and ensuring the integrity of financial systems represents a long-standing dilemma facing the authorities. Desegmentation has entailed a tendency towards "universalisation" of banking systems and contributed to sharpening competition, thereby putting pressures on profit margins.

While the stock of country experience is rapidly accumulating and evidence so far in the aftermath of the October 1987 stock market crash suggests that markets may be less "fragile" than feared, important questions remain in abeyance. As markets evolve, so will the need for adaptation to the challenges posed by liberalisation and deregulation. It is of crucial importance for the future prospects of the reform process that the prudential and regulatory frameworks adapt so as to provide greater resilience of the financial system in an environment marked by intensified competition and continuing macroeconomic imbalances at both the national and international levels.

Notes

1. The following *OECD Economic Surveys* have reviewed financial market developments:

Country	Review date
Japan	July 1984
Finland	May 1985
Australia	June 1985
New Zealand	July 1985
Greece	January 1986
Norway	January 1986
Germany	June 1986
Austria	July 1986
Yugoslavia	January 1987
France	January 1987
Switzerland	February 1987
Sweden	April 1987
Iceland	May 1987
United Kingdom	July 1987
Denmark	July 1987
Italy	August 1987
Canada	August 1987
Spain	January 1988
United States	May 1988

2. For a description of such innovations and a discussion of their implications, see Bank for International Settlements (1986) – the "Cross report".

3. Between 1970 and 1980 the share of goods and services exports in total OECD GDP rose from 11.4 to 19.6 per cent, but has since receded (to 16.9 per cent in 1986).

4. See Bryant (1987) for a detailed analysis of the growth of international banking and underlying commercial transactions.

5. See OECD (1985) for a comprehensive review of structural changes in financial markets and consideration of the issues to which these have given rise from the viewpoint of the banking sector.

6. Concerning selective credit controls in Greece, see, for instance, Molho (1986).

7. Most observers tend to view the trends toward de-specialisation of intermediaries and a growing role for capital markets as irreversible, being a consequence of the systemic changes alluded to above. However, De Cecco (1987) argues that securitisation and auction markets (particularly in the United States and the United Kingdom) are likely to prove merely a transitory phase of development.

8. For an analysis of the competitive environment in banking at the beginning of the 1980s, see OECD (1983).

9. See also the historical data for (slightly different) aggregates provided by Goldsmith (1985) for a number of industrial countries. These show financial assets/GDP ratios peaking for the most recent years.

10. The term "securitization" has two connotations: *(a)* In a general sense, the increased role of securities markets in the flow of funds; *(b)* More specifically, the issuing of securities backed by a pool of various type claims, such as mortgage and consumer loans.

11. Concerning economies of scale and scope in the banking sector, see, *inter alia*, Gilligan and Smirlock (1984). Concerning the relationship between concentration and profitability in the United States banking system, see Smirlock (1985).

12. The degree of comparability across countries is limited by the different fiscal and regulatory treatment of activities – including hidden reserves, off-balance sheet operations and the treatment of loan-loss provisions. Margins are also influenced by cross-subsidization of non-balance-sheet-related operations and by interbanking activities. Time-series analyses for a country pose less problems.

13. For details on country coverage and methodology applied, see OECD (1987a) and (1978,1983).

14. Interest rate margins (as recorded in banking-sector balance sheets) do not necessarily reflect given differentials between borrowing and lending rates; the composition of balance sheets, the existence and remuneration of reserve and/or liquidity requirements, and the general tax treatment of banks are key elements in determining actual spreads. While due caution is called for in interpreting absolute GEM levels in view of differences in accounting conventions, the highest (Denmark) and lowest (Austria) are found in Europe, with the United States and Japan near the top and the bottom of the scale respectively.

15. See Shiller (1981a) and (1981b). Concerning arguments against the "excessive variability" interpretation, see Kleidon, (1986).

16. Tentative support for this is provided by the INTERLINK investment equations, which show statistically-significant coefficients for short-run profits only in those countries where firms tend to be highly leveraged. See Helliwell *et. al.* (1986).

17. The following regression was run on the aggregate balance sheets of 18 national banking sectors for the period 1980-1985 (t-statistics in parenthesis):

$$GEM = \quad -.11 \quad +1.21 \ OC \quad +0.23 \ CR \quad -.11 \ TIME$$
$$\qquad\qquad (0.41) \quad (9.86) \qquad (4.90) \qquad (2.31)$$

$adj. R^2 = 0.70$
$S.E.E = 0.798$

where:

GEM = *gross* earnings margin of the banking sector (interest margin plus non-interest income as a percentage of assets)

OC = operating costs as a percentage of assets

CR = capital/asset ratio

$TIME$ = time trend

18. For an in-depth discussion of these issues, see OECD (1987a).

19. Individual shareholders are limited to a maximum holding of 10 per cent in Canadian banks, though exceptions are made for foreign banks and, for a period of 10 years, new banks.

Bibliography

Aliber, R.Z. (1986), "Financial markets and the growth of Europe", in Lawrence, R.Z. and C.L. Schultze, (eds.), *Barriers to European Growth – a Transatlantic View*, Brookings Institution, Washington.

Bank for International Settlements (1986), *Recent Innovations in International Banking*, Basle.

(1985, 1986, 1987), Annual reports.

Bryant, R.C. (1987), *International Financial Intermediation*, Brookings Institution, Washington D.C.

Cable, J. (1985), "Capital market information and industrial performance: the role of West German banks", *The Economic Journal*, March.

Committee of the Italian Treasury Ministry (1987), "Financial assets, public debt and monetary policy: an international integration perspective", *Banca Nazionale del Lavoro Quarterly Review*, No. 162, September.

Corrigan, E.G. (1987), *Financial Market Structure: A Longer View*, Federal Reserve Bank of New York, January.

Cottarelli *et. al.* (1986), "Monetary policy through ceilings on bank lending", *Economic Policy*, No. 3, October.

De Cecco, M. (ed.) (1987), *Changing Money – Financial Innovation in Developed Countries*, Basil Blackwell, Oxford.

Department of Finance Canada (1985), *The Regulation of Financial Institutions: Proposals for Discussion*, Ottawa, June.

Economic Council of Canada (1987), *A Framework for Financial Regulation*, Ottawa.

Fair, D.E. (1886), *Shifting Frontiers in Financial Markets*, Martinus Nijhoff Publishers, Dordrecht.

Fukao, M. and M. Hanazaki (1987), "Internationalisation of financial markets and the allocation of capital", *OECD Economic Studies*, No. 8, Spring.

Gilligan, T.W. and M. Smirlock (1984), "An empirical study of joint production and scale economies in commercial banking", *Journal of Banking and Finance*, 8, 67-77.

Goldsmith, R.W. (1985), *Comparative National Balance Sheets*, The University of Chicago Press, Chicago.

Goodhart, C. (1986), "Financial innovation and monetary control", *Oxford Review of Economic Policy*, Vol. 2, No. 4, November.

Hakim, J.R. (1985), "Securities markets", *IFC Occasional Papers, Capital Market Series*.

Helliwell *et. al.* (1986), "The supply side in OECD's macroeconomic model", *OECD Economic Studies*, No. 6, Spring.

Kleidon, A.W. (1986), "Variance bounds tests and stock price valuation models", *Journal of Political Economy*, Vol. 94.

Leigh-Pemberton, R. (1986), "Shifting frontiers in financial markets: their causes and consequences", in D.E. Fair (ed.), *Shifting Frontiers in Financial Markets*, Martinus Nijhoff Publishers, Dordrecht.

Molho, L.E. (1986), "Selective credit controls in Greece – a test of their effectiveness", *IMF Staff Papers*, September.

OECD (1978, 1983), *Costs and margins in banking*, Paris.

    (1983), *The Internationalisation of Banking – the Policy Issue*, Paris.

    (1985), *Trends in Banking in OECD Countries*, Paris

    (1987a), *Prudential Supervision in Banking*, Paris.

    (1987b), *Bank Profitability*, Paris.

    (forthcoming), *Competition in Banking*, Paris.

Revell, J. (1983), *Banking and Electronic Fund Transfer System*, OECD, Paris.

Shafer, J. (1987), Managing crises in the emerging financial landscape", *OECD Economic Studies*, No. 9, Autumn.

Shiller R. (1981a), "Do stock prices move too much to be justified by subsequent changes in dividends?", *American Economic Review*, June, pp. 421-36.

    (1981b), "The use of volatility measures in assessing market efficiency", *Journal of Finance*, Vol. 36, May.

Smirlock, M. (1985), "Evidence on the (non) relationship between concentration and profitability in banking", *Journal of Money, Credit and Banking*, Vol. 17 No. 1, February.

Sundararajan, V. (1987), "The debt-equity ratio of firms and the effectiveness of interest rate policy: analysis with a dynamic model of saving, investment and growth in Korea", *IMF Staff Papers*, June.

Suzuki, Y. (1986), "A comparative study of financial innovation, deregulation and reform in Japan and the United States", *BOJ Monetary and Economic Studies*, October.

Tobin, J. (1984), "On the efficiency of the financial system", *Lloyds Bank Review*, July.

Chapter 4

INDUSTRIAL ADJUSTMENT: FREEING INITIATIVE

Introduction

Special chapters on industrial adjustment have been included in the Economic Surveys of 16 Member countries[1]. These Surveys placed particular emphasis on the behaviour of manufacturing industry because of its importance in trade and total factor productivity, as well as to the evolving labour-market problems. The sectoral pressures for change facing the OECD economies have shown no signs of slackening in the course of the 1980s and to an extent that varies from one country to another, manufacturing is continuing to lose ground to the services sector. In large measure, this is a normal development characteristic of economies that have reached an advanced stage of development. However, in a context of slower growth, it has been accompanied by serious transitional problems which have become manifest since the 1970s.

Faced with these structural changes, governments in the 1970s responded in different ways. Some, like *Japan*, focused on promoting the expansion of "sunrise" industries. But in many other countries the authorities' initial response was to resort to defensive industrial policies. A change in policy direction is now under way, the aim of which is to stimulate economic growth by strengthening the role of competitive forces and establishing favourable conditions for the dissemination of technological progress. The consequences of this shift of policy, provided that it proves to be lasting, should be: *i)* a marked redistribution of factors of production among sectors and of incomes among economic agents and in particular away from those enjoying economic rents; *ii)* greater relative price and real-wage flexibility (see Chapter 2), thereby bolstering economies' capacity to respond to shocks; and *iii)* stronger growth due to the more rational allocation of resources and enhanced incentives to improve efficiency.

The evolving OECD economies

The relative decline of the manufacturing sector

Since the start of the 1970s the OECD economies have been undergoing profound change, the pace of which has not slackened in the course of the 1980s. The most visible of these changes has been the decline in the manufacturing sector's share of GDP relative to that of services. For the OECD area as a whole, this fall has accelerated, with the share amounting to less than 24 per cent during the first half of the 1980s, compared with averages of 26.1 per cent between 1974 and 1979 and 27.8 per cent between 1968 and 1973. This movement has been matched by a corresponding growth in market services and in the public sector. However, the trend has not been uniform across countries. In some countries it has been accentuated by the increasing importance of the extractive industries, exemplified by the development of mineral resources in *Australia*, and especially of oil in *Norway*, where the energy sector's share of GDP rose from 2½ per cent in 1975 to nearly 20 per cent in 1985. Although in *Germany* the relative share of manufacturing has receded in line with the average trend among its EEC partners, it remains appreciably higher than in most other OECD countries (Diagram 4.1). The rapidly-industrialising countries like *Finland* and *Greece* contrast somewhat with this general picture; in 1985 manufacturing still accounted for roughly the same share of GDP as at the beginning of the 1970s.

The decline in the manufacturing share of value-added has been accompanied almost everywhere by a fall in manufacturing employment, especially in the EC countries (down by a cumulative 20 per cent since 1973, compared with slightly under 10 per cent for the OECD area as a whole). However, in the most recent past this trend has reversed in *Japan* and appears to have weakened in *Canada, Germany* and the *United Kingdom*. Some smaller countries, such as *Denmark, Iceland, Norway, New Zealand, Sweden* and *Turkey*, have continued to experience employment increases (Table 4.1).

The factors underlying manufacturing's relative decline and services' corresponding growth are many and complex. Some form part of a normal trend in advanced economies. Given the differential in productivity gains (Table 4.2), relative prices of manufacturing industry are on an underlying downward trend. As a result, the decline in the weight of industry is less marked in "real" than in nominal terms. Higher real incomes also contribute to explaining the gradual shift in demand toward services. And with many traditional products approaching the end of their life cycle in

DIAGRAM 4.1

STRUCTURE OF NOMINAL GDP
AN INTERNATIONAL COMPARISON

1. Agriculture
2. Mining and quarrying
3. Manufacturing
4. Utilities and construction
5. Services
6. Government

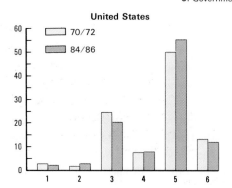

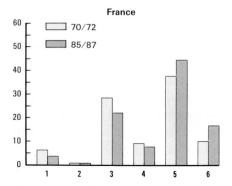

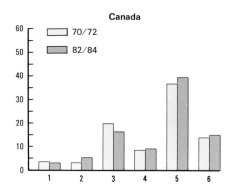

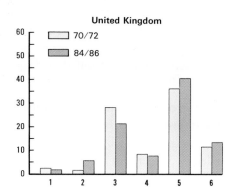

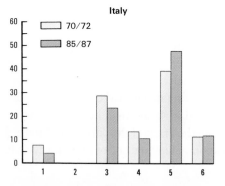

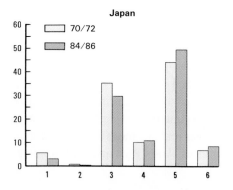

Note: Break in series in 1977 in France and 1980 in Italy.
Source: OECD, *National Accounts.*

DIAGRAM 4.1 (continued)

STRUCTURE OF NOMINAL GDP
AN INTERNATIONAL COMPARISON

1. Agriculture
2. Mining and quarrying
3. Manufacturing
4. Utilities and construction
5. Services
6. Government

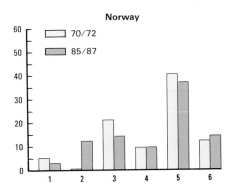

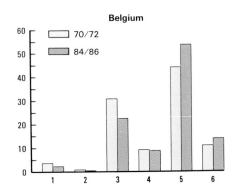

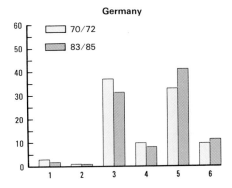

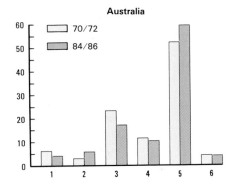

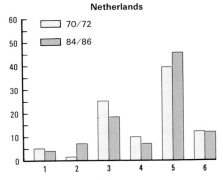

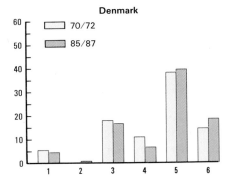

Source: OECD, *National Accounts.*

DIAGRAM 4.1 (continued)

STRUCTURE OF NOMINAL GDP
AN INTERNATIONAL COMPARISON

1. Agriculture
2. Mining and quarrying
3. Manufacturing
4. Utilities and construction
5. Services
6. Government

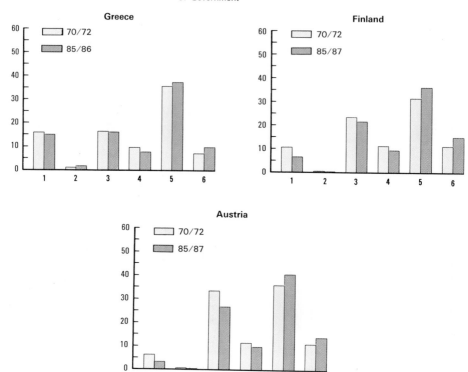

Source: OECD, *National Accounts.*

the most advanced industrialised countries, certain types of production have shifted – and technology transfers taken place – to lower-wage countries, in accordance with changes in patterns of comparative advantage.

In explaining the expansion of market services, a distinction may be made between services directly linked to goods production and "free-standing" services. An EC study (*European Economy*, September 1985) shows that, while in the major

Table 4.1. **Employment trends in services and manufacturing**[1]

	Services							Manufacturing						
	Average							Average						
	1960-1968	1968-1973	1973-1979	1979-1986	1984	1985	1986	1960-1968	1968-1973	1973-1979	1979-1986	1984	1985	1986
United States	2.5	3.4	3.2	2.4	3.8	3.0	2.9	2.3	0.2	1.1	−1.0	5.3	−0.6	0.4
Japan	2.8	2.4	2.2	1.8	1.2	0.8	2.0	4.1	2.0	−1.3	1.1	2.3	1.0	−0.6
Germany	1.0	1.7	1.1	0.9	1.1	1.4	1.4	0.3	0.9	−1.4	−1.1	−0.9	1.0	1.4
France	2.5	2.6	2.1	1.4	0.9	1.4	1.9	0.5	2.1	−0.9	−2.2	−2.7	−2.9	−2.1
United Kingdom	1.3	1.5	1.4	1.3	3.5	2.7	1.9	−0.3	−0.9	−1.3	−4.5	−2.1	−0.5	−2.3
Italy	1.4	1.3	2.7	2.9	4.5	3.4	2.1	0.8	0.4	0.2	−1.8	−3.9	−2.4	−1.0
Canada	4.2	4.0	3.6	2.5	2.2	3.6	3.3	2.8	2.1	1.5	−0.3	4.6	1.0	1.3
Total of above countries	2.3	2.7	2.5	2.0	2.8	2.3	2.4	1.7	0.8	−0.3	−1.0	1.6	−0.3	−0.2
Austria	1.3	1.8	2.4	1.3	0.8	1.5	1.7	−0.7	1.8	−0.7	−1.4	−0.5	−0.4	−0.8
Belgium	1.9	2.9	1.8	1.0	1.1	1.8	2.1	0.6	0.2	−3.3	−2.6	−1.0	−1.6	−1.6
Denmark	2.9	..	..	2.4	6.5	0.7	5.5	0.1	1.5	−1.5	0.9	5.0	7.1	2.0
Finland	2.9	3.7	2.2	2.5	2.9	3.4	0.7	1.0	4.8	−0.1	−0.8	−1.2	−1.4	−3.4
Greece	2.2	2.1	2.2	2.7	3.5	3.2	−0.3	1.9	5.0	1.6	1.6	0.0	0.0	5.7
Iceland	2.1	4.1	3.1	3.0	1.3	1.3	1.8	1.0	4.9	3.1	1.4	0.7	0.7	1.4
Ireland	0.9	1.2	2.5	1.3	−0.2	−0.8	1.4	1.6	1.8	1.2	−1.9	−4.6	−2.4	3.0
Luxembourg	1.3	..	3.2	2.6	2.5	3.2	4.6	0.7	..	−2.2	−1.5	−1.3	−0.5	1.3
Netherlands	2.2	1.8	1.8	2.5	2.0	2.2	3.2	0.3	−0.9	−1.9	−1.1	1.3	0.9	0.4
Norway	2.0	..	4.0	2.7	1.5	2.7	3.8	1.0	..	−0.2	−1.0	2.1	0.9	2.9
Portugal	4.1	2.2	..	..	−3.3	1.2	5.1	0.6	0.9	..	..	−0.4	2.9	−3.4
Spain	2.7	2.3	0.9	1.2	−0.8	3.2	6.3	2.5	..	..	−3.0	−2.6	−3.7	1.9
Sweden	2.0	3.2	2.9	1.2	..	1.3	0.8	0.1	−1.3	−0.6	−0.7	..	1.8	1.2
Switzerland	2.9	3.1	0.9	1.2	0.2	0.9	1.8	1.4	0.1	−2.6	−0.4	−1.0	1.4	1.6
Turkey	4.5	3.3	4.0	3.0	3.8	3.3	5.4	3.6	3.4	1.7	2.8	3.7	3.1	5.7
Smaller European	2.6	2.7	2.0	2.0	1.2	1.9	3.5	1.3	1.0	−0.6	−0.7	−0.1	0.4	1.4
Australia	3.6	3.9	2.2	..	4.1	3.9	..	1.1	1.6	−1.7	..	1.7	−3.3	..
New Zealand	2.7	3.8	2.5	..	1.5	3.3	..	2.7	0.8	0.7	..	0.0	5.3	..
Total smaller	2.7	2.9	2.1	2.2	1.6	2.1	4.1	1.3	1.0	−0.7	−0.7	−0.1	0.0	1.4
Total EEC	1.7	1.9	1.7	1.6	2.1	2.1	2.3	0.5	0.6	−1.0	−2.2	−1.9	−0.9	−0.4
Total OECD Europe	1.9	2.1	1.9	1.7	2.0	2.1	2.4	0.6	0.7	−0.9	−1.8	−1.5	−0.5	0.0
Total OECD less United States	2.3	2.4	2.0	1.8	1.9	1.9	2.6	1.4	1.1	−0.9	−1.0	−0.2	−0.1	−0.1
Total OECD	2.3	2.7	2.5	2.0	2.0	2.3	2.7	1.6	0.8	−0.4	−1.0	1.3	−0.2	0.1

1. Annual growth rates of civilian employment.
Source: OECD, *Historical Statistics, 1960-1986,* 1988.

Table 4.2. **Labour productivity and real growth in market services and manufacturing**

Average annual growth rate

A. Labour productivity

	1960-1968		1968-1973		1974-1979		1980-1985	
	Services	Manufac-turing	Services	Manufac-turing	Services	Manufac-turing	Services	Manufac-turing
United States	2.1	3.2	1.4	4.0	0.8	2.0	0.7	4.5
Japan	8.2	9.0	6.8	9.8	2.9	5.9	2.2	6.0
OECD-Europe	3.1	5.4	2.7	5.4	1.7	3.2	1.0	3.2

B. Real value added

	1960-1968		1968-1973		1974-1979		1980-1985	
	Services	Manufac-turing	Services	Manufac-turing	Services	Manufac-turing	Services	Manufac-turing
United States	4.6	5.5	4.4	3.8	3.9	3.3	3.2	3.5
Japan	11.2	13.5	9.8	11.8	5.3	4.4	3.9	7.6
OECD-Europe	4.7	5.8	4.9	5.5	3.6	2.0	2.5	0.8

Sources: OECD, *Historical Statistics, 1960-1985* and *National Accounts.*

Table 4.3. **Nature of service activities**[1]

Per cent, average 1980-1984

	Directly linked to goods production	Free-standing	Total
Wholesale and retail trade	13	0	13
Hotels and restaurants[2]	0.5	1.5	2
Transport[3]	2.5	2.5	5
Communications[4]	1	1	2
Financial institutions[4]	2	2	4
Insurance[4]	0.5	0.5	1
Real estate, except dwellings[5]	3	0	3
Dwellings[5]	0	6	6
Business services	3	0	3
Social and community services	0	3	3
Recreational and cultural services	0	1	1
Personal and household services	0	2	2
Total	25.5	19.5	45

1. Share of market services in total GDP, broken down into services directly linked to goods production and "free-standing" services.
2. It is assumed that three-quarters of expenditure on restaurants and hotels is by households for leisure purposes, and the remaining quarter for business entertainment.
3. Information is not available on the relative shares of goods and passenger transport. Road transport is assumed to be mainly freight, air transport mainly passengers, and other transport evenly divided between merchandise and passengers.
4. Arbitrarily divided 50/50 in the absence of other information.
5. Partial data suggest that dwellings (including "ownership of dwellings") is generally the largest part of total real estate.
Source: D. Blades: "Goods and services in OECD countries", *OECD Economic Studies,* Spring, No. 8, 1987.

European countries the share of market services in households' final consumption rose between 1975 and 1982, the growth of services bought-in by manufacturing clearly exceeded that of manufacturing value added. This seems to have been a major explanatory factor in the expansion of market services, reflecting partly industrial enterprises' withdrawal from various service activities that had previously been supplied in-house. A recent OECD study (Blades, 1987) shows that services directly linked to goods production are now of major importance, perhaps accounting for over 25 per cent of GDP during 1980-1984 in OECD countries for which data are available (Table 4.3).

The effect of the oil shocks

The oil shocks also contributed to reducing the share of manufacturing output. Not only was the cost of energy inputs raised, but the rigidity of real wages in some – especially European – countries also meant that industrial enterprises bore the brunt of the extra burden placed on national income by the higher oil bill, particularly after the first oil shock. Unlike protected sectors, manufacturing could pass on its higher costs through raising prices only at the expense of demand for its products and of competitiveness *vis-à-vis* countries less influenced by the oil shock. In many countries the rate of return in manufacturing thus proved more vulnerable to the medium-term effects of the oil shocks than in other sectors. In the *United States*, the positive differential between rates of return in the private sector as a whole and in manufacturing widened in 1973-1974 and after 1980 in the wake of the two oil shocks and other raw material price changes. This differential experienced a virtually continuous increase in *Canada* between 1974 and 1980, and has remained at a high level in *Japan* since 1975. The gap between rates of return, which had widened during the 1970s, began to narrow only from 1982 in *Germany* and from 1983 in the *United Kingdom* (Diagram 4.2). Thus, up to the early 1980s the rates of capital accumulation and output growth in manufacturing seem to have suffered more severely from the oil shocks than elsewhere in the economy. Various studies (e.g. Van Gemert, 1987) have confirmed this hypothesis; they show a negative differential emerging after the first oil shock between manufacturing's actual and "normal" shares of output – the latter being estimated econometrically by reference to a country's standard of living, size of domestic market, degree of openness of the economy, etc. However, these studies also suggest that the oil shocks' adverse impact was primarily a one-off effect on the share of manufacturing, the trend developments being little influenced.

DIAGRAM 4.2

RATES OF RETURN DIFFERENTIALS:
OVERALL BUSINESS SECTOR AND MANUFACTURING
Percentage points

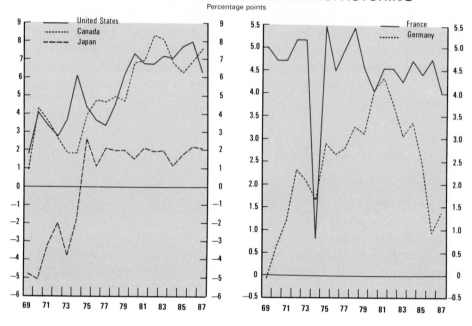

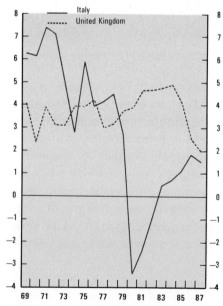

Source: OECD Secretariat estimates.

The decline in total factor productivity

These major structural changes have been accompanied by a disquieting slowdown in total factor productivity for the economy as a whole. The decline in total factor productivity growth in both manufacturing and the overall business sector has contributed to the slowdown in the growth of output and living standards. In the private sector, the slowdown in total factor productivity growth, which affected all countries between 1973 and 1979, was still evident in 1985 except in the *United States, Japan*, the United Kingdom and Finland (Table 4.4). While total factor productivity in manufacturing is now picking up in those four countries and in *Norway* and *Sweden*, the failure of most European countries during 1979-1985 to arrest the decline that began after the first oil shock reflected falling capital

Table 4.4. **Business-sector and manufacturing total factor productivity**[1]

Average annual growth rate

		Pre-1973[2]	1973-1979	1979-1985
United States	B	1.5	−0.1	0.0
	M	2.8	0.3	2.5
Japan	B	6.3	1.8	2.0
	M	6.5	2.2	4.5
Germany	B	2.8	1.8	0.8
	M	2.9	2.2	1.5
France	B	4.4	2.1	1.3
	M	4.9	2.4	1.2
United Kingdom	B	2.1	0.3	1.0
	M	2.9	−0.4	1.9
Italy	B	4.8	1.7	0.7
	M	4.4	1.9	1.9
Canada	B	2.2	1.1	−0.3
	M	3.0	0.4	0.1
Belgium	B	3.7	1.6	1.3
	M	5.8	4.1	3.5
Norway	B	1.6	2.6	1.1
	M	3.4	−0.4	1.5
Sweden	B	1.4	0.6	0.4
	M	2.6	−0.2	2.4
Finland	B	2.5	1.0	2.1
	M	3.9	1.0	3.3

1. B = Business sector; M = Manufacturing.
2. United States: 1960-1973; Japan: 1966-1973; Germany: 1961-1973; France: 1964-1973; United Kingdom: 1960-1973; Italy: 1960-1973; Canada: 1962-1973; Belgium: 1962-1973; Norway: 1964-1973; Sweden: 1964-1973; Finland: 1961-1973.
Source: Englander A.S. and A. Mittelstädt: "Total Factor Productivity: Macroeconomic and Structural Aspects of the Slowdown", *OECD Economic Studies*, No. 10, Spring 1988.

productivity. The decline in total factor productivity growth in the business sector to some extent reflects the loss in impetus of technological innovation and increased rigidities in goods and factor markets in response to major structural changes. The shift of activity away from industry has also contributed to the slowdown in total factor productivity growth in some countries, insofar as productivity gains in manufacturing have remained higher than elsewhere in the economy.

The emergence of persistent trade imbalances

The changes in OECD economies' structures have also been accompanied by the emergence of trade imbalances in the 1970s which have proved particularly tenacious in some countries. Although the imbalances can be explained in large part by cyclical demand differentials and movements in relative costs and exchange rates, structural rigidities in product, labour and financial markets and mismatches between domestic supply on the one hand and domestic and foreign demand on the other seem also to have played a role. This more structural aspect of countries' dependence on developments in partner countries can be gauged by comparing the elasticity of imports with respect to domestic demand and the elasticity of exports with respect to world income. The greater the difference between the two elasticities, the more likely it is that a country's export/import ratio[2] will worsen, under conditions of identical world and domestic growth and stable relative prices. The differences shown in Table 4.5 are derived from the OECD INTERLINK model's average elasticity values, which have generally been estimated over periods which do not include the most recent past[3]. The differential calculated with 1985 weights (Table 4.5, column C) seems particularly unfavourable for *the United States, Italy, the United Kingdom* and *Canada*. In contrast, the elasticity gap is extremely favourable in the case of *Japan, Germany, Finland, the Netherlands* and *Belgium*. The trend in these differentials for goods and services gives an indication of the favourable or unfavourable influence of shifts in both product and geographic market structures. The geographic structure of foreign trade has had a beneficial impact (column C compared with column B, Table 4.5). Changes in commodity composition (manufacturing, energy, services, raw materials, agro-food products) have, on the other hand, worsened the position of the *United Kingdom, Italy* and *Ireland* (column B compared with column A, Table 4.5), but improved that of *Finland, Norway* and *Canada* – in the latter two countries reflecting energy trade.

In most instances international disparities in trade elasticity differentials in respect to manufactures exceed those for total goods and services exports. This is illustrated by the differences between countries such as *Japan* and *Germany* on the

Table 4.5. **Import/export elasticity differentials**[1]

	Goods and services			Manufactures
	A[2]	B[3]	C[4]	D[5]
United States	0.32	0.28	0.11	0.18
Japan	− 0.30	− 0.30	− 0.29	− 0.32
Germany	− 0.18	− 0.17	− 0.25	− 0.24
France	− 0.06	− 0.04	− 0.11	− 0.01
United Kingdom	0.11	0.16	0.10	0.25
Italy	0.27	0.39	0.36	0.81
Canada	0.49	0.30	0.19	0.15
Australia	0.19	0.11	0.02	0.09
Austria	0.17	0.15	0.08	− 0.01
Belgium/Luxembourg	− 0.17	− 0.20	− 0.25	− 0.29
Denmark	0.11	0.11	0.01	0.23
Finland	− 0.07	− 0.12	− 0.22	− 0.24
Ireland	0.07	0.14	0.05	− 0.05
Norway	0.14	0.03	0.01	− 0.05
Netherlands	− 0.17	− 0.20	− 0.25	− 0.20
Sweden	0.03	0.03	− 0.05	− 0.15
Switzerland	0.05	0.04	− 0.12	− 0.08

1. Import elasticity with respect to domestic demand *minus* export elasticity with respect to world domestic demand. The domestic demand-elasticity of country *i* exports is the product of the export market-elasticity of exports and the average domestic demand-elasticity of country *j* imports weighted by country *j*'s share in country *i*'s exports. However, non-OECD countries need to be treated differently: it has been assumed that their income growth is the same as for their export earnings and that the propensity to import is equal to unity. The elasticities for goods and services are the averages of commodity elasticities (manufactures, energy products, agriculture/food processing, services and raw materials) weighted by each commodity's share in the foreign trade of the country concerned.
2. 1975 weighting for products and export areas.
3. 1985 weighting for products and 1975 for export areas.
4. 1985 weighting for products and export areas.
5. 1975 weighting for export areas.
Source: OECD Secretariat estimates.

one hand, whose industry would be in structural surplus in the event of uniform world growth and constant relative prices, and countries like *the United Kingdom, Italy* and *Denmark* on the other. The manufacturing sector's contribution to the aggregate elasticity gaps is all the more marked in that its weight in the OECD area's foreign trade has remained predominant. The share of manufactures in export volumes has even risen in most countries except for *the United States* and *Belgium* as well as for energy producers such as *Norway and the United Kingdom* (Table 4.6).

While the reduction in external imbalances will depend on macroeconomic policies aimed at ensuring an appropriate international pattern of demand and relative price levels, structural adjustment can reinforce the efficiency of such measures by, for example, improving the income elasticity of exports from countries with competitiveness problems stemming from structural weaknesses. Furthermore, competition policies aimed at promoting the adjustment of industrial structures will

Table 4.6. **Shares of manufactures and services in foreign trade**[1]

| | Manufactures | | | | Services | | | |
| | Exports | | Imports | | Exports | | Imports | |
	1975	1985	1975	1985	1975	1985	1975	1985
United States	61	57	37	59	19	18	16	14
Japan	85	88	13	22	13	11	14	19
Germany	74	76	37	49	16	15	22	20
France	53	54	35	46	29	27	23	20
United Kingdom	60	53	39	58	29	23	20	18
Italy	63	69	30	41	14	16	23	20
Canada	43	55	60	73	12	9	14	13
Australia	16	18	53	64	18	16	28	24
Austria	51	58	51	58	21	20	42	34
Belgium/Luxembourg	68	63	48	51	16	20	12	17
Denmark	38	42	42	52	29	23	21	20
Finland	73	66	57	53	11	15	7	18
Ireland	44	60	58	63	7	10	5	12
Netherlands	37	44	42	46	19	18	18	19
Norway	36	26	44	57	41	25	35	28
Sweden	68	67	48	58	18	18	20	17
Switzerland	74	73	55	63	22	23	21	19

1. Percentage share of volume trade in goods and services.
Source: OECD Secretariat estimates.

increase the responsiveness of demand to changes in relative prices, thereby reducing the size of exchange-rate adjustments needed to re-establish price competitiveness and limiting the effects on the price level of a devaluation.

The process of industrial adjustment

Differing intensity of inter-industry shifts across countries

The extent of industrial adjustment has varied from country to country depending on both the initial conditions and degree of exposure to international competition. An index of structural change (Table 4.7) reveals these shifts to have been relatively modest in *Germany* and *Italy*, but to have intensified considerably since 1976-78 in *Australia* and *the United Kingdom*. However, as the index is computed on the basis of a 22-sector subdivision of manufacturing industry, it is too

Table 4.7. **Index of structural change**[1]

	1970/1972 - 1976/1978		1976/1978 - 1983/1985	
	Index	Growth[2]	Index	Growth[2]
United States	0.18	3.1	0.33	3.2
Japan	0.22	6.8	0.25	7.3
Germany	0.17	2.0	0.18	1.3
France	0.19	3.6	0.27	1.4
United Kingdom	0.18	1.4	0.46	− 0.3
Italy	0.16	3.8	0.12	1.8
Canada	0.19	− 0.2	0.25	2.6
Australia	0.14	0.9	0.29	1.6
Belgium	0.25	3.0	0.26	2.0
Finland	0.21	2.3	0.22	4.1
Netherlands	0.23	2.6	0.38	1.1
Norway	0.21	0.8	0.32	1.4
Sweden	0.19	1.4	0.25	0.9

1. The index is computed as the average absolute change in the relative shares of 22 subsectors of manufacturing.
2. Average annual percentage change over the periods indicated.
Source: OECD Secretariat estimates.

highly aggregated to capture intra-sectoral changes. Nor does it provide a measure of manufacturing-sector performance. For example, the *United Kingdom* rates very highly on the index but suffered an overall decline in manufacturing output, whereas in *Italy*, the reverse holds. Furthermore, the index gives no information about the nature of the adjustments that have occurred.

A clearer indication of what lies behind the shifts in relative shares of various industries – retaining the same level of aggregation as the structural change index – emerges from comparing the commodity structure of output with that of world demand and with the rate of import penetration. In *Germany*, and to a lesser extent *Italy* during the 1970s, the low degree of structural change seems to reflect a stable high degree of correlation between domestic industrial structure and foreign demand, the composition of which – measured on a 22-products basis – is changing only slowly (Table 4.8). By contrast, the intensification of structural change in *Australia*, and to a lesser extent in *Japan* and *Canada*, since the mid-1970s seems partly to reflect certain domestic industries' shrinking participation in the home market, given that the negative correlation between a sector's share of output and domestic import penetration has become stronger. In *Australia* and *Japan* this trend might reflect the progressive adoption of a new approach to industrial policy aimed at reducing protection of the domestic market from import penetration.

131

Table 4.8. **Output structure: relationship to world demand structure and import penetration**[1]

| | Correlation between commodity structure of production and: | | | | | |
| | World demand[2] | | | Import penetration rate[3] | | |
	1970-1975	1975-1980	1980-1985	1970-1975	1975-1980	1980-1985
United States	0.73	0.70	0.63	−0.46	−0.26	−0.25
Japan	0.76	0.72	0.72	−0.28	−0.44	−0.43
Germany	0.87	0.88	0.88	−0.33	−0.33	−0.38
France	0.63	0.62	0.61	−0.65	−0.34	−0.33
United Kingdom	0.65	0.63	0.56	−0.53	−0.44	−0.44
Italy	0.74	0.73	0.69	−0.34	−0.29	−0.17
Canada	0.53	0.50	0.53	−0.22	−0.38	−0.41
Australia	0.55	0.49	0.42	−0.25	−0.55	−0.53
Belgium	0.72	0.75	0.74	−0.56	0.14	−0.25
Finland	0.32	0.27	0.23	−0.40	−0.65	−0.61
Norway	0.29	0.29	0.30	−0.22	−0.57	−0.50
Netherlands	0.43	0.40	0.40	−0.43	−0.35	−0.32
Sweden	0.60	0.56	0.52	−0.68	−0.55	−0.54

1. Based on a 22-sector subdivision of manufacturing industry. World demand is proxied by OECD exports.
2. Correlation coefficient between the percentage shares of product i in a country's domestic production and in total OECD exports. A coefficient of 1 implies complete correspondence between the two structures, while a value of 0 implies no relationship.
3. Correlation coefficient between the percentage share of product i in a country's domestic production and the products' import penetration rate. A coefficient of −1 implies that a products's share is inversely proportional to its import penetration rate, while a value of 0 implies no relationship between the two.
Source: OECD Secretariat estimates.

Diverse forms of specialisation

The adaptation of industrial structures to the changing conditions of international demand and competition takes two main forms, both of which may be found in the same country:

i) The development of "strong points" involving sectoral specialisation based on comparative advantage, the full exploitation of which may entail major inter-sectoral reallocations of production factors.

ii) Increased intra-sectoral specialisation based on product differentiation. This approach may yield economies of scale and possibly requires relatively low factor mobility, but renders export demand fairly sensitive to industries' competitiveness[4].

As regards inter-sectoral specialisation, analysis by major product category[5] based on "revealed" comparative advantage within the OECD shows the structure of *United States* output and exports to be geared to high-technology products. However, the country's comparative advantage in this area seems to have slipped slightly (Table 4.9). By way of contrast, *Japan* appears to be specialising increasingly in the

Table 4.9. **Relative production, import and export patterns[1]**

Products[2]		1970-1972					1977-1979					1984-1986				
		A	B	C	D	E	A	B	C	D	E	A	B	C	D	E
United States	Production	0.81	1.04	1.03	1.13	1.64	0.84	1.04	1.03	1.10	1.52	0.83	1.07	0.97	1.12	1.65
	Imports	1.09	0.95	1.16	0.82	0.52	1.07	0.88	1.11	0.98	0.84	1.03	1.02	1.10	1.14	0.77
	Exports	0.78	0.55	0.86	1.20	2.23	0.77	0.60	0.85	1.21	2.20	0.79	0.53	0.82	1.12	2.11
Japan	Production	0.71	1.07	1.14	0.85	0.86	0.76	1.09	1.13	1.31	0.89	0.72	1.02	1.08	1.55	0.98
	Imports	1.46	0.99	0.46	0.81	1.91	1.71	1.03	0.48	0.64	1.33	1.70	1.01	0.63	0.64	1.19
	Exports	0.29	1.20	1.43	1.12	0.40	0.22	0.74	1.45	1.33	0.44	0.17	0.61	1.28	1.62	0.63
Germany	Production	0.68	1.17	1.09	1.34	1.31	0.65	1.20	1.11	1.34	1.34	0.64	1.20	1.17	1.25	1.34
	Imports	1.14	1.26	0.87	0.81	0.91	1.12	1.22	0.84	0.84	1.06	1.18	1.14	0.85	0.86	1.11
	Exports	0.49	0.94	1.16	1.32	0.84	0.61	0.93	1.12	1.22	0.86	0.67	0.97	1.17	1.09	0.86
France	Production	1.03	0.96	0.92	1.04	1.22	0.99	0.96	0.93	1.09	1.30	1.00	0.94	0.91	1.09	1.31
	Imports	0.94	0.84	1.00	1.11	1.26	0.96	0.94	1.03	1.03	1.02	1.14	1.05	0.98	0.93	1.05
	Exports	0.98	1.15	1.09	0.79	1.03	1.01	1.00	1.10	0.81	1.09	1.10	1.03	1.07	0.76	1.11
United Kingdom	Production	0.81	1.19	1.03	1.13	1.16	0.85	1.15	1.02	1.10	1.26	0.93	1.06	0.90	1.13	1.43
	Imports	1.55	0.93	0.60	0.82	1.12	1.11	1.05	0.82	0.94	1.39	1.08	0.96	0.83	1.02	1.34
	Exports	0.76	1.16	0.92	1.11	1.33	0.83	1.29	0.85	1.00	1.54	0.91	1.06	0.80	0.96	1.75
Italy	Production	0.76	1.21	1.05	1.14	1.31	0.76	1.25	1.09	1.18	1.04	0.78	1.47	1.01	1.13	0.99
	Imports	1.14	0.79	0.94	1.02	1.08	1.19	0.77	1.00	0.92	1.00	1.35	0.74	0.95	0.85	1.03
	Exports	0.77	1.82	0.80	1.10	0.68	0.90	2.01	0.79	0.97	0.57	0.89	2.40	0.71	0.97	0.60
Canada	Production	1.11	1.01	0.98	0.75	0.99	1.04	1.01	1.00	0.65	0.89	1.09	0.96	1.13	0.59	0.87
	Imports	0.42	0.76	1.48	1.26	1.14	0.42	0.68	1.50	1.28	1.08	0.42	0.69	1.52	1.07	1.10
	Exports	1.97	0.30	1.18	0.44	0.65	2.02	0.32	1.20	0.44	0.48	1.69	0.36	1.42	0.47	0.46
Australia	Production	1.06	1.07	1.02	0.81	0.80	1.04	0.98	0.98	0.75	1.00	1.07	1.31	1.01	0.64	0.81
	Imports	0.53	1.04	1.08	1.34	1.54	0.67	0.99	0.99	1.37	1.39	0.68	0.93	0.93	1.35	1.37
	Exports	3.35	0.52	0.50	0.22	0.29	3.30	0.58	0.58	0.22	0.44	3.51	0.63	0.58	0.18	0.38
Belgium	Production	0.81	1.00	1.34	0.82	0.89	0.83	1.00	1.27	0.87	0.98	0.82	1.07	1.32	0.71	1.04
	Imports	0.89	1.25	1.04	0.91	0.93	0.91	1.27	1.11	0.79	0.84	1.13	1.21	1.11	0.65	0.72
	Exports	1.05	1.39	1.26	0.51	0.51	1.15	1.37	1.20	0.52	0.57	1.33	1.49	1.17	0.44	0.59
Finland	Production	1.60	0.78	0.66	0.68	0.37	1.49	0.77	0.74	0.74	0.40	1.42	0.80	0.82	0.74	0.42
	Imports	0.65	0.94	1.12	1.40	1.00	0.80	0.92	1.01	1.32	1.07	0.82	0.95	0.97	1.28	1.03
	Exports	2.97	0.79	0.51	0.44	0.08	2.57	0.90	0.66	0.57	0.19	2.55	0.87	0.72	0.64	0.27
Netherlands	Production	1.19	0.82	0.92	0.97	0.82	1.25	0.70	0.90	0.91	0.89	1.32	0.57	0.89	0.89	0.79
	Imports	0.85	1.23	0.94	1.10	1.07	0.99	1.15	0.94	1.01	0.96	1.16	1.01	0.91	0.92	1.05
	Exports	1.76	1.01	0.77	0.71	0.83	2.04	0.83	0.77	0.67	0.78	2.21	0.79	0.81	0.59	0.73
Norway	Production	1.42	0.80	0.86	0.64	0.54	1.38	0.76	0.84	0.76	0.54	1.38	0.67	0.78	1.01	0.51
	Imports	0.76	0.99	1.30	0.99	0.76	0.70	1.10	1.14	1.18	0.86	0.78	1.15	0.99	1.16	1.00
	Exports	2.29	0.43	1.02	0.47	0.21	2.03	0.43	1.15	0.46	0.31	2.28	0.43	1.10	0.51	0.37
Sweden	Production	1.02	0.86	0.97	1.13	1.09	0.88	0.95	1.21	1.25	0.95	1.00	0.86	1.02	1.14	0.87
	Imports	0.88	1.07	0.95	1.19	1.03	0.94	1.01	0.95	1.15	1.05	0.86	1.04	0.94	1.19	1.09
	Exports	1.44	0.59	0.96	1.07	0.60	1.41	0.71	0.94	1.04	0.64	1.52	0.74	0.94	0.98	0.68

1. *Production*: Share of product *i* in country *j* output relative to its share in output of the thirteen OECD countries listed in the Table.
   Imports : Share of product *i* in country *j*'s total imports relative to its share in total OECD area imports.
   Exports : Share of product *i* in country *j*'s total exports relative to its share in total OECD area exports.
2. Definition of products: A = Natural-resource-intensive; B = Labour-intensive; C = Scale-intensive; D = Differentiated goods; E = High-technology.
Source: OECD Secretariat estimates.

production of differentiated goods. *Germany*'s strong foreign trade performance stems primarily from the fact that its exports are concentrated in relatively "traditional" products where economies of scale play an important role. Thus, although *Germany*'s performance – like other European countries (apart from the *United Kingdom*) – in high-technology markets has not improved significantly over the years, its industry has managed to maintain poles of competitiveness in areas such as automobiles, engineering and chemicals. The robustness of these "strong points" lies primarily in the speed with which technological innovations are disseminated, thereby allowing German industry to outpace competitors in moving to up-market product niches. By contrast, *Australia, Norway* and *the Netherlands*, and to a lesser degree *Sweden*, seem until recently to have specialised increasingly in natural-resource intensive products for which demand is in relative decline. *Canada* and *Finland*, on the other hand, have sought progressively to reduce their export dependency on natural resources and to focus more on diversifying their output structures.

Smaller countries' industrial structures, with the exception of *Sweden*, are characterised by low proportions of differentiated goods (which lend themselves to intra-industry trade), whereas in some respects the contrary might have been expected, bearing in mind the potential advantages due to eventual economies of scale (Table 4.9). The index of intra-industry trade intensity (Table 4.10) is lower in *Australia* than elsewhere apart from *Japan*, and reflects in large measure the policy of import substitution pursued until the late 1970s. It also follows from the comparative advantage of *Australia* in natural-resource exports, and to a lesser extent from the country's geographic remoteness relative to the other industrialised economies. Indeed, in some instances transportation costs have been prohibitive, obliging *Australia* to manufacture a fairly wide range of products itself. *Belgium*, which is located at the centre of European trade flows, represents the opposite case of a small country that has developed its intra-industry trade.

Japan is similar to *Australia* in that trade in raw materials (as an importer and as an exporter respectively) depresses the intra-industry trade index. However, even if adjustment is made for this factor, intra-industry trade still remains unusually low. This circumstance is often ascribed to protectionist barriers (Lawrence, 1987b), which are not all of official origin, but could also stem from the way in which production and distribution are organised in *Japan*. The highly developed system of sub-contracting and major industrial groups' strategy of vertical integration may effectively limit the scope for import penetration. Moreover, as the 1987 *Economic Survey of Japan* noted, it is often more advantageous for foreign firms to conclude exclusive dealership agreements with major local distributors in Japan who, as sole

Table 4.10. **Intensity of intra-industry trade**[1]

	1964	1967	1973	1979	1985
United States	48	52	48	52	72
Japan	23	22	24	21	24
Germany	44	51	60	60	65
France	64	67	70	70	72
United Kingdom	46	55	71	80	76
Italy	49	45	54	48	55
Canada	37	49	57	56	68
Australia	18	17	29	22	25
Belgium/Luxembourg	62	66	69	73	74
Netherlands	65	66	63	65	67
Mean of above countries	46	49	55	55	60

1. The index of intra-industry trade is the Grubel-Lloyd trade balance-adjusted index:

$$\frac{\Sigma_i \left[(X_i + M_i) - |X_i - M_i|\right]}{\Sigma_i (X_i + M_i) - |\Sigma_i X_i - \Sigma_i M_i|}$$

with X_i and M_i, exports and imports of the industry i.

Source: OECD Secretariat estimates, computed from three digit SITC (Rev. 1) for all trade.

vendors, are then in a position to impose higher prices. However, such circumstances are changing somewhat, following the substantial shifts in major exchange-rate relationships which have taken place during 1988 and the Japanese authorities' resolve to open up the domestic market.

Varying degrees of success with adjustment

A number of Country Surveys incorporate constant-market-share analyses designed to show whether the change in industrial structure has improved manufacturing performance from the viewpoint of its export results. While for countries like *Australia* the commodity structure of exports has not helped performance, the European countries surveyed, with the exception of *Portugal*, seem to have benefited from a commodity structure conducive to export growth during the 1970s. However, industry's successful adaptation to changing international trade patterns depends not only on its effectiveness in product specialisation, but also on the geographic structure of its exports. In this respect, *Australia* has benefited from a favourable geographical pattern of exports, which are directed essentially to the Pacific region. In contrast, European countries have experienced a decline in the contribution of geographical specialisation to their market shares since the late 1970s (Table 4.11). However, *Finland* has experienced a favourable development in both the commodity and regional patterns of its exports since 1982.

Table 4.11. Constant market share analysis

Country/Period[1]	Growth of export values	Growth in world manu-facturing exports[2]	Difference	Effect on exports of:		Residual[5]
				Geographical pattern[3]	Commodity composition[4]	
Australia						
A	7.2	13.5	−6.2	−1.5	−3.2	−1.6
B	19.2	20.9	−1.7	0.7	−1.9	−0.6
C	12.7	15.7	−3.0	1.2	−0.3	−3.9
D	−4.0	2.9	−6.9	−1.1	−2.4	−3.4
Belgium						
A	13.6	13.4	0.2	1.4	0.1	−1.3
B	20.3	20.8	−0.5	0.3	0.0	−0.8
C	13.7	15.7	−2.0	0.3	0.3	−2.5
D	0.3	2.9	−2.6	−0.9	−0.7	−0.9
Finland						
A	10.3	13.4	−3.1	−0.6	−2.3	−0.2
B	20.5	20.8	−0.3	1.1	−0.9	−0.5
C	19.0	15.7	3.3	−2.5	−0.9	6.7
D	1.2	2.9	1.7	−1.6	−0.9	0.8
France						
A	13.9	13.2	0.6	0.7	0.5	−0.5
B	23.4	20.7	2.6	1.6	0.1	0.9
C	14.9	15.6	−0.8	0.8	−0.2	−1.4
D	0.1	3.0	−2.9	−1.4	−0.1	−1.4
Germany						
A	15.5	13.1	2.4	1.2	1.3	−0.1
B	21.3	21.0	0.3	0.9	0.5	−1.1
C	13.5	15.6	−2.1	0.0	−0.3	−1.8
D	3.2	3.0	0.3	−0.7	0.3	0.6
Italy						
A	14.9	13.4	1.5	0.9	0.6	0.0
B	20.6	20.8	−0.2	1.9	0.4	−2.5
C	16.8	15.7	1.1	0.6	0.0	0.4
D	2.9	2.9	0.0	−1.4	−0.2	1.6
Portugal						
A	12.2	13.4	−1.2	−0.8	−1.7	1.3
B	14.3	20.8	−6.6	−0.4	−1.0	−5.2
C	18.7	15.7	3.0	0.6	0.1	2.3
D	8.3	2.9	5.4	−0.9	0.0	6.2
Switzerland						
A	12.8	13.4	−0.5	1.0	0.3	−1.9
B	20.3	20.8	−0.5	0.5	0.0	−1.0
C	15.0	15.7	−0.7	0.4	0.6	−1.7
D	3.0	2.9	0.1	−0.3	−0.1	0.5

1. Periods are: $A = \frac{1970\text{-}71}{1965\text{-}66}$ $B = \frac{1975\text{-}76}{1970\text{-}71}$ $C = \frac{1980\text{-}81}{1975\text{-}76}$ $D = \frac{1985\text{-}86}{1980\text{-}81}$
2. Excluding the country under consideration.
3. Difference betwen the growth rate of a country's exports and that of world exports as a whole that is ascribable to the *geographic pattern* of the country's exports.
4. Difference betwen the growth rate of a country's exports and that of world exports as a whole that is ascribable to the *commodity structure* of the country's exports.
5. The residual term reflects *inter alia* the competitiveness effect.
Source: OECD Secretariat estimates, based on OECD, *Foreign Trade by Commodities.*

A new thrust to industrial policies

Industrial policies since the first oil shock

These sectoral changes, taking place in a context of slower growth after the first oil shock, have provoked social and economic strains to which governments have attempted to respond. The scope of intervention and the instruments used have varied widely from country to country. Indeed, the very concept of industrial policy is difficult to define, covering as it does both support to ailing sectors and promotion of "sunrise" industries. It has embraced both specific measures (such as sectoral aid) and general assistance (investment aid, trade policy), as well as direct intervention by the State as a producer or purchaser. Lastly, industrial policies have overlapped in many and varying ways with macroeconomic policy; at times they have been deployed to meet macroeconomic objectives – such as employment promotion – or, conversely, macroeconomic measures have been directed to industrial adjustment. Broadly speaking, the 1970s and the early 1980s were characterised by growing government intervention in the industrial adjustment process.

The proliferation of government intervention is illustrated by the rapid increase of subsidies (especially in Europe) till around 1984. Although their share in GDP is still small, such transfers appear much more significant in relation to corporate net operating surplus (Table 4.12). Subsidies nevertheless constitute only part of government aid to enterprises, which can also take the form of equity investments, credit on preferential terms or tax relief. These definitional problems often distort international comparisons; the national accounts record only subsidy disbursements, which are generally far from representing the most important form of aid. For example, in *Belgium* only 41 per cent of aid to private enterprises took the form of subsidies in 1984, tax relief being of an equivalent amount. Some studies also suggest that this latter form of aid has been gaining in importance over recent years. Although few estimates of the total amount of state aid are available, these confirm its importance. In *France*, for example, assistance more broadly defined than in the national accounts, increased from 2 per cent of manufacturing value added in 1970 to a peak of 5 per cent in 1983. *Belgium, Denmark, Ireland, the Netherlands,* and *Sweden* have experienced similar trends. Assistance has been largely concentrated in a small number of sectors, and consequently accounts in some cases for a very considerable share of value added in these industries. In *France* it averaged 20 per cent in the shipbuilding, aviation and arms industries over the period 1977/1981 and 17 per cent in the steel industry during the five years to 1983. In *Belgium*, aid to "national sectors"[6] increased from 15 per cent of value added in 1975 to 40 per cent in 1980; its

Table 4.12.   **Direct subsidy payments**

	1960	1970	1980	1982	1984	1986
	Percentage of GDP					
OECD	0.7	1.2	1.7	1.8	2.0	1.8
OECD-Europe	1.4	2.0	2.7	2.8	3.4	2.7
EEC	1.3	1.8	2.6	2.7	3.0	2.8
	Percentage of net operating surplus					
OECD	2.6	4.6	7.9	8.4	8.2	7.2
OECD-Europe	4.2	7.0	11.7	11.5	11.3	9.4
EEC	4.0	6.6	11.4	11.5	11.8	10.4

Source: OECD, *National Accounts.*

share has also grown in other industries, but remains small (up from 3 to 6 per cent of value added over the same period).

Although ailing sectors have been the prime beneficiaries of industry aid in many countries, governments have also tried to foster the development of new activities. For example, *Ireland* has sought to speed up its industrial development by providing tax concessions to enterprises. Many countries have implemented programmes of aid for investment and R & D. In particular, in response to competition from the NIEs in markets for mature products, several small European countries have endeavoured to encourage new activities, especially in small and medium-sized companies and to promote the dissemination of technology within enterprises. *Denmark, Belgium, the Netherlands* and *Sweden* are notable examples. This increased emphasis on support to R & D-related activities has usually taken the form of supplementing, rather than attempting to replace, private-sector R & D, and in most countries (with the major exceptions of *Italy*, the *Netherlands* and *Canada*) the share of government funding in R & D outlays has remained stable or even fallen (Table 4.13).

Another area where government intervention has played an important role is foreign trade. Admittedly, tariff barriers have been coming down steadily; the Tokyo Round cut tariffs by about 30 per cent to 6 per cent on average in the *EEC*, 5.4 per cent in *Japan* and 4.9 per cent in the *United States*. But at the same time non-tariff barriers have increased and their relative impact on trade flows is all the greater in that customs tariffs are now very low. Like financial assistance, quantitative non-tariff barriers are concentrated in a relatively small number of traditional sectors – in particular steel, textiles and clothing. But within these sectors they concern a growing number of products; the share of steel imports to which non-tariff measures

Table 4.13.   **Structure of R&D expenditure**

| | Total expenditure | | Business-sector R&D expenditure (BERD) | | Share of BERD financed by industry | |
| | Per cent of GDP | | Per cent of total | | Per cent | |
	1981	1985	1981	1985	1981	1985
United States	2.45	2.83	70.3	71.7	68.4	66.4
Japan	2.32	2.81	60.7	66.8	97.9	98.0
Germany	2.45	2.66	69.5	72.2	81.7	82.2
France	2.01	2.31	58.9	58.7	68.2	69.6
United Kingdom	2.42	2.33	61.8	63.1	61.3	65.6
Italy	1.01	1.33	56.4	56.9	86.9	77.0
Canada	1.23	1.38	48.9	51.0	83.4	79.3
Australia	1.01	1.14	24.2	33.9	78.8	90.9
Austria	1.17	1.28	55.8	—	88.4	—
Belgium	—	—	—	—	94.5	94.8
Denmark	1.10	1.25	49.8	55.3	83.6	87.2
Finland	1.19	1.50	54.7	60.9	90.1	92.2
Ireland	0.73	0.80	43.6	51.4	80.5	79.6
Netherlands	1.99	2.11	50.3	56.2	84.3	81.1
New Zealand	1.01	1.01	21.7	35.0	83.6	—
Norway	1.29	1.63	52.9	62.7	73.0	77.7
Spain	0.40	—	48.8	—	93.6	—
Sweden	2.22	2.78	66.6	70.8	84.6	87.0
Switzerland	2.29	—	74.2	—	89.6	—

Source: OECD, *Main Science and Technology Indicators, 1981-1987,* Paris 1988.

apply rose from 29 per cent in 1981 to 64 per cent in 1986. Among other sectors, it is essentially the automobile industry that is subject to major and growing restrictions; half of its trade was subject to non-tariff barriers in 1983 (Noguès et al., 1986), compared with less than 1 per cent ten years earlier. However, these quantitative restrictions are clearly not the only instruments applied to restrict imports. In addition, trade can also be impeded by technical specifications (e.g. health and safety standards), price regulations (anti-dumping provisions) or preference for domestic producers in public procurement. Trade distortions also arose until the early 1980s through the export subsidies given by a number of countries.

By their very nature, it is difficult to assess the impact of non-tariff barriers; quantifying the actual degree to which they restrict trade would require determining the *ad valorem* tariff equivalent for each measure. Various studies have, therefore, sought to determine at an aggregate level the extent of trade distortion by comparing actual import penetration rates with what could be considered "normal" on the basis of a country's particular characteristics (size, distance from main centres of economic activity, membership of customs unions). Their findings suggest that the effective degree of protection, whether of an official regulatory nature or resulting from economic agents' spontaneous behaviour, may differ from measures which report the frequency of quantitative restrictions (Table 4.14). Import penetration in *France* is slightly lower than that "warranted" by the country's macroeconomic and geographic situation, but the difference is far smaller than the country's exceptionally large number of non-tariff barriers would imply[7]. The *United States* would seem to have a low effective rate of protection, which contrasts with its numerous non-tariff barriers to trade in goods and services. Lastly, *Japan* would seem to be an "underimporter" in respect to manufactures, but not to trade as a whole. However, the basis for this type of analysis is rather tenuous, as the findings depend heavily on model specifications.

Other aspects of government intervention – regulation, public procurement policies, state-owned enterprise operations – do not lend themselves readily to quantitative assessment. It seems, however, that even where government intervention

Table 4.14.   **Extent of non-tariff barriers in OECD countries**[1]

Per cent

	All products	Manufactures	Change 1980-1983	
			All products	From industrialised countries
EEC	18.9	18.3	2.8	4.1
Germany	14.7	17.7	2.6	3.9
Belgium/Luxembourg	21.0	19.1	2.1	3.0
Denmark	13.3	14.5	2.7	3.7
France	44.2	29.1	2.8	3.8
Greece	19.0	23.3	5.9	8.7
Ireland	13.0	16.1	2.8	4.3
Italy	10.0	9.6	1.5	2.3
Netherlands	21.4	19.8	2.6	4.2
United Kingdom	13.9	16.5	2.4	3.1
Australia	44.4	24.8	2.8	3.7
Austria	7.5	2.4	0.2	0
United States	34.3	12.3	0.5	0.6
Finland	34.3	8.8	− 3.1	− 4.2
Japan	9.0	5.4	0.1	0.1
Norway	6.1	2.9	− 0.2	− 0.3
Switzerland	42.9	16.1	2.5	3.1
Average	21.8	14.9	1.8	2.8

1.   Share of import categories subject to non-tariff barriers in 1983.
Source: Nogués J., A. Olechowski and L.A. Winters (1986): "The Extent of Non-tariff Barriers to Imports of Industrial Countries". *World Bank staff Working Paper* 789, Washington, p. 44.

is considered to be on a small scale, highly-regulated sectors play an important and probably growing role in the economy (about a third of total output in *Germany* and *Canada*). It is also estimated that the share of productive activities subject to specific regulation increased in the *United States* from 10 per cent in 1965 to 20 per cent in 1980. It is also clear that in some countries, like *France*, government procurement is an important industrial-policy instrument, and is used to promote activities regarded as having growth potential, especially in high-tech sectors. Likewise, state-owned enterprises have been used as a vehicle for macroeconomic policy, particularly for employment promotion. This policy of direct intervention in industrial supply reached a peak in *France* in 1982 with the nationalisation of the major groups in the competitive sector.

Criticism of industrial policy

Industrial policies have, however, often yielded disappointing results compared with the efforts deployed. Several hypotheses have been put forward to explain this. Policies have often failed to match targets and means; for example, sectoral aid has been directed toward regional-policy objectives. Rather than aiming to promote better resource allocation between sectors, policies have been directed toward social or political objectives, such as maintaining sector specific incomes and employment or developing advanced technologies. Broadly speaking, the growth of subsidies and other protective measures has distorted competition and blurred market signals, thereby delaying the necessary adjustments and creating unexpected distortions. Lastly, these policies have often proved costly in budgetary terms, and have made for additional rigidity in the management of public finances. Thus, at a time when efforts are being made to achieve fiscal consolidation, their appropriateness is being increasingly challenged.

In fact, industrial policies have proved largely ineffective in safeguarding jobs. The employment trend in declining sectors has not differed significantly between countries, irrespective of the policy options adopted (Table 4.15). Indeed, state aid to industry may have helped maintain excessively high wage levels in heavily unionised sectors – such as steel and automobiles – and, by thus distorting relative factor prices, may have accentuated the substitution of capital for labour. Since increased assistance may accordingly have retarded rather than facilitated the process of trimming over-capacity, unprofitable activities have been preserved in sectors enjoying no obvious comparative advantage. This problem has been particularly stressed in the Surveys of *Austria, Belgium, Norway* and *Sweden*. By contrast, excess

Table 4.15. **Employment in three ailing sectors**

	Steel 1985 (1974 = 100)	Textiles 1984 (1974 = 100)	Shipbuilding 1985 (1975 = 100)
United States	46	64	..
Japan	80	63	52
Germany	66	60	45
Belgium/Luxembourg	60	49	56[3]
France	52	64[1]	57
Italy	76	81	35
United Kingdom	31	42	25[3]
Austria	71	62	..
Norway	53	65[1]	29
Sweden	62	62[2]	11
Switzerland	50	..	..

1. 1983.
2. 1982.
3. 1984.
Source: OECD, *Structural Adjustment and Economic Performance*, Paris 1987.

capacity has been trimmed to a remarkable extent in *Japan*, and this without the help of subsidies.

Success in promoting new activities has also fallen far short of expectations. The Survey of *Ireland* remarks that industrial policy there has attracted multinational companies to invest in the country as a base for exporting to Europe, but that most of the net income so earned is repatriated overseas and domestic value added has been rather small. Thus, both the impact on local job creation and the extent of technological spin-off for the economy as a whole have been limited. Similarly, the Report on *Structural Adjustment and Economic Performance* concluded that efforts in *France* and *the United Kingdom* to create competitive advantages in sectors regarded as strategic by the authorities have proved successful only when backed up by government procurement.

Growing attention is being focused on the impact of protectionist policies on countries' production structures. The Survey of *Australia* clearly demonstrates how such policies can have unforeseen adverse effects. High levels of protection have helped to foster a highly diversified industrial structure with little involvement in international trade. Protection of the domestic market has inhibited intra-industry trade to a certain extent, and thereby also the scope for exploiting scale economies as much as other countries. Furthermore, the sectoral dispersion in rates of protection has distorted relative prices and attracted resources into sectors where this country enjoys no particular comparative advantage. Similarly, the Survey of *Greece* suggests that the high degree of protection which manufacturing enjoyed prior to the country's accession to the *EC* was largely responsible for the difficulties that Greek industry had in adjusting to changing international-trade patterns in the aftermath of the oil shocks. On the other hand, in *Germany* the overall level of tariff protection is low, with individual sectoral rates inversely proportional to sectors' comparative advantage.

Various studies have sought to quantify the costs and benefits of policy measures, especially in the area of protection. An OECD study of the automobile sector suggests that the restrictions imposed on imports of Japanese cars, which may have raised vehicle prices by 6 to 15 per cent in *the United States, Canada, the United Kingdom* and *France*, created economic rents for both domestic and foreign manufacturers. These higher prices have not been offset by any significant effect on employment; between 20 000 and 35 000 jobs were preserved in *the United States,* but practically no effect whatsoever was discernible in *France* and *the United Kingdom*. In its 1987 *World Development Report*, the World Bank has summarised the findings of various studies on the costs of protection. A few figures are eloquent in this respect. The cost to United States consumers of preserving one job in the steel and automobile industries was estimated at more than $100 000. In *the United Kingdom,* the cost of preserving one job in the automobile industry is estimated at $50 000, and at over $100 000 in the video-recorder industry. At a more general level, the OECD report on the *Costs and Benefits of Protection* noted that restrictive trade policies are likely to redistribute income and employment rather than improve overall performance, to adversely affect investment and business confidence, and to jeopardise efforts by indebted less-developed countries to stabilise their debt and growth situations.

However, criticism is not limited to the way in which interventionist policies are being implemented. Their theoretical justification is also being increasingly called into question. The ability of governments to conduct interventionist industrial policies is challenged on the grounds of uncertainty in respect to the theoretical criteria for both determining policy and measuring performance (Krugman, 1987). The justifications for regulatory control have also come under scrutiny, especially in sectors such as telecommunications and transportation which have traditionally been regarded as providing a public service and which are now of crucial importance for the growth of modern economies. Studies have shown not only that regulation has been widely abused by firms in regulated sectors as a protective device to the detriment of consumer interests, but also that such control is not necessarily warranted by conditions of imperfect competition. Some sectors that have been traditionally regarded as natural monopolies, owing to the magnitude of non-recoverable (sunk) fixed costs, were nevertheless "contestable" – in other words, the threat of entry by new competitors which have been held back by regulation suffices to modify firms' behaviour. In line with such reasoning are suggestions to open up "infrastructure" sectors like telecommunications and transportation to competition. The concept of "contestability" is central to the reforms that are currently underway in *New Zealand*.

New trends in industrial policy and their limitations

With the effectiveness of interventionist measures being called into question, adjustment policies have placed growing emphasis on the need to strengthen market mechanisms and achieve greater flexibility. As in the case of interventionist measures, experience varies from country to country depending on the policies previously pursued and the nature of the problems confronting individual governments. However, two broad complementary thrusts can be distinguished: reducing government intervention in product markets and bolstering adjustment capacity in factor markets. The instruments deployed to these ends – reducing border protection and subsidies, privatisation and deregulation – have varied across countries. Greater emphasis is being placed on achieving policy coherence as well as on making aid less discretionary, and on ensuring its compatibility with macroeconomic objectives. However, although these new policies have met with general acceptance internationally, in many countries they are still being applied only very gradually.

One field where the change in policy orientation seems most clear-cut is deregulation. This trend originates in part in technological progress, particularly in the transport and telecommunications sectors, which has lowered the natural barriers to entry to many of these markets and has increased the scope for competition between different types of service. The *United States*[8], *the United Kingdom, Japan* and *Canada* have all deregulated the telecommunications sector. Regulatory change is also underway in *Australia* and *Germany* as well as in a number of other countries. In the *United States*, new entry is restricted to the long distance networks but in both *Japan* and *the United Kingdom* there are no such restrictions. These changes have led to major revisions in the price structures, the relative price for long distance communications falling. In *Japan*, several new carriers have entered the basic telecommunications market while the complete deregulation of Value Added Network Services has led to the entry of around 500 new enterprises. In the *United Kingdom*, British Telecom has been privatised but only one additional license for short and long distance services will be issued until 1990. A wide range of peripheral activities have, however, been deregulated.

The transport sector has also been extensively deregulated in the *United States* and the *United Kingdom* and to a somewhat lesser extent in many other countries. A number of studies have highlighted the advantages gained from these measures. Deregulation of air transport in the *United States* is calculated to save air travellers $11 billion a year and the opening up of routes between the *United Kingdom* and the *Netherlands* has resulted in sizeable benefits to consumers and producers alike. Similar efficiency gains have been observed for surface transport.

Privatisation has been embraced in similar spirit, being designed to strengthen market forces in activities which, as long as they remained in the public sector, were at least partly sheltered, while the privatisation proceeds contribute to public budget finance. Programmes have been implemented on a particularly large scale in the *United Kingdom* and *France*. In the *United Kingdom* no public enterprise or public service has been excluded *a priori* from privatisation. So far, fifteen major companies and a number of smaller enterprises have been transferred to private ownership; their combined workforce, totalling about 650 000, represents one-third of workers employed in the industrial public sector in 1979. The proceeds of future sales are expected to exceed 1 per cent of GDP per year until 1990. Efforts have also been made to improve the management of public enterprises; as a result, British Steel, for example, is now showing a profit and has been returned to the private sector at the end of 1988. These initiatives – privatisation plus reorganisation – have allowed budget expenditure on aid to public enterprises to be cut from £3 billion in 1978-79 to less than £0.5 billion. However, an extremely cautious aproach was initially adopted in the *United Kingdom* towards injecting competition into industries dominated by major monopolies, followed more recently by more ambitious plans for the privatisation of the electricity industry. In *France*, the privatisation programme is more recent and limited to a list of statutory designated companies which together accounted for around one-half of industrial public-sector employment in 1982. Thirteen enterprises had been privatised by the end of 1987, the proceeds amounting to FF 89 billion (about 1¾ per cent of GDP). Privatisation of public-service monopolies is not currently envisaged in *France*. Substantial progress has been made in *Japan* where both the telephone and railway systems have been privatised. In *New Zealand*, the initial approach was to "corporatise" public enterprises (that is, convert them into share companies with ownership retained by the Government). However, more recently the authorities have embarked on a large-scale programme of privatisation. Privatisation programmes are also under consideration in *Austria* and *Portugal*, while a few companies have transferred to private ownership in *Italy* and *Germany*.

In the foreign trade area, the 1987 OECD Ministerial Council meeting

145

reaffirmed Member countries' commitment to "reverse recent trends towards restrictive trade measures, notably of a bilateral or a discriminatory nature". Multilateral negotiations are now underway within the framework of the Uruguay Round. *Australia* provides a good example of where policy has been re-oriented in the right direction. The effective rate of protection for the manufacturing sector as a whole fell from 22 per cent in FY 1984-85 to 19 per cent in FY 1986-87. This decline was almost entirely accounted for by the reduced assistance afforded by quotas in the textile, clothing and footwear and passenger motor vehicle sectors. Assistance to non-quota-protected manufacturing sectors remained broadly unchanged at around 14 per cent, although the disparities in effective rates of protection may have declined marginally. But the level of protection should now begin to fall again, following decisions to reduce tariffs in a number of specific sectors and the abolition of the 2 per cent revenue duty imposed on duty-free imports since 1979. Moreover, a general lowering of manufacturing tariffs was announced in May 1988. As a result of these measures, the average effective rate of assistance to manufacturing should fall to 14 per cent by FY 1992-93 and the dispersion of assistance among manufacturing industries is expected to be reduced by about 30 per cent. In *New Zealand* customs duties have been lowered substantially on products not covered by specific industry plans, which set timetables for the reduction of aid to "trade-sensitive" industries. Furthermore, import quotas will be phased out. Notwithstanding these measures, the unweighted average of nominal customs tariff rates on all products will still be well above the average in other industrialised countries.

Progress has also been made in the area of bilateral trade. A major free trade agreement has been signed by the *United States* and *Canada* that provides for the abolition of all customs duties and of most non-tariff barriers in trade between the two countries, open tendering for government contracts and the liberalisation of services and foreign investment. Studies carried out in *Canada* indicate that the agreement could boost GDP by about 2½ per cent and permit the creation of between 100 000 and 150 000 new jobs in Canada, thanks primarily to the economies of scale made possible. Creation of the European Single Market from the beginning of 1993 should also be of considerable importance from the viewpoint not only of the potential for exploiting scale economies, but also for the accompanying amendments to national legislation which could bring greater flexibility.

However, this has been accompanied at the multilateral level by increased protectionist pressures during recent years, which have heightened uncertainties surrounding investment decisions. There has been a sharp increase in the incidence of restrictive measures, which have spread to new sectors, especially high-technology goods and certain services. The most important of these measures are the new anti-dumping regulations introduced by the *EC*, the semiconductor agreement between *Japan* and the *United States* in 1986 and the new trade legislation recently adopted in the *United States* in autumn 1988.

A widespread effort is underway to both cut and retarget government subsidies (see above). However, although the rising trend has been contained, the outlays in relation to GDP have not been substantially reduced. The revival in profits from 1985-1988 has led to their share in gross operating surplus falling appreciably in *Denmark, Norway, United Kingdom* and *Sweden*. The employment cost of cutting assistance has been relatively limited in *Norway* and *Sweden*, thanks to the implementation, especially in *Sweden*, of regional development programmes to promote new activities. In some countries, such as *Germany* and *Belgium*, the decentralised nature of decision-making may have retarded the process of cutting assistance, and ailing sectors in *Belgium* continue to absorb the bulk of government and quasi-public aid. The policy of retargeting subsidies has been taken further in some countries than in others. In the *Netherlands*, "defensive" intervention has been halved since 1982 and investment subsidies (WIR programme) have now been abolished (1988). Aid is henceforth geared primarily to supporting R & D and technological innovation.

Macroeconomic consequences of policies to strengthen competition

The increased competition expected to ensue from reductions in protectionist barriers and state aid will have three main effects – reallocation of resources, enhanced macroeconomic flexibility in responding to changes in the economic environment and stronger long-term growth. The first-mentioned effect, which is of microeconomic nature, concerns the redistribution of factors between sectors and of income between individuals. Domestically, the relative profitability of previously protected sectors will be threatened by the strengthening of competition, thereby inducing transfers of capital and labour to industries not favoured by earlier policies but whose prospects will henceforth be enhanced. Similarly, privileged categories of wage-earners will see their relative advantages challenged. And the budget savings accruing from the withdrawal of State assistance will release resources for use elsewhere. Internationally, the abolition of certain protectionist barriers in OECD countries could have a favourable net impact on the developing countries.

147

Industrial adjustment and economic flexibility

The second – macroeconomic – effect of enhanced competition will be to reinforce economies' capacity to respond to supply shocks, thanks to enhanced price and real-wage flexibility. An economy's resilience seems determined to a fairly large extent by its type of international specialisation and by the degree of protection enjoyed by its industry from international competition. The greater an economy's exposure to competition, the more sensitive its prices will be to foreign competitors' prices and to demand conditions. Similarly, the degree of tolerable real-wage rigidity will diminish and, as the factor-price elasticity of labour demand increases, the sensitivity of wage-earners to the threat of unemployment will intensify (Lawrence (1987a). It is the competitive nature of wage and price formation which partly determines the speed with which the growth opportunities offered by technological innovation can be exploited via lower prices and increased purchasing power. It also determines how rapidly *relative* prices respond and how quickly an economy reverts to an "equilibrium" growth path following supply shocks – such as the oil price shocks or intensified competition from the NIEs. The shorter response time of the adjustment will result in smaller overall losses in output and employment. Thus, strengthening competition through product-market deregulation and the removal of support to industry can be expected to result not only in a more rational allocation of resources but also in an improved capacity to respond to changes in the economic climate. The less flexible economies were initially, the greater will be the expected macroeconomic gains.

From this viewpoint, the *United States* may be contrasted, on the basis of empirical evidence, with the major European countries. Despite a manufacturing sector which tends to be a price-setter abroad (Table 4.16, column 1) on account of its dominance in high technology, *United States'* producer prices for the corporate sector as a whole seem much more sensitive to competitive conditions (measured by their response to import prices and demand/supply pressures) than in *Germany, France* or *Italy* (Table 4.16, columns 3 and 2). Long-run real-wage rigidity also appears to be much lower there than in *France*, the *United Kingdom* or *Italy*.

France and *Italy* seem to have accumulated handicaps *vis-à-vis* foreign competitors; their domestic prices and real wages are comparatively inflexible, while their exporters take close account of prices in foreign markets. Real-wage rigidity in the *United Kingdom*, which is also very marked, penalises local manufacturers during a domestic economic downturn given competitive conditions in the home market. In *Germany*, which combines long-run real-wage flexibility with pronounced price rigidity, the corporate sector as a whole has demonstrated a remarkable ability to

Table 4.16. **Price and real-wage sensitivity to market conditions**

	Weight of foreign prices in export price formation[1]	Long-term responsiveness of producer prices to[2]:		Long-term real-wage rigidity[3]
		Business cycles	Import prices	
United States	0.13	2.28	0.46	1.15
Japan	0.56	1.13	0.27	0.72
Germany	0.16	0.69	0.11	1.27
France	0.42	1.40	0.14	3.03
United Kingdom	0.26	1.97	0.62	6.66
Italy	0.61	0.38	0.26	1.67
Canada	0.32	1.75	0.45	1.96

1. Elasticity of manufacturing export prices with respect to competitors' prices. The specification of the export price equation is described in R. Herd, "Import and Export Price Equations for Manufactures", *ESD Working Papers,* 43, 1987.
2. Concerning specification of the equation on which these estimates are based, see U. Stiehler, "Price Determination in the major seven country models in Interlink", *ESD Working Papers,* 44, 1987. The coefficients are those of the current version of INTERLINK. The coefficients are:
   — *Business cycles:* Semi-elasticity of producer prices in the non-energy enterprise sector with respect to the index of capacity utilisation.
   — *Import prices:* Elasticity of producer prices with respect to non-energy import prices.
3. Ratio of long-term price-elasticity of wages to semi-elasticity of wages with respect to the unemployment rate. The elasticities are from Chan-Lee, Coe and Prywes, "Microeconomic Changes and Macroeconomic Wage Desinflation in the 1980s", *OECD Economic Studies,* Spring 1987. For some countries the wage equation is not linear with respect to the unemployment rate and sometimes also includes a productivity term; in these cases, the semi-elasticities with respect to the unemployment rate have been obtained using the method and assumptions set out in Coe and Gagliardi, "Nominal Wage Determination in Ten OECD Economies", *ESD Working Papers,* 19, 1985.
Source: OECD Secretariat estimates.

maintain overall profit ratios in the face of short-term shocks and movements in foreign competitors' prices. This can be partly explained by the fact that the country's manufacturing industry is able to set export prices without much weight being given to competitors' prices (Table 4.16). This probably reflects the entrenched positions that German exporters have built up in certain markets, as referred to above. Thus, price rigidity has not handicapped *Germany*'s external performance.

As regards price flexibility, *Japan* exhibits unique features. Econometric estimates covering the period 1972-1983, suggest that its manufacturing export prices are comparatively very sensitive to competitors' prices and the degree of flexibility of Japanese firms' export margins has been frequently noted. This flexibility derives partly from exporters' specialisation in differentiated product markets where price competition is keen, but also from importing countries' imposition of quantitative restrictions on Japanese exports. This latter allows exporters to reap additional profits by aligning prices to the higher levels prevailing in the importer's domestic market. On the other hand, in *Japan's* domestic market business-sector producer prices as a whole seem to respond primarily and rapidly to movements in domestic costs, implying that corporate profit margins are relatively inelastic with respect to both cyclical conditions and foreign competitors' prices. A tentative explanation for this apparent asymmetry in price behaviour is that the relative weakness of effective foreign competition in the domestic market makes for the price elasticity of domestic demand being lower than that of world demand for Japanese products[9].

Since the major European countries on average seem less flexible than the *United States* or *Japan*, they will be the most affected by deregulation. They will probably also be among the main ultimate beneficiaries of the gains expected to accrue from greater macroeconomic flexibility, although this may also have its negative aspects. Increased relative-price and real-wage flexibility may lead to greater uncertainty with respect to profit and employee-compensation prospects, with possible adverse consequences for the economy's vitality. Some authors (e.g. De Long and Summers, 1986) even contend that greater price volatility could induce paralysing swings in real interest rates. Furthermore, a number of studies suggest that a certain amount of price inertia is warranted on rational economic grounds, based on firms' need to foster customer loyalty in order to minimise transactions costs[10]. However, such practices should not be threatened insofar as policies to strengthen competition aim solely at improving market signals. It may also be noted that, to the extent enhanced price flexibility reduces the number of sectors operating below full capacity, monetary and fiscal demand management policies will impact more on the general price level and less on the volume of output than earlier[11].

Industrial adjustment and economic growth

Stimulating competition should reinforce not only countries' capacity to respond flexibly to real shocks, but also economic growth over the longer term. The estimated impact on growth depends on whether a static or dynamic modelling approach is adopted. Many studies of the consequences of abolishing protectionist barriers and subsidies based on applied general equilibrium models conclude that there would be net gains in welfare, although their estimated magnitude varies widely. Since these are nearly always comparative-static models which show once-for-all shifts in the level of output, they are by definition unable to throw light on possible favourable effects on the equilibrium growth rate.

The magnitude of the long-term gains when true dynamic effects are taken into account is potentially higher but more uncertain. It is sometimes argued that too much competition will reduce the planning horizon and hence the expected profitability to firms of R & D and product innovation. This viewpoint, associated with a structural approach to competition, further argues that monopolistic markets with large firms are a necessary condition for growth. On the other hand, viewed as a process and not as a structure, competition forces firms to innovate and to improve efficiency so that increased competition is beneficial. Moreover, this view is behind the contestable market approach and has been supported by the favourable effects of increased competition following deregulation in fields such as transport and telecommunications (see above). Size does not appear to be an absolute determinant of the propensity to innovate. The advantages associated with size may depend on the market in which firms are operating. Some tests (e.g. Acs and Audretsch, 1987) suggest that relatively small companies can be more innovative and out-perform large firms in the creation of new products, essentially in the first stages of a product's life cycle and in markets where professional skills are of key importance.

Moreover, the speed with which economies adjust to change in the economic environment has a major dynamic impact on growth. The accumulated losses in jobs and investment will be greater where impediments to the free play of market forces retard adjustment. If adjustment occurs swiftly, long-term unemployment and the associated losses in human capital will be curtailed, and investment, which is a main vehicle of technical progress, will be stimulated. These two effects will combine to enhance the economy's potential growth rate[12].

Conclusions

A comparative study of industrial adjustment reveals how experience has differed from country to country. The pace of structural adjustment has varied according to the pressures exerted by international competition. It has taken different forms according to sector and country, involving for example exploitation of comparative advantages deriving from factor endowment in certain industries or the development of trade in differentiated products. These developments have been many and varied but in the long term generally in line with market forces, and have been only marginally affected by the sometimes highly selective industrial objectives of governments.

As strongly interventionist industrial policies have proved ineffective, in many countries governments' declared intentions, and increasingly their actions, are now mainly directed towards strengthening the play of competitive forces in absorbing tensions. Numerous types of state aid have been reduced and certain contestable markets have been deregulated. Thus, industrial policies are now being deployed to facilitate, rather than delay, necessary adjustments by enhancing their social acceptability and by rendering them economically less hazardous for those concerned. Promoting occupational mobility by improved training systems, devising appropriate instruments for financing innovative firms, and tackling discrimination between sectors by removing barriers to entry in over-protected markets, can all contribute to these objectives. In this respect, the role of macroeconomic policies is itself under review. Such policies can and must promote the emergence of a more stable macroeconomic environment which is a prerequisite for fostering private initiatives and economic growth. They should also strive for greater neutrality and transparency with respect to their impact on the intersectoral allocation of resources.

Reinforcing the role of relative prices and wages in matching supply and demand by promoting competition will subject markets to more rigorous constraints. It will also call for stricter discipline in government macroeconomic policies. As foreign trade, and certainly import demand, will become more responsive to relative price movements with the dismantling of protectionist barriers, exchange rate policies will have more immediate and more marked consequences. At the same time, the need for expansionary policy measures will decrease, as prices approximate more closely market-clearing levels and production capacity is thereby more fully utilised. Furthermore, the process of consolidating public finances by reducing expenditure, on which many countries have now embarked, will depress the level of activity less within the framework of a more competitive economy driven by a dynamic private sector.

Notes

1. The following *OECD Economic Surveys* have reviewed industrial adjustment developments:

Country	Review date
Switzerland	October 1984
Norway	December 1984
Austria	January 1985
Iceland	March 1985
Ireland	March 1985
Sweden	April 1985
New Zealand	May 1985
Japan	July 1985
Netherlands	February 1986
Denmark	February 1986
Belgium	July 1986
Luxembourg	July 1986
Australia	January 1987
Germany	June 1987
Finland	February 1988
Canada	June 1988

2. See Goldstein and Khan (1985) for a discussion of the methodology of measuring elasticity differentials. The effect of a change in the export/import ratio on the trade balance depends on the latter's initial level.

3. The income-elasticity values may in fact have changed recently, precisely because of the adjustments described below. Estimating the magnitude of the possible changes is, however, still difficult, pending completion of the Secretariat's re-estimation of the foreign trade equations and its analysis of their stability.

4. For a discussion of the consequences of both types of specialisation for factor adjustment, see Lundberg and Hansson (1986). For econometric testing of the various factors (endowment with production factors, demand similarity, existence of economies of scale, etc.) which determine the place which a country or a given industry takes in international trade, see Belassa and Bauwens (1988) and Bowen *et al.* (1987).

5. In *Structural Adjustment and Economic Performance*, OECD, 1987 a new classification of industries was proposed: *i)* high R & D-intensive; *ii)* differentiated goods; *iii)* scale-intensive; *iv)* labour-intensive; *v)* natural-resource intensive. This breakdown has some advantages over the classification used hitherto in OECD studies which had grouped extremely heterogeneous industries under the headings of low- and medium-technology products.

6. The "national" sectors are: steel, coal, shipbuilding, textiles and glass containers. Although they consist of private enterprises, they are labelled "national" because responsibility for industrial policy towards them was not transferred to the regions under the institutional reform of 1980. Their critical situation required an appeal to national solidarity.

7. See, for example, Lawrence (1987b), Hazart and Khong (1987) and Barbone (1988).

8. E.E. Bailey (1986) gives a preliminary assessment of United States experience.

9. The apparent inertia of domestic prices may also be in part a statistical illusion insofar as it is costs, and primarily wage costs, that may adjust more or less directly and rapidly to both foreign and domestic competitive pressures. In fact, the indicator of real-wage rigidity is comparatively very low in *Japan.*

10. Stiglitz (1984) contains a theoretical survey of the macroeconomic rationality of price inertia. Recent tests (Bradburd and Caves, 1987) confirm the hypothesis that the closer buyer-seller relationships are, the more inert prices will be.

11. For a review of the literature on the effects of monetary policy, given varying degrees of price flexibility, see Bailey *et al.* (1987) and Chouraqui *et al.* (1988).

12. Econometric studies do not invalidate the hypothesis that rigidities in the functioning of markets may be detrimental to long-term growth. A study by Heitger (1987) suggests, for example, that the effective rate of protection has a strongly negative impact on economic growth. The tests were conducted by pooling data for two periods (the 1960s and 1970s) and fifty countries.

Bibliography

Acs Z.J. and D.B. Audretsch (1987): "Innovation, market structure and firm size", *Review of Economics and Statistics*, No. 4, (November).

Bailey E.E. (1986): "Price and productivity change following regulation: the US experience", *The Economic Journal*, No. 96, (March).

Bailey R.W., Ch. Bordes M.J. Driscoll, M.O. Strauss-Kahn (1987): "Monnaie, demande globale et inertie des rythmes d'inflation dans les principaux pays européens", *Economie Appliquée*, XL, No. 3.

Barbone L. (1988): "Trade imbalances and import barriers", *OECD Economic Studies*, (Autumn).

Belassa B. and Bauwens L. (1988): "Inter-industry and intra-industry specialisation in manufactured goods", *Weltwirtschaftliches Archiv*, Vol. 124, No. 1.

Bradburd R.M. and R.E. Caves (1987): "Transaction-cost influences on the adjustment of industries prices and outputs", *Review of Economics and Statistics*, No. 4, (November).

Blades D. (1987): "Goods and services in OECD countries", *OECD Economic Studies* No. 8, (Spring).

Bowen H.P., Leamer E.E. and Sveikaurhaus L. (1987): "Multicountry, multifactor tests of the factor abundance theory", *American Economic Review*, (December).

Chouraqui J.C., M. Driscoll and M.O. Strauss-Kahn (1988): "The effects of monetary policy on the real sector: an overview of empirical evidence for selected OECD economies", *OECD Working Papers* No. 51, (April).

De Long J. and L.H. Summers (1986): "Is increased price flexibility stabilising?", *American Economic Review*, (December).

Donges J.B. and H.H. Glismann (1987): "Industrial adjustment in Western Europe – retrospect and prospect", *Kiel Working Paper* No. 280, (March).

Goldstein M. and M.S. Khan (1985): "Income and price effects on foreign trade" in *Handbook of International Economics*, vol. II, ed. by R.W. Jones and P.B. Kenen, Elsevier Science Publishers, 1985.

Hazart P. and V. Khong (1987): "Les importations françaises: une analyse statistique", *Revue de l'Ipecode*, No. 17, (November).

Heitger B. (1987): "Import protection and export performance. their impact on economic growth", *Weltwirtschaftliches Archiv*, Volume 123.

Krugman P.R. (1987): "Is free trade passé?", *The Journal of Economic Perspectives*, vol. 1, 2, (Autumn).

Lawrence R.Z. (1987a): "Product market rigidities and macroeconomic performance: issue in theory and measurement", OECD unpublished paper, (May).

Lawrence R.Z. (1987b): "Imports in Japan: Closed Markets or Minds?", *Brookings Papers on Economic Activity*, No. 2, (Autumn).

Lundberg L. and P. Hansson (1986): "Intra-industry trade and its consequences for adjustment" in *Imperfect Competition and International Trade*. Ed. by Greenaway and P.K.M. Tharakan, Wheatsheaf Books.

Nogues J., A. Olechowski and L.A. Winters (1986): "The extent of non-tariff barriers to imports of industrial countries", *World Bank Staff Working Paper* No. 789, Washington.

OECD (1987): *The Cost of Restricting Imports. The Automobile Industry.*

Stiglitz J. (1984): "Price rigidities and market structure", *American Economic Review*, No. 74(2), (May).

Van Gemert H.G. (1987): "Structural change in OECD countries: a normal pattern analysis", *De Economist*, vol. 135, No. 1.

Chapter 5

THE PUBLIC SECTOR:
RESTORING THE BALANCE

Introduction

The following review of fiscal trends describes the process of budgetary reform documented in *OECD Economic Surveys* in recent years and the thinking behind it[1]. Rationales for reform developed to a large extent from the experiences of the 1970s, when the coincidence of slowing economic growth, rising structural unemployment and accelerating inflation began to persuade governments that the usual goals of economic policy were no longer being served by a continuing expansion of the public sector. Governments turned towards greater self-restraint as evidence accumulated that higher taxes and budget deficits could contribute to allocative distortions which reduced long-run growth potential. There have been differences in priorities (in particular between the United States and the rest of the OECD over the need to raise taxes to cut the Federal deficit), but there has, in general, been a remarkable degree of agreement among OECD countries on the issues involved. The 1980s have been characterised by the pursuit of a smaller and more efficient public sector and greater private choice; a more coherent tax structure and better control over government borrowing.

The chapter begins with a discussion of public spending issues and the progress made in OECD economies towards better public expenditure control. The second section discusses the progress towards tax reform and the rationales for it. Structural issues arising from persistent budget deficits are discussed in Section three.

156

Public expenditure: containing the expansion

The welfare state in crisis

In the two decades from 1960 the average share of government outlays in OECD GNP increased by a third, from just under 30 to 40 per cent (Diagram 5.1, Table 5.1). In a number of economies it practically doubled (Table 5.2). The reasons for the expansion were complex, involving problems of planning and control, difficulties in containing rising costs and measuring government output, the high income elasticity of demand for some services, demographic pressures and political constraints. The rapid growth of the public sector up to 1980 was not wholly planned, as can be seen from how much slower the government share of resources was expected to grow in the 1970s (see OECD 1972). But over-expansion was facilitated by a widespread attachment to the view that the secular growth of the public sector was an

DIAGRAM 5.1

TOTAL PUBLIC EXPENDITURE (1)
Per cent of GDP/GNP

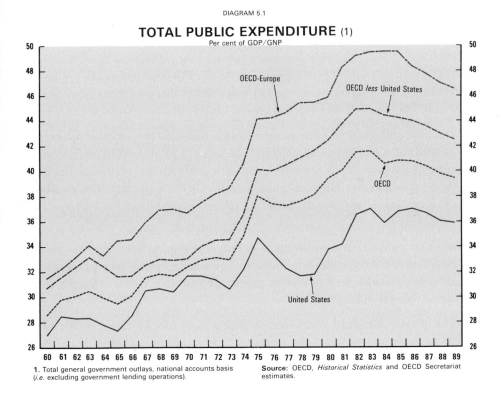

1. Total general government outlays, national accounts basis (*i.e.* excluding government lending operations).

Source: OECD, *Historical Statistics* and OECD Secretariat estimates.

Table 5.1. **Structure and growth of general government outlays**[1]

	Relative to total government outlays					Relative to GDP				
	1960	1975	1980	1983	1986	1960	1975	1980	1983	1986
Final consumption	56.7	46.2	43.8	42.4	47.0	14.9	17.2	17.0	17.6	17.1
Social security transfers	24.6	33.2	34.1	34.5	32.3	6.7	12.8	13.4	14.3	13.0
Other current outlays	11.5	10.6	13.2	15.7	13.1	3.4	4.6	5.4	6.5	7.0
Capital outlays	7.2	10.0	8.9	7.5	7.6	3.6	3.8	3.5	3.1	3.1
Total	100.0	100.0	100.0	100.0	100.0	28.6	38.4	39.3	41.5	40.2

Source: OECD Secretariat estimates.

essential element in economic growth and stability. Public expenditure policies tended to be characterised by optimism about the external benefits accruing from public sector involvement in the economy, combined with a belief in the need to correct pervasive market failure (including employment shortfalls caused by deficient private sector demand).

As productivity growth declined and inflation accelerated, views about the role of the public sector began to change during the late 1970s. The increasing concentration of resources on a sector not subject to the discipline of market forces came to be seen as harmful to efficiency. The basis of the new consensus can be seen emerging from a conference convened in late 1980 to discuss "the welfare state in crisis" (OECD 1981). It had become clear:

> "that the real social progress we can achieve is limited by economic means; that methods of achieving social objectives should not be allowed to undermine the economic system which produces the means; and that we live in societies based on the principle that individual consumers are, in the main, the ultimate arbiters for allocating means to ends" (*Opening address of the Secretary General,* OECD 1981, p.9).

Concern that public sector involvement in the economy was leading to the relative over-provision of public goods with consequent allocative inefficiencies has turned the consensus towards the need to restore greater private sector choice and enhanced reliance on market outcomes.

The growth of transfers was seen as posing particular efficiency problems. As doubts grew about the gains in terms of fairer income distribution, evidence accumulated that the economic costs of welfare programmes could be quite high, particularly with respect to lower labour-force participation and higher structural

Table 5.2. **General government claims on resources**[1]

Per cent

	Total outlays as a ratio of GNP						Government employment share				
	1960	1975	1980	1982	1986	1988[2]	1960	1975	1980	1982	1986
United States	27.0	34.6	33.7	36.5	36.9	36.0	15.7	17.8	16.5	16.5	15.8
Japan	..	27.3	32.6	33.7	33.1	32.6	..	6.5	6.7	6.7	6.4[3]
Germany	32.4	48.9	48.3	49.4	46.6	46.3	8.0	13.9	14.9	15.6	16.1
France	34.6	43.5	46.4	51.1	51.8	50.9	13.1	14.3	15.6	16.4	18.1
United Kingdom	32.3	46.3	45.1	47.4	46.2	42.8	14.8	20.8	21.1	22.0	21.8
Italy	30.1	43.2	41.6	47.6	50.5	50.6	8.7	14.0	15.0	15.5	15.7
Canada	28.9	40.1	40.5	46.4	46.2	45.5	..	20.3	18.8	19.9	20.0[4]
Total of above countries	28.8	37.7	38.4	40.4	40.0	39.5	11.5	14.7	14.6	14.8	14.7
Austria	35.7	46.1	48.9	50.9	51.9	51.7	10.5	16.4	18.2	19.3	20.5[3]
Belgium	30.3	44.5	50.8	55.7	53.2	51.4	12.2	15.7	18.6	19.5	20.2
Denmark	24.8	48.2	56.2	61.2	55.4	59.1	..	23.6	28.3	30.8	29.4
Finland	26.6	36.1	36.5	39.0	42.3	42.0	7.7	14.6	17.8	18.9	20.8
Greece	17.4	26.7	30.5	37.0	42.8	46.2	..	..	..	..	..
Iceland	28.2	38.5	31.4	34.1	36.6	37.4	..	13.9	15.7	16.7	16.9
Ireland	28.0	46.5	50.9	55.3	55.7	52.7	..	13.3	14.5	15.2	16.0[3]
Luxembourg	30.5	48.6	54.8	56.4	..	..	..	9.7	10.8	11.0	12.0[3]
Netherlands	33.7	52.8	57.5	61.6	59.1	59.1	11.7	13.6	14.9	15.9	15.8
Norway	29.9	48.4	50.7	50.8	52.0	54.4	..	19.3	21.9	22.9	23.3
Portugal	17.0	30.3	25.9	46.2	45.5	42.8	3.9	8.1	10.3	..	..
Spain	..	24.7	32.9	37.5	42.2	42.2	..	10.0	11.9	12.6	14.6
Sweden	31.0	48.9	61.6	66.6	63.5	60.4	12.8	25.5	30.7	31.9	33.0
Switzerland	17.2	28.7	29.3	30.1	30.4	..	6.4	9.5	10.7	10.9	11.2
Turkey	21.1	24.6	28.5	26.4	..	..					
Smaller European	28.1	40.3	45.6	49.3	49.3	51.5	8.9	14.2	16.7	17.6	18.5
Australia	21.4	33.7	34.5	37.6	38.3	35.2	23.0	26.2	26.0	26.0	26.7
New Zealand	..	..	30.7	31.3	29.9	28.4	17.9	18.9	19.2	19.0	18.1[3]
Total smaller	26.8	39.3	44.2	47.4	47.8	48.3	10.4	15.8	17.9	18.7	19.6
Total EEC	32.0	44.4	45.7	49.2	49.1	48.1	10.5	15.1	16.3	17.0	17.6
Total OECD Europe	31.5	44.1	45.8	49.1	48.9	48.6	10.4	15.4	16.7	17.5	18.1
Total OECD less United States	30.8	40.1	42.4	44.8	43.6	42.6	9.6	13.5	14.4	14.8	15.2
Total OECD	28.6	38.0	39.3	41.4	41.0	39.9	11.3	14.9	15.1	15.4	15.4

1. Total general government outlays, SNA definition.
2. Estimations.
3. 1985.
4. 1984.
Sources: OECD 1988i and OECD Secretariat estimates.

unemployment. Many *United States* studies, for example, began to find a strong negative link between unemployment insurance and work incentives. Evidence has not been as conclusive for other countries. The difference between replacement ratios in *Europe* and the *United States* has narrowed in the 1980s while the gap in

DIAGRAM 5.2

PUBLIC EXPENDITURE
EXCLUDING INTEREST PAYMENTS (1)
Per cent of GDP/GNP

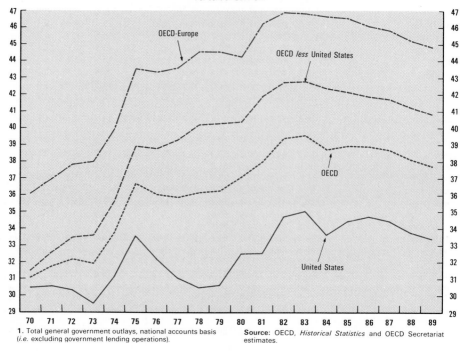

1. Total general government outlays, national accounts basis (*i.e.* excluding government lending operations).

Source: OECD, *Historical Statistics* and OECD Secretariat estimates.

unemployment rates has widened. But nevertheless, it is apparent that, in conjunction with the tax system, unemployment and related social welfare benefits can create a "poverty trap" at the lower end of the income distribution, where the combination of lower benefits and higher taxes discourages the take-up of employment. In this respect, social policy came to be seen as creating obstacles to economic growth, particularly where it added to labour market rigidities (OECD 1981, p.31).

Public spending restraint 1980-88

The restraint applied to public spending is immediately evident from the fact that the average share of government outlays in OECD GDP has fallen since 1982, and in *Germany*, the *United Kingdom* and *Sweden* it is now below its 1980 level (Diagram 5.1 and Table 5.2). Where it is still above, it often reflects a failure to meet stated objectives. But most governments had to cope with decelerating GNP growth in the early years of the 1980s, and with a rising trend in debt interest payments. Excluding debt interest payments the the government share of resources has fallen more sharply (Diagram 5.2) and as economic growth has recovered in recent years the shift in resources away from the public sector has become more marked.

a)   Controlling the costs of public services

Three factors illustrate the break with previous trends: the cut-back in public investment; the brake on recruitment; and closer control of public sector costs. The ratio of government investment to GNP has fallen as cost/benefit criteria applied to public projects have been tightened and governments have exploited the greater short-term flexibility of investment spending compared to other types of spending (Table 5.1). The average ratio of government final consumption to GNP has levelled off (and fallen outside the *United States*) by virtue of closer control over government wages and a stable government employment share (Tables 5.1 and 5.2). The fact that productivity gains tend to be lower in the government than the private sector means that the cost of public services rises faster than average unless the wages of public servants rise more slowly (the so-called "relative price effect")[2]. The average increase in the price of government consumption (as measured in the national accounts, which may be biased upwards because they generally assume zero productivity gains) exceeded that of private consumption by about 1¾ per cent a year from 1968 to 1979 (Table 5.3). Since 1979 the trend has been reversed. Because of curbs on public sector pay awards, the relative price of public services has risen much more slowly than was previously the case. And although government employment has generally continued to rise, it has done so more slowly than before. The relative labour intensiveness of public services and the tendency to equate government output increases with higher labour inputs tended to lead to a growing government employment share in the 1960s and 1970s, whereas greater emphasis is now given to improvements in efficiency (see below). As a result the share of government employment in total employment has been fairly stable in the 1980s and has tended to fall recently in the *United States, Japan, the United Kingdom* and *Denmark*.

Retrenchment began somewhat earlier in *Japan, Germany,* and the *United Kingdom* than elsewhere, and has been a persistent feature of budget-making in the 1980s. Apart from these countries, it has been particularly marked since 1982 in those smaller economies, such as *Belgium,* the *Netherlands, Denmark, Norway* and *Sweden,* where the ratio of public spending to GNP was relatively high (OECD, 1988b). Cut-backs were delayed in some other economies. In the *United States,* cuts

Table 5.3. **Change in the relative price of public services**

Annual average percentage change

	Implicit price deflator						Change in the relative price of government consumption		
	Private consumption			Public consumption					
	1968-73	1973-79	1979-86	1968-73	1973-79	1979-86	1968-73	1973-79	1979-86
United States	4.5	7.9	5.5	6.8	8.5	6.0	2.2	0.6	0.5
Japan	7.1	9.4	2.9	12.7	9.7	2.7	5.2	0.3	−0.2
Germany	4.6	4.6	3.4	9.5	5.8	3.3	4.7	1.1	−2.0
France	6.0	10.4	9.0	8.2	12.5	9.2	2.1	1.9	0.2
United Kingdom	7.0	15.6	7.7	9.3	17.2	9.7	2.1	1.4	1.9
Italy	6.4	17.1	13.6	9.6	18.2	15.1	3.0	0.9	1.3
Canada	4.1	8.6	7.1	7.1	11.0	7.7	2.9	2.2	0.6
Total of above countries	5.2	8.9	6.1	8.0	9.7	6.8	2.7	0.7	0.7
Austria	5.0	6.4	4.9	9.1	8.1	5.2	3.9	1.6	0.3
Belgium	4.4	8.0	5.8	7.3	9.9	5.3	2.8	1.8	−0.5
Denmark	7.8	10.8	7.8	9.6	10.9	7.3	1.7	0.1	−0.4
Finland	6.2	12.7	8.2	8.3	13.2	9.6	2.0	0.4	1.3
Greece	5.4	15.1	20.5	6.3	18.3	21.4	0.9	2.8	0.7
Iceland	16.2	40.1	45.9	20.7	41.6	42.7	3.9	1.1	−2.2
Ireland	9.2	15.7	11.2	12.1	16.5	11.5	2.7	0.7	0.3
Luxembourg	4.2	7.3	6.7	8.2	11.4	7.0	3.8	3.8	0.3
Netherlands	7.0	7.2	3.7	10.4	9.3	1.6	3.2	2.0	−2.0
Norway	6.8	8.6	8.9	8.2	9.0	7.4	1.3	0.4	−1.4
Portugal	5.4	22.1	21.0	6.6	14.8	19.9	1.1	−6.0	−0.9
Spain	7.3	18.1	12.2	10.5	19.6	11.6	2.9	1.3	−0.5
Sweden	6.0	10.4	9.2	7.7	12.6	8.2	1.6	2.0	−0.9
Switzerland	6.0	4.1	3.8	8.9	4.3	4.0	2.7	0.2	0.2
Turkey	14.2	33.1	47.4	13.5	30.8	36.6	−0.6	−1.7	−7.3
Smaller European	6.1	10.4	12.7	8.7	11.1	9.7	2.5	0.6	−2.7
Australia	6.0	12.5	9.1	8.7	13.1	9.2	2.5	0.5	0.1
New Zealand	6.7	14.6	12.7	10.7	15.1	13.5	3.7	0.4	0.7
Total smaller	6.1	10.7	12.3	8.8	11.3	9.7	2.5	0.5	−2.3
Total EEC	5.9	10.5	8.5	9.4	11.3	8.5	3.3	0.7	0.0
Total OECD Europe	5.9	10.3	9.6	9.3	11.1	8.8	3.2	0.7	−0.7
Total OECD less United States	6.1	10.1	8.2	9.5	11.0	8.1	3.2	0.8	−0.1
Total OECD	5.3	9.2	7.2	8.0	10.0	7.3	2.6	0.7	0.1

Source: OECD 1988i.

in non-defence spending were more than offset by increases in defence outlays up to 1985. Other countries, such as *France* and *Italy*, together with some smaller economies such as *Spain, Ireland, Austria, Finland* and *Greece*, pursued an expansionary fiscal policy further into the recession, with the result that the ratio of government consumption to GNP continued to rise up to the middle of the decade. In *Greece*, contrary to the general trend, there was a relatively fast rate of growth of public sector salaries and this was the reason why the growth in the general government share of current spending was the most rapid in the OECD area during the first half of the decade (OECD, 1987c).

b) *Reform of income maintenance programmes*

Social security transfers have been the most powerful influence of all on the growth of government expenditure (Table 5.4). There has been a tendency for those sections of the population dependent on benefits to increase, because of demographic trends (still continuing and discussed below) and towards a higher rate of "take-up" in benefits (Table 5.5)[3]. These pressures were compounded in the 1970s by a further trend towards a higher real rate of benefits per recipient, exacerbated in some instances because rising energy costs caused consumer prices – to which benefits are normally indexed – to increase relative to other domestic prices. During the early 1980s, the oil price shock and the appreciation of the dollar meant that the consumption deflator rose faster than the GDP deflator, serving further to raise the real value of indexed transfer payments in European economies such as *Belgium* (OECD, 1988b). However, from 1985 pressure began to be reduced, as this differential inverted.

As a result of tighter control of real benefit rates, the growth of transfers has been restricted in the 1980s, despite adverse demographic and unemployment trends which have generally continued to increase the number of claimants. Efforts to remedy growing shortfalls in social security funds have led to reductions in the purchasing power of pensions, family allowances and education benefits in many OECD countries in the 1980s. State pensions have declined by 0.8 per cent a year in real per capita terms in *Belgium*, compared with a real wage decline of 0.1 per cent a year and the real value of family allowances has fallen by 3 per cent a year. *Luxembourg* instituted major cuts in welfare spending in 1982 and pegged expenditure growth to nominal GDP growth from 1984. *Austria* trimmed pension rights and tightened indexation rules. There have been similar developments in *Germany, Denmark, Spain, Sweden, Ireland* and the *United Kingdom*.

Table 5.4. **Social security transfers**

Per cent of GDP

	Average			1960	1980	1986	1988[1]
	1968-73	1974-79	1980-86				
United States	7.7	10.3	11.3	5.0	10.9	11.0	10.6
Japan	4.8	8.4	10.9	3.8	10.1	11.4	11.5
Germany	13.2	16.7	16.7	12.0	16.5	15.8	15.7
France	17.2	21.0	24.6	13.5	23.2	26.0	26.0
United Kingdom	8.7	10.5	13.5	6.8	11.5	14.1	12.8
Italy	13.0	15.4	16.4	9.8	14.1	17.2	17.3
Canada	8.2	9.9	11.5	7.9	9.9	12.3	12.2
Total of above countries	9.0	12.1	13.2	6.7	13.0	13.8	13.5
Austria	15.6	17.8	19.9	12.9	19.0	20.3	20.5
Belgium	14.4	19.2	22.0	11.3	20.8	21.2	21.0
Denmark	11.1	14.0	17.0	7.4	16.6	15.5	17.5
Finland	7.4	8.9	9.9	5.1	8.7	11.1	11.0
Greece	7.8	8.1	12.9	5.3	9.2	14.6	14.4
Iceland	9.4	9.8	4.6	7.1	4.6	4.6	4.5
Ireland	8.6	11.9	14.8	5.5	12.6	16.9	16.5
Luxembourg	14.7	19.9	..	11.6	22.7	..	..
Netherlands	17.7	23.5	27.1	..	25.9	25.9	26.3
Norway	12.4	14.2	15.0	7.6	14.4	15.8	16.8
Portugal	3.5	9.3	12.0	2.9	10.6	13.3	15.2
Spain	8.9	11.7	15.8	2.3	14.2	16.6	16.5
Sweden	11.6	15.9	18.3	8.0	17.8	18.6	19.4
Switzerland	8.5	12.6	13.3	5.7	12.7	13.7	12.1
Smaller European	11.2	15.5	18.0	7.3	17.0	18.1	18.3
Australia	5.6	8.3	9.2	5.5	8.3	..	9.3
New Zealand	..	..	11.8	..	11.4	12.1	12.4
Total smaller	10.4	14.5	16.8	6.9	15.9	16.7	16.8
Total EEC	13.0	16.4	18.2	10.0	17.1	19.1	18.8
Total OECD Europe	12.6	16.2	17.9	9.7	16.8	16.6	15.6
Total OECD less United States	10.6	13.8	15.4	8.8	14.8	16.2	16.1
Total OECD	9.2	12.4	13.6	6.7	13.4	14.2	14.0

1. Estimates.
Sources: OECD 1988i and OECD Secretariat estimates.

Table 5.5. Determinants of the growth of state retirement pensions

1960-1985

	Changes in expenditure ratio[1]	Due to changes in:		
		Dependency ratio	Eligibility ratio	Benefit level ratio
Basic systems				
Australia (1961-1985)	1.49	1.11	1.37	0.98
New Zealand	2.39	1.06	1.40	1.62
Average	1.89	1.08	1.38	1.26
Contribution to change[2]	..	12.2	51.1	36.7
Mixed systems				
Canada	2.33	1.18	1.57	1.43
Denmark (1960-1984)	1.38	1.37	0.90	1.19
Finland (1960-1984)	3.28	1.55	1.04	1.94
Ireland	2.33	0.96	1.19	1.61
Norway	2.61	1.42	1.45	1.55
Sweden	2.72	1.50	1.22	1.62
United Kingdom	1.75	1.28	1.23	1.04
Average	2.26	1.31	1.21	1.45
Contribution to change[2]	..	33.2	23.4	45.8
Insurance systems				
Austria	3.03	1.14	1.78	1.36
Belgium	2.10	0.95	1.42	1.39
Germany	2.10	1.32	1.72	0.78
France	1.57	0.95	n.a.	n.a.
Italy	2.92	1.39	1.57	1.13
Japan	7.53	1.54	2.99	1.56
Luxembourg	1.57	1.18	1.64	0.82
Netherlands	2.28	1.20	1.22	1.34
Portugal	40.62	1.44	59.29	0.52
Spain	2.54	1.14	1.01	1.59
Switzerland	2.28	1.15	1.55	1.40
Average[1]	2.82	1.27	1.60	1.29
Contribution to change[2]	..	23.7	45.6	24.7
Average of all countries	2.46	1.26	1.41	1.35
Contribution to change[2]	..	25.6	38.0	33.2

Memorandum item:				
Public pension expenditure as a % of GDP	1960	1975	1980	1985
OECD average	4.3	7.1	8.2	8.9

1. The change in the expenditure ratio for pensions is the pension share of GDP in 1985 divided by the corresponding share in 1960. This change is itself the product of the demographic, beneficiary and benefit level ratio. Any figure over 1 indicates a positive impact. The percentage contribution to the overall change indicates the relative contributions of each factor.
2. Per cent.
Source: OECD 1988f.

The real value of unemployment benefits has also fallen in many economies, particularly in Europe (see Chapter 2). The *Netherlands* is an example of a country with a large allocation of resources to income-maintenance, and relatively generous eligibility rules – an extensive safety net benefiting the unemployed on exhaustion of entitlements (OECD, 1987d). To reduce labour market rigidities, the replacement-ratio in the Netherlands has been cut and the duration of benefits made more work-related from the beginning of 1987. Average benefits to the unemployed already tended to be low by international standards in the *United States* (a factor which may have helped to keep unemployment rates relatively low). Nevertheless, a tightening of job-search requirements in recent years has meant a reduction in those eligible. Benefits are higher in *Japan* than in Europe, although coverage is more limited (the number of beneficiaries accounts for less than 60 per cent of the unemployed). A special bonus was introduced in 1984 for beneficiaries who find a job before the termination of their benefit periods. *Australia* has followed a somewhat different approach. Since 1982, real benefits have been increased while total programme costs have been contained by income tests. While this has raised replacement ratios at lower income levels, the problem of the poverty trap has been mitigated by giving additional family benefits to lower-paid workers actually in employment.

Improving government efficiency

Scepticism about the ability of governments to ensure the efficient use of resources, together with the tendency for the relative price of public services to rise has led to the search for improved management techniques, with the aim of promoting productivity and efficiency gains in the government sector. (For a discussion of public sector management and control issues see OECD 1987(l).) In the *Scandinavian* economies and the *United States* there have been campaigns to identify and enhance opportunities for such gains. The new system of expenditure control in *Denmark* directly imposes productivity goals via reduced budget allocations which incorporate productivity gains; decision-making has become more decentralised, and spending units more directly responsible for productivity improvements and costs. Similarly, budget allocations in *Sweden* are set 2 per cent below inflation in order to allow for productivity improvement, with agencies being subjected to performance review. In *Norway* efficiency gains have been sought by giving ministries and other spending units greater discretion in determining the allocation of resources. Savings in one category of expenditure can be transferred to other categories within the same agency and to some extent between financial years (OECD 1988e). Better productivity measurement has been seen as a pre-requisite of greater government efficiency in the *United States*. The output indicators developed over a number of years are being used to embark on a major government productivity improvement programme.

A related, but alternative, approach has been to specify "performance" measures by which to judge the effective use of resources. The principle of defining objectives and then setting performance targets for their achievement has a long history, but has received fresh impetus in the 1980s. In the *United Kingdom* performance measures are now integrated into the public expenditure survey and control system (PESC). In *Canada*, departments have been required to measure and report performance since the early 1970s but compliance has been limited. The requirement has been given substantially greater prominence by the Increased Ministerial Authority and Accountability (IMAA) reforms now being introduced. The development of performance indicators is also proceeding in *Australia* under the aegis of the financial management improvement program (FMIP). However, the pace of development in this area is determined by the ability to set objectives, place them in an agreed administrative framework and then to set performance targets for managers. Better resource utilisation may involve more use of "user fees". Under a wide-ranging expenditure reform, government departments in *New Zealand*, for example, now price some services provided to users on a full cost-recovery basis, including an allowance for depreciation and an imputed 10 per cent return on capital (OECD, 1987b).

Governments have also been encouraging greater private sector involvement in public projects. This has been particularly true for road projects. *Norway* uses private finance, paid for by tolls, for about one-quarter of the Ministry of Transport's construction programme, while the *Netherlands* has welcomed "off-budget" partnerships for tunnel and related projects. However, there has been concern as to whether entrepreneurial risks are actually being borne by the private sector. The *United Kingdom* approach has probably been the most radical, via the "contracting out" of public services where possible. In pursuit of greater efficiency the government has being willing to build up private sector participation in most sectors – including some areas of health and education.

The search for greater efficiency has also involved a process of government disengagement from activities considered best undertaken by the private sector. This "privatisation" process has been taken furthest in the *United Kingdom, France, Japan* and *Canada* and is discussed in Chapter 4. Controversy still exists as to whether state monoplies can be subjected to sufficient competition once privatised. An alternative approach, followed in *New Zealand*, is to maintain public ownership while stemming the drain on resources caused by loss-making public corporations by making them more profit-oriented ("corporatisation"). Some state-owned enterprises are now issuing equity to the general public. As in the *United Kingdom*, quasi-autonomous non-governmental organisations (Quangos) have been subject to detailed review in *New Zealand*, with the objective of streamlining operations and eliminating those whose functions are no longer considered justified.

Governments can also exercise substantial indirect influence over industrial efficiency through regulations stemming from competition, social and environmental policies. Such regulations may often be justified as imposing an implicit "user charge" to cover the social cost of air pollution etc. But concern that costs of complying with government regulations may be under-estimated has led to a campaign to improve the cost-effectiveness of government social regulations in the *United States*. All agencies now have to have their cost-benefit analyses of additional regulations approved[4]. Since non-regulation may also have costs, in terms of safety, trading standards and environment pollution, the trend is still towards greater rather than less regulation in some areas. OECD governments in general face dilemmas in this respect. But the cost-effectiveness of government regulatory activity has become an important issue.

Tax reform: motivation and design[5]

Tax neutrality

Parallel to the growing concern that bigger government has implied worse economic performance, a concern has also developed that the economic distortions resulting from higher taxes have imposed additional and unacceptably high efficiency costs on OECD economies. The pursuit of more economically-neutral (i.e less discriminatory) tax systems has been as important a budgetary influence as controlling the overall burden of taxation. In principle, this implies movement towards a system of revenue-raising which minimises the impact of taxation on economic behaviour; in practical terms there have been three basic characteristics of this reform movement (for a more complete description see OECD, 1987m):

i) The reduction of income tax rates via a broadening of the income tax base, a reduction in the number of marginal rates and a lowering of top rates relative to the standard rate. In some countries there have also been moves to integrate income and social security taxes;

ii) A rationalising and broadening of the consumption tax base, through a switch to a general expenditure tax (usually VAT);

iii) A trend to base-broadening and greater neutrality in the corporate tax system, often accompanied by a switch from household to corporate taxation and/or a better integration of corporate and personal income taxes (including capital gains).

The prevailing rationales for such reform have been that high marginal tax rates threaten work incentives and aggravate problems of tax avoidance and evasion and that accumulated tax concessions have rendered tax systems overly complex and inequitable, distorting consumption/saving decisions as well as patterns of investment, corporate finance and production (issues discussed further below).

Up to a point, the pursuit of tax neutrality has followed the principles of "optimal taxation", as to the need for base-broadening and standardisation of rates (Pechman, 1987). But the results of dismantling a tax or removing an allowance are not necessarily equivalent to not introducing it in the first place: tax-favoured activities attract capital and labour resources which may be costly to reallocate in the short run. And withdrawal of tax reliefs or exemptions can often have arbitrary and inequitable distributional consequences. An interest rate subsidy, such as a tax-exempt bond, may give a capital gain to a bond-holder when introduced (a process known as "tax capitalization") but a subsequent purchaser of that bond would not gain from the concession because he would be paying a higher price. If the concession were withrawn, he would lose. Governments have had to remain eclectic, making better and more efficient use of existing tax systems, which have developed in an *ad hoc* and unsystematic way. The shift towards expenditure taxation and/or towards a broader income tax base, for example, has been less marked than might have been expected *a priori*, not just for administrative reasons but because the distributional consequences have been deemed to be unacceptable.

The roots of the reform movement can be traced to the 1970s, when pressure arose to index tax systems for inflation. The trend towards more radical reform began in the early 1980s, with the fundamental overhaul of the British and American tax structures. It has gained further momentum since the 1986 Tax Reform Act in the *United States*, partly because of evidence that high rates of tax in one country can lead to an exodus of labour and capital to another. In *Switzerland* there is evidence of wealthy taxpayers moving residence in response to high income and wealth taxes, for instance, while high tax rates in *Ireland* have contributed to the emigration of young qualified workers. Although there are widely differing degrees of change and implementation, the freer movement of labour and capital between OECD economies has meant that reforms have been to an important degree international.

The need for reform

a) Inflation and fiscal indexation

Up to the mid-1970s tax receipts grew in line with public expenditures (Diagram 5.3 and Tables 5.6 and 5.7). The existence of progressive income tax schedules in most OECD countries meant that an increase in income could push taxpayers into higher income brackets, automatically raising their real tax burden (see OECD 1986b and 1986c). This mechanism provided an important additional source of tax revenue, which increased more than proportionally as nominal incomes rose with inflation[6] (Table 5.8). Only *Iceland, Luxembourg* and *France* had formal provisions for indexing tax brackets to inflation prior to 1970.

Because of the erosion of the real value of tax allowances fixed in nominal terms, average *marginal* income tax rates also tended to rise. In the case of the *United States*,

DIAGRAM 5.3

GENERAL GOVERNMENT RECEIPTS (1)
Per cent of GDP/GNP

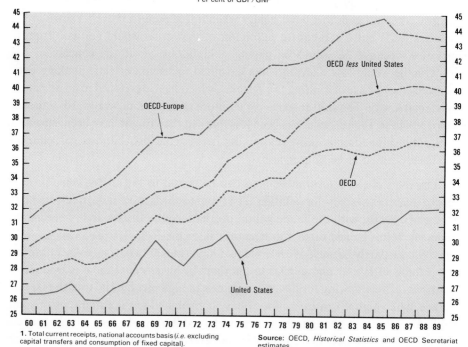

1. Total current receipts, national accounts basis (*i.e.* excluding capital transfers and consumption of fixed capital).

Source: OECD, *Historical Statistics* and OECD Secretariat estimates.

Table 5.6.   **Structure and growth of general government tax receipts**

Tax	Relative to total tax receipts					Relative to GDP				
	1965	1975	1980	1983	1986	1965	1975	1980	1983	1986
Personal income	26.3	31.4	32.7	32.0	31.5	7.3	10.7	11.6	11.7	12.1
Corporate income	9.2	7.7	7.7	7.3	7.9	2.4	2.4	2.7	2.7	3.0
Social security	18.2	23.7	24.3	24.6	24.2	5.0	7.7	8.6	9.2	9.3
Payroll taxes	1.1	1.2	1.1	1.2	1.0	0.3	0.4	0.4	0.5	0.4
Property taxes	7.9	6.1	5.2	5.2	4.9	2.0	1.9	1.7	1.8	1.8
Goods and services	37.1	30.1	29.2	29.8	30.0	9.7	9.8	10.3	11.0	11.5
Total taxes	100	100	100	100	100	26.6	32.7	35.1	36.8	38.1

Source: OECD 1988h.

which is probably fairly typical, the aggregate marginal rate of income tax rose from 14 per cent in the mid 1950s to 23 per cent at the end of the 1970s – an increase of two-thirds – while the average rate increased by almost a half (Diagram 5.4). A similar trend occurred in other economies, with marginal income tax rates on labour income (including payroll and social security taxes) reaching over 50 per cent, on average, in OECD Europe in the early 1980s (Table 5.9). (In *Finland*, for example, the last twenty years have seen the number of tax-payers facing a marginal rate of 50 per cent or above rise from a few thousand to around one million (OECD, 1988c)). Effective rates of corporation tax also tended to rise with inflation, as the real value of (nominally-fixed) depreciation allowances fell (CBO, 1985, p.37).

The proportion of tax receipts accruing from the personal income tax tended to increase up to 1975 because of the combination of inflation and progressivity and to stabilize with the spread of fiscal indexation thereafter. By the end of the 1970s about a half of OECD economies had introduced indexation of tax brackets, the *United States* being an exception until 1985 and *Belgium* until 1986 (Table 5.10). Indexation and the reduction in inflation having checked the tendency for the real tax base to expand automatically with rising prices, attention has subsequently focused on the erosion of the tax base via special exemptions, during which process some governments have abandoned or altered indexation procedures (*Denmark, Canada* and *Sweden*).

b)   *Tax expenditures and the erosion of the income tax base*

Inflation had consequences for the structure of the tax system as well as for the overall yield, since a search began for other methods of tax avoidance, to compensate

Table 5.7. **General government current receipts**[1]

Per cent of GDP

	1960	1975	1980	1983	1986	1988[2]
United States	26.3	28.8	30.8	30.7	31.3	32.1
Japan	20.7	24.0	27.6	29.8	31.3	32.5
Germany	35.0	42.7	44.7	45.1	44.7	43.5
France	34.9	40.3	45.5	47.7	48.2	48.6
United Kingdom	30.0	40.2	40.1	42.7	41.9	40.7
Italy	28.8	31.2	32.9	37.8	38.9	40.2
Canada	26.0	36.1	36.2	38.7	39.2	40.2
Total of above countries	27.8	32.2	34.6	34.8	34.3	36.2
Austria	34.4	42.9	46.4	46.4	47.6	47.0
Belgium	27.5	40.4	42.8	44.7	44.8	44.8
Denmark	27.3	46.1	52.2	53.6	58.0	59.9
Finland	29.7	37.8	35.8	37.4	41.8	41.6
Greece	21.1	27.4	30.5	33.6	36.4	36.8
Iceland	36.4	34.6	32.3	33.3	32.1	33.9
Ireland	24.8	34.6	38.8	43.5	44.3	46.1
Luxembourg	32.5	48.6	53.2	..	..	..
Netherlands	33.9	49.2	52.8	55.3	52.8	52.1
Norway	33.1	49.6	54.2	53.1	56.3	55.2
Portugal	17.6	24.8	31.4	38.0	38.0	38.6
Spain	18.1	24.3	29.7	33.5	35.9	38.9
Sweden	32.1	50.5	56.6	59.9	61.5	62.8
Switzerland	23.3	32.1	32.8	33.9	35.0	..
Turkey	..	25.7	25.1	25.8	..	..
Smaller European	27.9	39.2	42.8	45.1	46.4	48.1
Australia	24.6	29.3	31.3	31.9	34.1	33.8
New Zealand	..	..	38.8	41.0	43.0	41.9
Total smaller	27.3	37.7	41.3	42.8	44.5	45.6
EEC	31.5	39.0	41.5	43.8	42.9	44.8
OECD-Europe	31.3	39.5	42.0	44.1	43.7	44.9
OECD less United States	29.5	35.8	38.3	39.7	40.0	41.4
Total OECD	27.7	33.1	35.7	35.8	36.0	37.5

1. Tax and non-tax receipts excluding capital taxes.
2. Estimates.
Sources: OECD 1988i and OECD Secretariat estimates.

DIAGRAM 5.4

THE EFFECTS OF INFLATION ON INCOME TAX RATES
AND ALLOWANCES
IN THE UNITED STATES

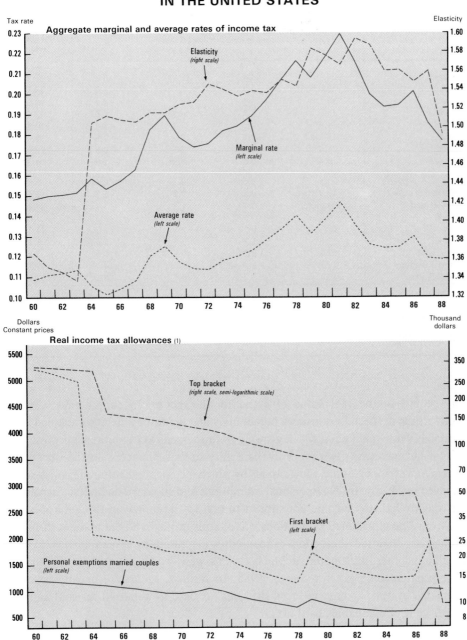

Tax rate

Aggregate marginal and average rates of income tax

Elasticity
(right scale)

Marginal rate
(left scale)

Average rate
(left scale)

Elasticity

Dollars
Constant prices

Thousand
dollars

Real income tax allowances (1)

Top bracket
(right scale, semi-logarithmic scale)

First bracket
(left scale)

Personal exemptions married couples
(left scale)

1. Personal exemption for married couples, ceiling of first tax
bracket and threshold of top rate bracket, respectively, deflated
by the consumption deflator and based on 1960 prices.

Source: J. Pechman, *Federal Tax Policy* (Fifth Edition, 1987)
and OECD Secretariat estimates.

Table 5.8. **Fiscal drag and inflation**[1]

As percentage of tax liabilities to income

| Country | Effective central government income tax rates in 1975 | Changes in tax rates accounted for by | | | Effective central government income tax rates in early 1980s[1] |
		(a) Effect of change in real income	(b) Inflationary fiscal drag	(c) The effect of formal indexation and changes in legislation	
Australia	20.1	−0.4	11.7	−10.2	21.3
Belgium	25.0	0.9	5.2	−2.4	28.7
Canada	10.1	0.3	4.5	−4.7	10.2
Denmark	15.6	−2.7	6.5	−6.0	13.4
Finland	11.8	—	7.4	−8.4	10.8
France	14.2	−0.1	8.9	−7.6	15.4
Ireland	21.5	−0.4	2.3	−0.8	22.6
Italy	9.8	0.8	5.9	−1.9	14.6
Japan	3.6	0.4	2.2	−0.4	5.8
Netherlands	17.9	−0.5	5.2	−5.5	17.1
New Zealand	23.5	−0.4	11.5	−7.2	27.4
Norway	6.1	−0.5	7.7	−8.3	5.0
Spain	10.1	0.5	2.3	−1.2	11.7
Sweden	12.8	−1.7	9.6	−12.6	8.1
Switzerland	2.8	−0.3	0.3	0.0	2.9
United Kingdom	19.7	0.4	11.0	−14.1	17.1
United States	13.1	0.7	4.5	4.1	14.2

Key:

a) Automatic change in the effective tax rate due to the interaction of progressive rate structure and real income changes.
b) Automatic change in the effective tax rate due to inflation-induced income changes.
c) Discretionary change in effective tax rate due to legislation, including formal indexation provisions.
1. End year varies from 1981 to 1983.
Source: OECD 1986c.

for the fall in the real value of standard allowances. In conjunction with the proliferation of special exclusions, higher marginal tax rates were accompanied by an erosion of "horizontal equity" – a growing unfairness, as tax liabilities for those with similar incomes came to vary with the ability to find loopholes. In the case of the United States, for example, the methods by which income was sheltered from taxation changed markedly. In 1947 personal exemptions and standard deductions accounted for roughly half the income not subject to tax. In the following three decades, the relative value of personal exemptions was sharply eroded and the number of special exclusions, itemised deductions and credits increased to three-quarters of non-taxable income. In Belgium such concessions were worth as much as 40 per cent of personal income tax revenue in 1985. In Iceland, successive exemptions were estimated by 1987 to have reduced the sales tax base by about 40 per cent and only 10 per cent of companies paid tax.

Table 5.9. **Total marginal tax rates on labour income**[1]

Per cent of total compensation in 1983

	Effective tax rate	Payroll tax	Employers' contribution	Employees' contribution	Personal income tax	Indirect tax
Australia	42.31	4.76	0.00	0.00	28.57	8.98
Austria	63.99	1.61	17.87	12.40	22.48	9.63
Belgium	61.65	0.00	19.40	8.72	25.29	8.24
Canada	42.72	0.00	0.00	0.00	29.40	13.32
Denmark	71.24	0.00	0.00	4.50	55.90	10.84
Finland	62.48	0.00	5.17	2.61	43.78	10.92
France	59.70	4.64	30.24	9.68	5.61	9.53
Germany	57.02	0.00	15.61	14.60	18.57	8.25
Ireland	63.80	0.00	10.40	7.62	31.36	14.41
Italy	62.66	0.00	31.33	5.94	18.19	7.20
Japan	39.93	0.00	10.15	9.07	16.15	4.55
Luxembourg	50.61	0.64	16.30	10.07	13.83	9.78
Netherlands	73.47	0.00	19.68	31.17	16.99	5.63
New Zealand	55.50	0.00	0.00	0.00	48.75	6.75
Norway	63.00	0.00	13.94	8.69	23.24	17.13
Portugal	44.29	0.00	17.70	9.47	4.37	12.76
Spain	46.66	0.00	23.55	4.20	14.36	4.54
Sweden	73.02	4.22	22.38	0.00	39.01	7.41
Switzerland	40.21	0.00	9.30	9.21	15.60	6.10
United Kingdom	54.53	1.25	9.34	8.05	26.82	9.07
United States	42.64	0.00	7.83	6.18	24.29	4.34
Average	55.80				25.00	9.00

1. Per cent of total compensation including payroll taxes for a single-earner married couple with two children, with income equal to that of the average production worker.
Source: McKee *et al.* (1986).

As the importance of "tax expenditures" (tax allowances used instead of direct subsidies and grants to achieve economic and social goals) increased, so did the need for their better control (OECD 1984). Almost a half of OECD countries now provide for tax expenditures to be reviewed in their Budgets. In the *United States*, this has been required by law since 1974, and in *Germany* a comprehensive listing of tax subsidies has been presented every other year since 1967. "Tax expenditures" are now regularly identified in *Australia, Austria, Canada, Finland, France* and *Spain*, and the cost of all tax reliefs – some of which may be seen as part of the normal tax structure – is now regularly published in *Ireland, Portugal* and the *United Kingdom*. Substantial controversy surrounds the measurement of tax expenditures, because tax concessions directly affect both the marginal tax rate and the tax base used to calculate forgone revenue[7]. But the concept has been useful in focusing attention on the fact that deviations from a neutral tax system may have substantial, if uncertain, costs which can only be brought under control through radical tax reform. The *United States* tax

Table 5.10. **Indexation provisions in OECD countries**

	Income tax		Public spending
	Date of operation	Index[1]	Automatic indexation of pension benefits
Australia	1976-1981[2]	CPX	Yes - CPI
Austria	—	—	Yes - Wages
Belgium	1986	—	Yes - CPI
Canada	1974[3]	CPI − 3%	Yes - CPI
Denmark	1970-1984[3]	CPX[4]	Yes - CPI
Finland	1977	CPI	Yes - CPI
France	1968	CPI	Yes - Expected wage increase
Germany	—	—	Yes - Wages
Iceland	1966	CPI	Yes - Wages
Ireland	—	—	No
Italy	—	—	Yes - Prices and wages
Japan	—	—	Yes - CPI
Luxembourg	1968	CPI	Yes - CPI
Netherlands	1972	CPX	Yes - Minimum wage
New Zealand	—	—	Yes - Wages
Norway	—	—	Yes - CPI
Portugal	—	—	No
Spain	—	—	Yes - Expected CPI
Sweden	1979-1982	CPI	Yes - CPI
Switzerland	1985	—	Yes - Average of CPI and salary index
United Kingdom	1978	CPI	Yes - CPI
United States	1985[5]	CPI	Yes - CPI

1. CPI = Consumer price index, including indirect taxes.
   CPX = Consumer price index, excluding indirect taxes.
2. Suspended in 1979, abandoned 1982.
3. Applies to local incomes taxes.
4. From 1975 to 1979 indexation was operated by reference to hourly earnings.
5. Indexation was introduced in nine states between 1978 and 1980.
Sources: OECD 1986b; OECD 1988f.

reform, for example, cut the revenue losses from the largest tax expenditures quite substantially (CBO 1988).

Tax reform in the 1980s

a) Reforming personal income taxation

Although the reforms differ in scope and intensity, measures already implemented or planned for 1989 have reduced marginal income tax rates in the great majority of OECD countries. Top marginal rates have typically been aligned at around 50 per cent (Table 5.11), but the *United States, United Kingdom, New Zealand, Portugal* and *Iceland* have gone further, bringing the maximum rate down to between 30 and 40 per cent. Only in *Denmark, Sweden* and *the Netherlands* is the highest rate of income tax now above sixty per cent (incorporating local taxes where these exist) and in the latter two countries there are plans to bring it down. The impact of income-tax reform on marginal rates faced by tax-payers with average rather than high incomes is more difficult to identify. It has generally been less dramatic (progressivity higher up the income scale being sacrificed for greater economic neutrality), but has nevertheless often been substantial.

Table 5.11. **Changes in personal income tax rates**

	Central government taxes				State and local tax	Overall top rate
	Lowest and highest marginal rates			Number of brackets[1]	1988-1989	
	1975	1983	1988-1989			
Australia	20-65	30-60	24-49	3	—	49
Austria	23-62	21-62	10-50[2]	5	—	50
Belgium	17-60	17-72	25-55[2]	7	6-8	59
Canada	9-47	6-34	17-29	3	16	45
Denmark	19-44	19-44	22-40	3	28	68
Finland	10-51	6-51	11-44[2]	6	16	60
France	5-60	5-65	5-57	12	—	57
Germany	22-56	22-56	19-53[3]	Formula[4]	—	53
Greece	3-63	11-63	18-50	9	—	50
Iceland	—	25-50	28	1	7	35
Ireland	26-77	25-60	35-58	3	—	58
Italy	10-72	18-65	10-50[2]	7	—	50
Japan	10-75	10-70	10-50[2]	5	5-15	65
Luxembourg	18-57	12-57	10-56	24	—	56
Netherlands	20-71	17-72	35[5]-60	3	—	60
New Zealand	19-57	20-66	24-33	2	—	33
Norway	6-48	4-41	10-29[2, 6]	3	25	54
Portugal	4-80	4-80	16-40[2]	5	—	40
Spain	15-62	16-65	25-56[2]	16	—	56
Sweden	7-56	3-54	5-42[2, 7]	3	30	72
Switzerland	1-13	1-13	1-13	6	5-34	47
Turkey	10-68	25-65	25-50	6	—	50
United Kingdom	35-83	30-60	25-40	2	—	40
United States	14-70	11-50	15-28/33	3	2-14	38

1. Not including zero-rate band.
2. From 1989.
3. From 1990.
4. The tax rate increases by linear progression.
5. Including employee social security contribution of 28 per cent.
6. Including a surcharge of 6 per cent on income above 180 000 kronur.
7. The government has proposed to reduce the overall (central plus local) tax rate to a range of either 30 to 50 or 30 to 60 per cent by 1991.
Sources: OECD 1987k, 1987m and information supplied to the OECD Secretariat.

In the *United States*, the process of tax reform began with the 1981 Economic Recovery Tax Act (ERTA), which cut most marginal tax rates, in stages, by 23 per cent across-the-board and reduced the top tax rate from 70 to 50 per cent (C.B.O., 1983). However, the problem of the narrowing income tax base was not tackled until the 1986 Tax Reform Act, which eliminated a large number of exemptions and allowances while transferring part of the tax burden to corporate income and taxing realised capital gains at the equivalent income tax rate. This enabled the Act to remain revenue-neutral, while further cutting the top federal tax rate to 33 per cent and the number of rates to three (a basic two-bracket system consisting of 15 and 28 per cent rates, with a surcharge of 5 per cent in the middle-income ranges) (Table 5.11). For families on average earnings, the marginal rate was effectively cut from 22 per cent to 15 per cent. At the same time, the elimination of tax exemptions and allowances meant that the Act increased progressivity, by raising the slope of the effective rate schedule in the lower half of the income scale more than it lowered it in the top half (Musgrave, 1987).

Reform has been equally substantial in the *United Kingdom*. The basic rate of personal income tax has been brought down from 35 per cent in the mid-1970s to 25 per cent, with a single higher rate of 40 per cent instead of 83 per cent. Although the *Canadian* income tax system offered fewer opportunities for base-broadening than in the *United States,* the rate structure has been simplified, reducing the top federal rate from 47 to 29 per cent, giving a combined federal-and-provincial maximum of 45 per cent. Base-broadening has allowed a similar rationalisation of the *Australian* income tax. Marginal rates have been cut from a range of 25-60 to 24-49 per cent, reducing the number of brackets to five. The *New Zealand* reform has been radical still. The number of tax rates has been reduced from eight, ranging from 8 to 66 per cent, to two of 24 and 33 per cent – the latter being the lowest maximum income tax rate in the OECD area.

Reforms have been more modest in the major continental European economies, but still significant. Because a progressive rate structure is still regarded as desirable, income tax reform along *United States* lines has been ruled out in *Germany* (Pechman 1988). However, under the 1986-88 Tax Reduction Law, the top marginal rate will be cut from 56 to 53 per cent from 1990. In *France*, where the income tax is relatively low-yielding (forming only 6 per cent of tax receipts) the top marginal rate has been cut from 65 to 56.8 per cent. However, an extension of the tax base appears difficult for political reasons. In *Italy* the longer-run trend has been for the proportion of income tax in total taxation to increase because of failure to adjust for inflation and the need to control the budget deficit. To reverse this trend, the tax rate schedule has been amended, first reducing most marginal rates by 1 to 3 percentage points and bringing the top rate down from 62 to 60 per cent and then introducing a maximum rate of 50 per cent from 1989. A 50 per cent maximum central government income tax rate has also been introduced in *Japan,* although local taxes may raise this to as much as 65 per cent.

With the exception of *Denmark*, the tax reforms implemented or planned by the Nordic economies have been fairly sweeping. The Danish tax reform, which took effect in 1987, broadened the income tax base by restricting the value of deductions and reduced the higher rates of tax. However, the highest (central-plus-local) rate remains is still a rather high 68 per cent (reached at an income only 20 per cent above average annual income for white-collar workers), and the reduction in marginal rates has been modest compared with some other OECD economies (partly because priority has been given to cutting public borrowing). Similarly, although marginal tax rates for those on average incomes in *Sweden* have been reduced by 20 percentage points (a reform accompanied by abolition of indexation), the maximum rate remains for the moment at 72 per cent. Attention has turned towards further rate reduction, however, and the government proposes to introduce either a 30 to 50 per cent or a 30 to 60 per cent tax scale by 1991. In *Norway*, the government has implemented its tax reform programme, aimed at streamlining the previously complicated system, broadening the tax base, lowering rates and stimulating saving. Tax allowances, including interest-payment deductibility, have been cut back and tax rates significantly reduced. Personal income tax deductions have been cut back by nearly a half in *Finland,* permitting a reduction in the top marginal tax rate to 60 per cent. *Iceland*, which does not depend very heavily on income taxes for revenues, introduced a single-rate income tax at 35 per cent (the only flat-rate system in the OECD area) as part of a sweeping tax reform in 1988.

Marginal rates are also still high in the *Netherlands*, with a wide range of special deductions narrowing the tax base and raising marginal tax rates perhaps by as much as 5 percentage points (OECD, 1987d). However, following the report of a tax commission, parliament has approved a proposal to simplify the income tax system by 1990, reducing the number of special allowances and lowering marginal rates to a 60 per cent maximum. The *Belgian* government's tax reform proposal, put forward in August 1987, finally passed in late 1988, reducing the number of tax brackets to seven and the maximum rate from 72 to 55 per cent. *Austria* has also introduced a major reform, effective from 1989, aimed at broadening the tax base and cutting the top rate from 62 to 50 per cent, resulting in a reduction in the number of brackets from 11 to 5.

After enacting measures to steepen the rate structure up to 1983, *Spain* closed a number of loopholes and cut the rates of income tax in 1986, following this with a further reduction in top rates to 56 per cent in 1988. *Portugal* is also moving toward a more efficient and equitable income tax system, combining a broadening of the tax base and lower rates, currently with a maximum of 40 per cent. *Turkey* has successively lowered marginal rates of income tax since 1981 (partly to compensate for inflation) and currently has a maximum rate of 50 per cent. Partly in order to limit tax evasion, the tax system has also been simplified and the top rate reduced to 50 per cent in *Greece.*

b)   Increasing the scope of indirect taxes

As the need to reduce the income tax burden has increased, a trend towards greater reliance on general consumption taxes is discernible in several OECD countries (especially *Denmark, Spain, Portugal, Turkey, New Zealand, Canada* and the *United Kingdom*) (Table 5.12). This includes the introduction of new consumption taxes in some countries, while in others the expenditure tax base has been broadened and the number of rates reduced. As part of its tax reform, *Denmark* introduced a new tax on the VAT base as a substitute for a large part of the non-wage labour costs borne by employers. *Spain, Portugal* and *Greece* introduced a value added tax on joining the Common Market. Rates among European Community members currently vary quite widely, and in order to avoid trade distortions once border controls are dismantled, it is proposed to harmonise the rate between 14 and 20 per cent for most goods and services by 1992, with a lower rate of 4 to 9 per cent on food, heating and lighting etc. The 1989 *French* budget included a proposal to reduce the number of rates from five to three, as step towards achievement of the Common Market VAT harmonisation programme.

Outside the European Community, progress towards greater reliance on sales taxes has been mixed. As part of the major overhaul undertaken in 1987, *Iceland* adopted a Value Added Tax (to be introduced in January 1990), lowering import duties in the process. *Turkey* introduced a VAT system in 1985, with a view to reducing dependence on income taxes. *New Zealand* has also had a value added type tax – a general goods and services tax – since 1986, which has raised the proportion of indirect taxes from one-quarter to one-third of tax revenues. *Canada* intends to introduce a value added tax as part of a wide-ranging tax reform. However, despite discussion of VAT as a means of reducing the federal deficit, such a reform appears politically difficult to implement in the *United States*. The implementation of a broad based consumption tax was also proposed in *Australia* in 1985, but was not proceeded with because it failed to gain widespread support. Similarly, the proposal for a value added tax in *Switzerland* has twice been rejected by referenda. Attempts to introduce

Table 5.12. **General consumption taxes**

	General consumption taxes			Tax structure in 1988				
	1975	1980	1986	Type of tax[1]	No. of rates[2]	Rates		
						Standard	Low	High
	Per cent of total tax revenue					Per cent		
Australia	6.6	5.2	7.8	WST	3	20	10	30
Austria	19.8	20.1	20.7	VAT	3	20	10	32
Belgium	15.9	16.8	15.5	VAT	5	19	6	33.3
Canada	12.5	11.5	14.6	RST	1	12	—	—
Denmark	16.9	22.2	19.5	VAT	1	22	—	—
Finland	17.8	20.6	21.5	VAT	1	16	—	—
France	23.3	21.0	19.5	VAT	5	18.6	5.5[3]	33.3[3]
Germany	14.7	16.6	15.3	VAT	2	14	7	—
Greece	18.9	22.9	17.0	VAT	3	18	9	36
Iceland	35.1	34.8	37.9	VAT[4]	1	22	—	—
Ireland	14.7	14.8	20.8	VAT	3	25	2	2
Italy	14.3	15.6	14.6	VAT	4	18	38	2
Japan	—	—	—	GST[4]	—	3	—	—
Luxembourg	12.0	10.8	13.3	VAT	3	12	3	—
Netherlands	14.4	15.8	16.5	VAT	2	19	5	—
New Zealand	9.0	10.2	12.9	GST	1	10	—	—
Norway	20.5	18.1	19.7	VAT	1	20	—	—
Portugal	11.2	16.2	21.0	VAT	3	17	8	30
Spain	15.3	10.2	18.0	VAT	3	12	6	33
Sweden	12.0	13.4	13.4	VAT	2	23.5	11	—
Switzerland	7.7	9.1	9.3	RST	1	6	—	—
Turkey	—	—	23.0	VAT	4	12	0	—
United Kingdom	8.8	10.5	15.5	VAT	2	15	0	—
United States	6.7	6.6	7.6	—	—	—	—	—
Overall average[5]	15.0	15.9	16.5					

1. WST = wholesale sales tax;   GST = general sales tax;   RST = retail sales tax.
2. Excluding zero rate.
3. From 1989 the top rate will be 28 per cent and the lowest 7 per cent.
4. With effect from 1st January 1989 for Japan and 1st January 1990 for Iceland.
5. Unweighted.
Sources: OECD 1988h Paris, 1988, Hagemann *et al.* (1988), and OECD Secretariat estimates.

a general consumption tax in *Japan* also failed until 1988, when such a tax was introduced (at 3 per cent) to pay for income tax reductions.

c) *Developments in corporate taxation*

In most OECD economies, after-tax rates of return differ widely between various assets (see Table 3.11). Reforms adopted or proposed in *Australia, Belgium, Canada, Finland, Japan,* the *Netherlands, New Zealand,* the *United Kingdom* and the

United States have aimed to give greater uniformity to post-tax returns, often reducing the statutory corporation tax rate, while removing special allowances and credits and switching the burden of tax from the personal to the corporate sector (Tables 5.13 and 5.14). Earlier reforms having given preferential treatment to machinery and equipment investment in the *United States*, the 1986 Tax Reform Act attempted to apply more uniform rates, by abolishing the investment tax credit, eliminating tax shelters which encouraged investment in commercial property and reducing the top tax rate from 46 to 34 per cent (CBO, 1985; OECD, 1986a; Auerbach, 1987). The share of corporate taxes in total revenues is expected to increase as a result, following a steady decline over the last decade. In the February 1986 Budget *Canada* also announced first steps towards the realisation of company tax reform, aimed at reducing tax rates over a three-year period, accompanied by the elimination of the inventory allowance and a phasing-out of the general investment tax credit.

Table 5.13.   **Changes in corporate income tax rates**[1]

Country	1972	1983	1986	1988-1989	Treatment of dividends
Australia	47.5	46	46	39	→ Imputation
Austria	58	55	55	30	→ Imputation[2]
Belgium	48	45	45	43	→ Classical
Canada[1]	50	51	53	44	Imputation
Denmark	36	40	50	50	Imputation
Finland[1]	58	59	50	45[3]	→ Imputation[2]
France	50	50	45	42	Imputation
Germany	52.5	56	56	50[3]	Imputation
Iceland	..	65	51	51	Classical (p)
Ireland	50	50	50	43	Imputation
Italy[1]	44	46	46	46	Imputation
Japan[1, 4]	47	53	53	50	→ Classical[2]
Luxembourg	40	40	40	36	Classical
Netherlands	48	48	42	35	Classical
Norway	51	51	51	51	→ Imputation[2]
Spain	..	35	35	35	Classical (p)
Sweden	54	52	52	52	Classical (p)
New Zealand	45	45	48	28	→ Imputation
United Kingdom	52	52	40	35	Imputation
United States	48	46	46	34	Classical

Key: Classical system: economic double taxation;   p : partial deduction for dividends paid.
      Imputation system: credit for company tax withheld.
1. Combined national and local tax rates.
2. Formerly split rate system: lower tax rate on distributed income.
      → = recent change.
3. From 1990.
4. 40 per cent national tax in 1989, to be reduced to 37 1/2 per cent in 1990.
Sources: OECD 1975; OECD 1987m; Pechman, 1988 and national sources.

Table 5.14. **Corporate tax allowances**

	Normal depreciation method	Investment allowance or credit (1986)	Total allowance[2,3] in 1983	
			Equipment	Structures
Australia	SL or AD*	IA removed	38.3	7.7
Austria	SL or AD*	IA	47.3	31.3
Belgium	DB	IA	44.8	29.2
Canada	DB, AD	IC*	31.8	18.1
Denmark	DB (M), SL (S)	—	22.2	12.9
Finland	DB	—	22.4	12.0
France	SL, DB (M)	—	34.5	22.2
Germany	DB or SL	—	48.4	27.5
Ireland	AD*	—	55.0	55.0
Italy	SL, AD	—	24.2	12.9
Japan	DB or SL	—	36.0	16.1
Netherlands	DB or SL	—	41.0	24.0
New Zealand	DB (M), SL (S)	—	24.1	5.4
Norway	DB	—	36.7	20.6
Spain	DB or SL	IC	32.9	26.2
Sweden	DB (M), SL (S)	IA (m)	34.5	22.4
Switzerland	DB or SL	—	12.3	6.9
United Kingdom	DB or SL (S)	(AD abolished 1983)	52.0	41.4
United States	AD	(IC abolished 1986)	44.3	25.3

1. SL = straight line; AD = accelerated depreciation; DB = declining balance; M = machinery; S = structures; * being cut back.
2. At "average" inflation per dollar of investment.
3. The difference between the tax rate and allowances indicates the degree to which the system of capital allowances by itself is distortionary. Allowances smaller than the tax rate indicate that capital formation is *ceteris paribus* taxed; allowances greater than the tax rate imply that it is subsidised. The standard formulation of the neoclassical user cost of capital is: $c = q \left[(r(1-t) + d)^* (1 - k - t^*Z) \right] / (1 - t)$ where c is the real cost of capital, per dollar of investment (which is equated in equilibrium with the present value of the net income stream generated by the asset); q is the relative price of capital goods; r (1 − t) is the after tax cost of funds; d is the true economic depreciation rate on new assets; k is the rate of the investment tax credit; t is the statutory corporate income taxe rate, and Z is the present discounted value (in dollars of the year of investment) of depreciation deductions stemming from the investment. The last term on the right hand side summarises the effect of the corporate tax system, where $(k + t^*Z)$ is the value of the tax concession given by the government to the company. It can be seen that if $(k + t^*Z)$ equals the statutory corporate tax rate t then $(1 - k - t^*Z) / (1 - t) = 1$ and the after-tax return is the same as the pre-tax one and the effective marginal tax rate is zero.
Sources: OECD 1987m, and McKee *et al.*, 1986.

In the *United Kingdom*, the corporation tax reform introduced in 1984 has now been fully implemented, with a major reduction in tax rates from 52 to 35 per cent, together with a widening of the tax base by the abolition of stock relief and accelerated depreciation allowances. Corporation tax rates have been reduced in *Germany* and *France* (the rate to be cut from 42 to 39 per cent for income reinvested according to the 1989 Budget proposal), while in the *Netherlands*, the investment tax credit has been abolished and corporate tax rates and employers' social security contributions have also been reduced. In *New Zealand*, a comprehensive reform of the business tax system is being undertaken, and a broader tax base and lower tax rate has also been introduced in *Australia*. The *Austrian* tax reform also aims to remove incentive-distorting exemptions. In *Ireland*, where the yield of corporation taxes is low, reform of the company tax system is linked to the need to reduce the bias in favour of capital-intensive production. The objective of *Swiss* tax reform, aimed for 1990, is to eliminate double taxation of investment income.

Solutions to the problem of economic double taxation of dividend income remain diverse (Table 5.13), but a trend seems to have emerged in favour of regimes mitigating or avoiding the double taxation inherent in the so-called "classical system" (whereby interest paid on debt can be deducted from taxable profits, while dividends are taxed) (OECD, 1987m). Both *Australia* and *New Zealand* have introduced full imputation systems in recent years, in order to eliminate the implied discrimination against equity and in favour of debt finance and *Finland* intends doing so from 1990. This leaves only *Belgium, Luxembourg,* the *Netherlands, Switzerland* and the *United States* operating a pure classical system, with no alleviation for double taxation, with *Iceland, Sweden, Portugal* and *Spain* having only slight alleviation. Most other OECD economies have imputation systems which give partial relief against double taxation of dividends, with *Greece, Turkey, Italy, Norway* and *Germany*, giving total alleviation.

Treatment of capital gains remains similarly diverse. Some countries fully tax the gain from the sale of capital assets, whether they are due purely to inflation or not. This is true of the U.S. tax system under the 1986 Reform Act. Partial taxation and even the complete exemption of capital gains are sometimes justified on the grounds that inflationary gains should not be taxed, but these *ad hoc* arrangements can only be approximate. The recent *Australian* reform introduced taxation of capital gains at the same time as it removed double taxation of dividends. Overall, however, the field of capital gains taxation remains a difficult and controversial area.

Rationales and effects of reform

The pursuit of greater neutrality has been based on the growing acceptance of the fact that a proportional tax system is more likely to be optimal from an efficiency point of view than one which is graduated and selective, since it does not affect relative prices and minimises substitution effects (see Sandmo (1976) for a résumé of the optimal taxation literature dealing with this issue). The alternative of selective taxation formerly held wide appeal. It could be justifed on the basis that taxing price-inelastic goods was non-distortionary (although taxing "necessities" has unacceptable redistributional consequences which put practical limits on the amount of revenue raised in this way). Also, the idea of minimising the impact of the tax structure on economic behaviour has been a distinctly unfamiliar idea to many

OECD governments until recently. Governments have often used the tax system deliberately, to alter consumption or investment patterns. But tax shifts of the complexity and magnitude described began to persuade governments that the marginal costs of raising extra revenue could imply an excessive marginal "excess burden" or "deadweight loss" from the tax system, quite out of proportion to the marginal social benefits of government interventionism.

A marginal excess burden of 1 cent implies that every extra dollar of public spending requires a net sacrifice of 1 cent in economic welfare because private spending is reduced by $1.01[8]. The efficiency loss can be of several kinds: the substitution of leisure for work; of consumption for saving (lowering potential output): of capital for labour (creating structural unemployment): of one type of capital asset for another; of one consumption good for another. Whatever the distortion, the effect is to switch resources into areas where they are less efficiently used, thereby reducing capital and labour productivity. Although marginal excess burdens are difficult to measure, the factors on which they depend can be clearly identified. They depend on the elasticities of substitution between taxed and untaxed sectors, on the height and dispersion of marginal tax rates (increasing as the marginal tax rate rises) and on the ratio of the marginal to the average rate. In the case of taxes on labour income they depend both on the inter-reaction between the tax rate and the labour supply and demand elasticities[9], which determine the incidence of these taxes. The burden of taxes on investment income would be heavier the greater the elasticity of saving with respect to after-tax interest rates.

Measurements of these elasticities remain controversial, but the thrust of recent research has been that distortions can be large, particularly where marginal tax rates are relatively high and there are large variations between them. In this respect, a bad *tax structure* may lead to welfare costs which can compound the efficiency loss arising from an increase in the overall tax burden. OECD governments have been influenced as much by the perception that there are efficiency gains to be made by making the tax system more *neutral* in its effect on different activities as by the belief that the costs imposed by raising any extra dollar of taxation, howsoever financed, are now prohibitively large in comparison with the marginal benefits of most public sector projects.

a) Reducing labour market distortions

Until fairly recently, empirical studies of the impact of marginal tax rates on labour supply tended to point, if anything, to the conclusion that the impact was not large enough to be of great economic or sociological significance (Saunders and Klau,

1985). The overall impact may be quite complex: an increase in marginal tax rates would make it less costly not to work (i.e reduce the opportunity cost of leisure), but any accompanying rise in the average tax rate might well induce greater work effort to compensate for lost income, offsetting all or part of the work/leisure substitution effect.

More recent research has shown notably larger effects than previously, for the broad middle spectrum of workers, as well as for the lower-income earners, who would be most affected by the benefit system and "poverty trap" phenomenon noted above. These "second-generation" studies point to a higher labour supply responsiveness for men than previously estimated, although married women appear to be the most sensitive to tax changes. Much of the evidence relates to the *United States*, where by one estimate a reduction in the labour supply of 5 to 12 per cent could be attributed to the existing combination of taxes and transfers (OECD 1987a). The 1986 U.S. reform is estimated to raise the labour supply by about 1 per cent in the long run (following the ½ per cent increase as a result of the 1981 reform). Supporting evidence is available in the *United Kingdom*, *Canada* and *Sweden* and *Switzerland* (although the impact in the last-mentioned country is rather small because of the relatively low weight of the *Swiss* tax burden)[10]. In *Iceland* the transition to a PAYE system in 1987 meant that incomes earned during that year were untaxed. The resultant surge in labour force participation adds anecdotal support to the conclusion from research work that cutting the average rate of income tax could have labour supply effects large enough to affect economic performance measurably.

Justification for the two other features of tax reform, namely the shift towards a proportional tax, with larger rate reductions for higher income earners, can also be found in available research (although, once again, there is controversy). Some researchers have estimated that much of the adverse impact on work incentives could be eliminated by a move to proportional taxation. And some survey evidence does show that highly-taxed individuals spend a significant amount of time seeking ways to avoid tax even if high taxes do not seem to result in a significant reduction in work effort.

Taxation may also affect the demand for labour, helping to create structural unemployment problems. Post-war economic policies tended not to recognise this possibility, being based on the belief that a tax-financed increase in public spending would increase the demand for labour (expressed in the so-called "balanced budget multiplier"). But as the focus of attention has shifted to real wage rigidities as a cause of unemployment, it has come to be recognised that taxes can raise the relative price of labour, so reducing labour demand and helping to sustain a "real wage gap". In particular, if higher taxes and social security contributions are shifted forward into higher wages (as some wage-bargaining models imply), the relative price of labour could rise and labour demand would fall as public spending and taxation rise. The precise impact will depend on the type of spending undertaken, with transfers having a lower multiplier than some types of infrastructure spending. Some research has suggested that the size of the public sector may have reached the point where a long-run negative balanced-budget multiplier now exists for *Germany*, the *Netherlands*, the *United Kingdom*, and (despite the fact that its public sector is much smaller) the *United States* (Knoester and Van der Windt, 1987). Again, the issue remains controversial, but *OECD Surveys* show that tax pressure has pushed up the cost of labour (in *Belgium* for example, where the cost of labour relative to capital rose faster than in other countries during the 1970s), depressing profits and distorting relative factor costs (see Chapter 2). Since by some estimates the elasticity of substitution between factors tends to be high, the employment situation may have been worsened by the expansion of the public sector (OECD, 1988b).

b) Increasing saving and improving the efficiency of capital

In principle, income taxes weaken the incentive to save, because they tax investment income twice (first as earnings, then as interest income). Because of this, the most favoured non-distortionary tax is a flat rate consumption tax, which would tax income only when it was spent, and this provides the rationale for the greater reliance on general consumption taxes. Although the effects of income taxes on saving is another controversial area empirically, they could be substantial according to some recent estimates. A 1 per cent increase in real after-tax yields in the *United States* appears (ceteris paribus) to raise the saving ratio by about 0.5 percentage points in the long run (Table 5.15). And a recent study identified a significant and substantial negative relationship between tax rates and saving ratios in European countries, ranging from 0.3 to 1.2 percentage points for a 1 percentage point increase in nominal interest rates (European Community, 1987). Bank of Italy calculations have shown that real interest rates have had a positive and major effect on financial savings, while private consumption may also be very sensitive to interest rates in *Denmark* (OECD, 1988e).

However, the effects of taxation on saving behaviour may be blurred by the income and wealth effects of interest rate changes, which can be quite powerful[11]. Capital gains may be counted as saving by recipients, who will reduce their saving out of current income if the value of their assets rise. An interest rate fall, for example, would increase the wealth of stock- and bond-holders and house-owners[12], reinforcing the incentive to consume given by the lower returns on saving (or lower cost

Table 5.15. **Effects of interest rate on personal saving**

| | Effect of a 1 percentage point increase in after-tax interest rates on[1]: | |
| | Consumption | Saving ratio |
	Per cent change	Percentage point change
Belgium	−0.6	+0.5
France	−0.3	+0.3
Germany	−0.7	+0.6
Japan	−1.2	+1.0
Sweden	−1.2	+1.2
United Kingdom	−0.8	+0.7
United States		
EC estimates	−0.7	+0.6
OECD estimates	−0.5	+0.5

1. Column 2 is equal to column 1*(c/y), where c = consumption and y = disposable income and the consumption function is of the form: lnc = $\alpha + \beta_1 \ln y + \beta_2 \ln w + \beta_3 r$, etc., where w is the net worth of households and r is the real (or nominal) after-tax interest rate.
Sources: Commission of the European Communities, *Economic Paper* No. 51, December 1986 and OECD 1988d.

of borrowing). But substitution and wealth effects may be offsetting so far as a tax change is concerned. In the *United States*, for example, part of the motivation for the 1981 tax reform was that it would increase personal saving by increasing after-tax returns. In the event the saving ratio fell over the following six years, partly because the stock market boomed and consumers substituted capital gains for other forms of saving. The stock market boom may have been partially induced by the tax reform package, which improved company profitability. In this case, the net effect of the ERTA on saving appears to have been negative. Indeed, the influence of changing tax rates on saving may be complex and unpredictable, depending on the effect of the tax cut on asset values.

The bias against saving exerted by many tax systems may be offset by special provisions which allow saving to escape taxation (owner-occupied housing; life-insurance and private pension funds etc.). These provisions mean that OECD income tax structures are somewhere between a comprehensive income tax system and a consumption tax. However, concern that the tax system may deter saving has been heightened in those countries (*Denmark, Luxembourg,* the *Netherlands, New Zealand, Norway, Portugal, Switzerland* and the *United States*) where interest payments on consumer loans have been fully deductible. (They are also partially deductible in *Belgium, Finland* and *Ireland.*) The deduction of interest payments often represents the largest itemised deduction for tax purposes; in the case of *Norway* deductions rose from 3¼ per cent of GDP in 1976 to 5½ per cent in the mid 1980s. This practice has had adverse effects on the saving ratio (OECD, 1987i). The need to introduce greater symmetry into the taxation of capital income was one rationale for the *Danish* reform; as part of a drive to increase saving, a 20 per cent tax on interest on consumer loans has been introduced and interest costs are now deductible only against capital income. *Sweden* has also restricted the tax deduction for interest payments, with the tax value now limited to 50 per cent. The 1986 *United States* reform phased out interest relief on consumer credit, but the Act is expected to have a small negative effect on saving, partly because it abolished the investment tax credit but also because it made it easier for tax-payers to deduct interest on consumer debt if secured by a mortgage (Hausman and Poterba, 1987).

On the other hand, the 1988 reform in *Japan* intentionally reduced the bias in favour of saving. In conjunction with reductions in higher tax rates, most formerly tax-exempt savings (which left 70 per cent of interest income untaxed) were made subject to a withholding tax of 20 per cent. Similarly, in the case of *Italy*, non-taxation of interest payments on government securities may have given an incentive to save until partly removed in 1986.

The net impact of taxes on saving patterns is also complicated by capital gains taxes and the combination of depreciation provisions and relief for interest payments which have tended to cause corporation taxes to favour certain forms of asset accumulation over others and debt-finance over equity-finance. Capital gains taxation can often imply substantial negative post-tax real rates of return, while the inter-action of income and corporation taxes has reduced yields on dividends compared with other forms of investment (see above). Together with the ability of firms to deduct interest payments from taxes and profits, the effect has been to encourage a build-up of corporate debt. In the United States this has been associated with the phenomenon of the "leveraged buy-out", which has begun to cause the regulatory and fiscal authorities some concern.

In the OECD at large, corporation taxes have generally favoured machinery over other assets, encouraging machinery-intensive production and distorting the allocation of capital (see Chapter 3). Because the asset mix (and hence the rate of economic depreciation) varies widely with the production process, after-tax rates of return have varied widely from industry to industry, with little reason to suppose the resulting pattern is optimal. Since there is reasonably strong evidence that private investment is sensitive to after-tax returns, corporate tax systems have ensured that investment has been strongest in tax-favoured sectors, reducing the marginal efficiency of investment from what it would be in the absence of taxation. Estimates of the resultant efficiency losses vary (Boskin, 1988), but this has only served to emphasise that tax structures had become too complicated to know what their precise effects on national and international resource allocation actually were.

c)   Aggregate welfare effects of tax reform

Under elasticity assumptions which are generally plausible in the light of the above discussion, estimates of the marginal cost of financing government expenditure on goods and services have been put at $1.17 to $1.56 per dollar in the *United States* (i.e. excess burdens of $0.17 to $0.56 plus the $1 private spending displaced by the of extra revenue raised), depending on the tax (Ballard et al, 1985). The welfare loss arising from the tax will vary with the height and number of tax rates so that, as noted, an existing tax *structure* may impose an extra efficiency loss compared with a similar average tax burden with more uniform rates. Indeed, research with general equilibrium models confirms that the greater the degree of variance in tax rates the greater the estimated welfare loss[13]. Moving towards a more economically-neutral system (represented by a revenue-neutral change to a more comprehensive base with greater proportionality) thus offers significant potential economic benefits. One estimate has put the plausible range of the effects of "levelling the playing field" on the level of GNP at ½ to nearly 2 per cent so far as the U.S. tax reform was concerned[14]. Estimates for *Canada* put the marginal excess burden of the tax system at 24 cents per dollar of tax for commodity taxes and within a range of 9 to 24 cents for labour taxes, while those for *Sweden* are more dramatic; the welfare gain from reducing the local income tax may be as high as $1.84 per dollar of tax eliminated according to one estimate, while replacing the current progressive tax system with a distributionally neutral tax on labour and capital would itself give a marginal welfare gain of $1.33 per dollar[15].

The implications of such estimates, even though they remain controversial, are both that tax-neutrality is efficiency-enhancing and that the cost-benefit standards applied to public spending should be more stringent than hitherto. If the deadweight loss is even nearly as large as the lowest of these estimates, public spending, to be welfare-improving, has to produce significant marginal benefits. On that basis, many public sector spending commitments probably should not have been undertaken, and there is the implication that gains can be made by cutting back transfer spending in particular[16]. On the other hand, each reform has to be judged on its merits. The introduction of a tax may sometimes reduce distortions caused by taxes in other sectors, implying a negative excess burden. By some calculations, a tax on gasoline would have such an effect in the *United States*, since it would alter relative prices to reflect pollution and congestion costs (French, 1988). More generally, a tax may, in a "second best" situation reduce distortions by offsetting biases caused by subsidised user costs or taxation elsewhere in the system[17].

Medium-term strategy: controlling government indebtedness

The problem of growing government indebtedness

The pace of tax reform has been in part determined by the need to contain the accumulation of government debt – the legacy of persistent budget deficits (Diagram 5.5 and Table 5.16). Increased taxpayer resistance led many OECD governments to have growing recourse to deficit finance from the mid-1970s and government debt increased accordingly (Chouraqui and Price, 1984). The average gross public debt/GNP ratio rose by about 10 percentage points in the 1970s, tending to gain momentum towards the end of the decade as real interest rates rose (Diagram 5.6 and Table 5.17). With inflation accelerating and economic growth slowing, moves to bring budget deficits back under control were generally given

DIAGRAM 5.5

GENERAL GOVERNMENT FINANCIAL BALANCES (1)
Per cent of GDP/GNP

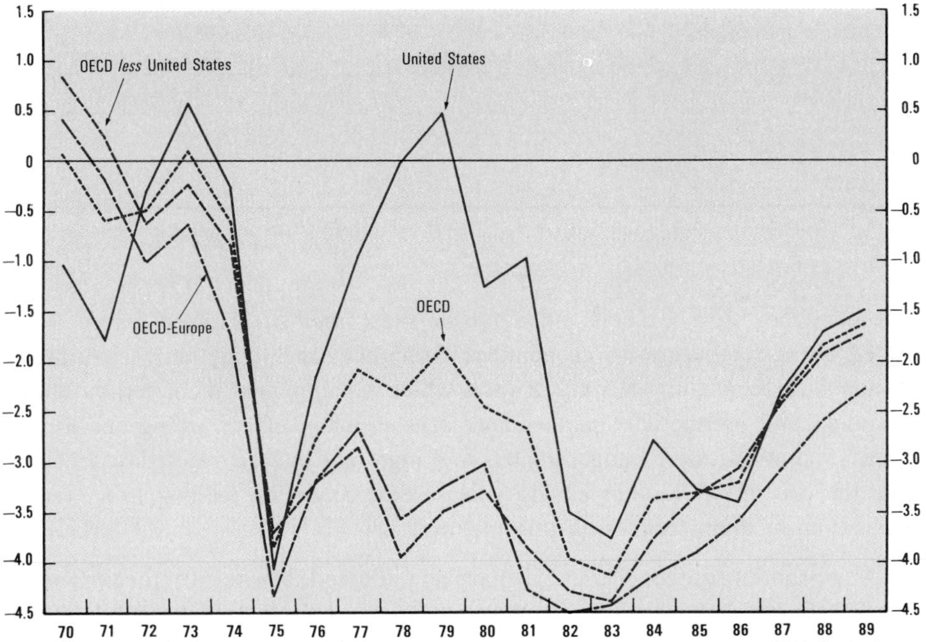

1. General government net lending on an SNA basis except for the United States, United Kingdom, Australia and Greece, which are on a national accounts basis.

Source: OECD, *Historical Statistics* and OECD Secretariat estimates.

191

Table 5.16. **General government financial balances**[1]

Surplus (+) or deficit (−) as a percentage of nominal GNP/GDP

	1970	1975	1980	1982	1986	1988[2]
United States	− 1.0	− 4.1	− 1.3	− 3.5	− 3.4	− 1.7
Japan	1.8	− 2.7	− 4.4	− 3.6	− 1.1	− 0.2
Germany	0.2	− 5.7	− 2.9	− 3.3	− 1.3	− 2.0
France	0.9	− 2.2	0.0	− 2.8	− 2.9	− 1.6
United Kingdom	2.5	− 4.7	− 3.5	− 2.5	− 2.4	+ 0.3
Italy	− 3.7	− 12.4	− 8.5	− 11.3	− 11.4	− 10.0
Canada	0.9	− 2.4	− 2.8	− 5.9	− 5.4	− 3.3
Total of above countries[3]	− 0.1	− 4.3	− 2.5	− 3.9	− 3.3	− 1.9
Australia	2.9	− 0.6	+ 1.6	− 0.5	− 2.2	+ 1.2
Austria	1.0	− 2.5	− 1.7	− 3.4	− 3.6	− 3.6
Belgium	− 2.0	− 4.7	− 9.2	− 11.3	− 9.2	− 6.9
Denmark	3.2	− 1.4	− 3.3	− 9.1	+ 3.1	+ 1.2
Finland	4.3	2.6	0.3	− 0.6	+ 0.7	+ 1.2
Greece	− 0.1	− 3.4	− 2.9	− 7.6	− 10.5	− 13.0
Netherlands	− 0.8	− 3.0	− 4.0	− 7.1	− 5.9	− 5.9
Norway	+ 3.2	+ 3.8	+ 5.7	+ 4.4	+ 6.0	+ 2.3
Spain	0.7	0.0	− 2.6	− 5.6	− 6.1	− 3.3
Sweden	4.4	2.7	− 3.7	− 6.3	− 0.7	+ 3.7
Total of smaller countries[3]	1.7	0.7	− 2.3	− 4.8	− 3.5	− 2.1
Total of European countries[3]	0.6	− 4.4	− 2.9	− 4.8	− 3.9	− 2.9
Total of above countries[3]	0.1	− 3.9	− 2.5	− 4.1	− 3.3	− 1.9

1. On an SNA basis except for the United States, the United Kingdom, Greece and the Netherlands which are on a national income account basis.
2. OECD estimates and forecasts.
3. 1982 GNP/GDP weights and exchange rates.
Source: OECD Secretariat estimates.

greater urgency than tax cuts, since outside the *United States* they tended to be blamed for the deterioration in economic performance – including the acceleration in inflation and the rise in real interest rates which accompanied the deterioration in investment and productivity performance (the problem of "crowding out"). The combination of excessive budget deficits and high real interest rates threatened to make the rise in public debt explosive in several countries, leading to a greater emphasis on medium-term budgetary planning.

A substantial number of countries have now adopted some form of medium-term financial planning in order to control and/or monitor the growth of public sector borrowing and indebtedness. This approach has been partially successful. Overall, the OECD-area general government deficit is now close to that at the beginning of the

GROSS PUBLIC DEBT (1)
Per cent of GDP/GNP

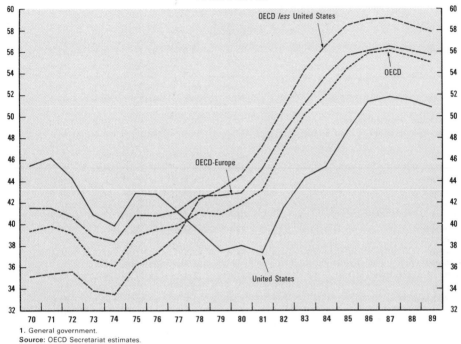

1. General government.
Source: OECD Secretariat estimates.

decade (at 2 per cent of GNP), and significantly lower than its 1982 peak of 4 per cent (Table 5.16). The containment of public sector borrowing has been particularly successful in *Japan*, the *United Kingdom, Denmark, Sweden, Australia,* and *New Zealand*, which have all made considerable progress in bringing down their budget deficits, and it has also had significant results in *Germany, Canada* and *Belgium.* The effectiveness of the broad commitment to "budget consolidation" is reflected in the fact that excluding debt interest the aggregate OECD structural deficit (general government) has moved sharply towards surplus (Table 5.18). If the *United States* is excluded, this represents a discretionary tightening of fiscal policy amounting to 3 per cent of GNP in the last ten years. Nevertheless, the difficulties involved in rolling back public indebtedness are illustrated by the continuing increase in government debt and debt interest as proportions of both public spending and GNP in a significant number of OECD economies (although the rate of increase has slowed).

193

Table 5.17. **Gross public debt**[1]

Per cent of nominal GNP/GDP

	1970	1975	1980	1983	1986	1988[2]
United States	45.3	42.6	37.9	44.1	51.3	51.3
Japan	12.1	22.4	52.0	66.9	69.3	67.3
Germany	18.4	25.0	32.5	40.9	42.3	44.1
France	52.9	41.1	37.3	41.4	46.2	47.3
United Kingdom	86.2	65.3	54.7	53.6	53.0	46.1
Italy	44.4	66.8	58.5	72.1	88.0	94.2
Canada	39.5	44.8	44.7	54.5	67.2	69.5
Total major seven countries	40.8	40.3	42.4	50.2	56.0	56.0
Total major seven less United States	37.7	38.3	46.5	55.6	60.4	60.0
Australia	41.7	28.5	25.1	24.3	26.9	20.7
Austria	19.4	23.9	37.2	46.0	49.0	52.3
Belgium	73.3	68.8	77.4	106.9	122.0	126.6
Denmark	11.3	11.9	33.5	62.6	59.3	54.9
Finland	15.5	8.6	13.8	18.7	18.1	17.7
Greece	21.3	22.4	27.7	41.2	58.3	64.5
Ireland	66.8	72.3	87.7	109.5	128.4	..
Netherlands	51.4	41.3	45.9	61.9	74.3	84.2
Norway	48.4	48.2	55.9	42.5	38.4	34.4
Portugal	..	26.3	38.7	56.9	..	..
Spain	14.4	12.9	18.5	34.4	47.6	48.5
Sweden	30.7	29.5	44.7	66.1	68.3	58.5
Switzerland	37.1	42.2	42.6	38.3	24.0	..
Turkey	..	20.6	28.1	37.2	51.1	..
Total of smaller countries[3]	32.0	30.0	36.4	49.1	55.9	55.9
Total of above countries[3]	39.5	39.0	41.6	50.0	55.9	55.9
Total OECD less United States[3]	35.7	36.6	44.3	54.2	59.4	59.4

1. For definition see note 26 of the text.
2. Estimates.
3. Excluding Ireland, Portugal, Switzerland and Turkey.
Source: OECD Secretariat estimates.

The need to pay for growing interest payments has been one of the most widespread impediments to cutting tax burdens. But the choice between cutting taxes or borrowing has also entailed judgements about the relative importance of tax distortions and the interest rate effects of public sector borrowing. In deciding on relative priorities, *European countries* and *Japan* have often taken the view that the long-run costs of higher public indebtedness are greater, on the grounds that deficits may be inflationary and where they are not, they involve government competition for credit which raises interest rates and reduces capital accumulation. The *United States* has been the major exception, the Reagan administration choosing to cut taxes at the

Table 5.18. **Structural budget balances net of debt interest payments**

Per cent of nominal potential GNP/GDP

	1972	1975	1980	1983	1986
United States	1.0	0.3	1.6	1.7	1.5
Japan	−0.1	−1.8	−2.5	−0.8	2.1
Germany	−0.7	−3.5	−1.6	1.8	2.3
France	1.1	0.5	1.8	0.6	2.1
United Kingdom	1.6	0.6	3.3	5.2	3.8
Italy	−6.6	−6.7	−2.9	−1.7	−3.0
Canada	0.2	−2.0	−0.4	−0.4	0.3
Total of above countries	0.3	−0.9	0.4	1.2	1.6
Total of above countries less United States	−0.4	−1.9	−0.7	0.7	1.7
Australia	4.2	1.4	1.8	0.4	−0.5
Austria	2.6	−0.2	0.4	−0.1	1.4
Belgium	−1.9	−1.4	−2.8	−0.4	4.3
Denmark	1.9	0.7	0.2	0.8	8.5
Finland	4.3	2.5	−0.6	−2.0	−0.3
Greece	1.2	−0.1	1.4	−2.0	0.5
Ireland	0.3	−6.8	−6.3	1.2	4.6
Netherlands	1.5	0.7	0.6	1.9	0.9
Norway	4.8	4.8	5.7	3.4	−8.8
Spain	0.1	0.0	−0.9	−2.3	−0.8
Sweden	3.2	−0.4	−3.4	−0.4	2.5
Total of smaller countries	2.0	0.5	−0.1	−0.1	0.7
Total OECD	0.5	−0.7	0.4	1.0	1.5
Total OECD less United States	0.1	−1.4	−0.5	0.6	1.5

Source: OECD Secretariat estimates.

expense of increasing the federal deficit in 1981. This was partly to pressure Congress into cutting spending, but it also reflected the belief that (given an independent central bank) government borrowing has little or no impact on either inflation or interest rates.

a) Budget deficits, monetisation and inflation

The second half of the 1970s saw substantial wealth losses imposed on domestic lenders in many OECD economies, because of the erosion of the purchasing power of fixed-income assets. This "inflation tax" on bond holders is reflected in the fact that real yields on government bonds tended to become negative (Price and Chouraqui, 1983) (Diagram 5.7)[18]. The decision to "accommodate" the first oil price shock appears to have been partly responsible. As a result, the OECD monetary base expanded strongly, inflation expectations became entrenched and the importance of "seigniorage" (i.e. of inflation as a tax on money balances) rose (Table 5.19)[19]. Although borrowing from the central bank was only a temporary source of finance in most countries (with the exception of *Italy, Portugal* and *Iceland*), the association of large budget deficits with monetary expansion and inflation from the mid-1970s has tended to turn public attitudes against deficit finance during the 1980s. Governments have had to convince lenders that they are willing to finance deficits in a non-inflationary way. To do so, they have had to pay *ex post* real interest rates 5 to 7 per cent, with consequences for resource allocation generally. The increasing sensitivity of bond and exchange markets to signs of monetary laxity and/or debt monetisation has been an important constraint on budgetary policy in the last decade.

DIAGRAM 5.7

REAL RATE OF RETURN ON GOVERNMENT DEBT
AND THE "INFLATION TAX"
IN THE UNITED STATES (1)

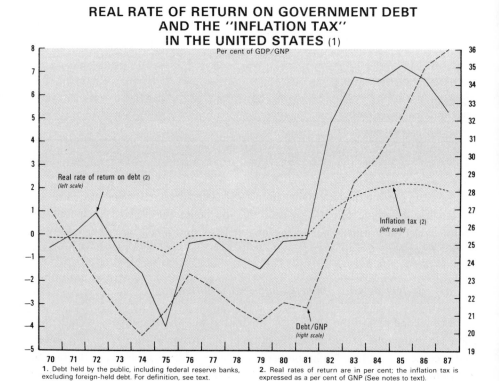

1. Debt held by the public, including federal reserve banks, excluding foreign-held debt. For definition, see text.
2. Real rates of return are in per cent; the inflation tax is expressed as a per cent of GNP (See notes to text).
Source: OECD Secretariat estimates.

Table 5.19. **Seigniorage and tax revenues**

	Tax revenues as a percentage of GDP 1986	Change in the monetary base as a percentage of:		
		GDP		Total tax revenue
		1973-1978	1979-1986	1979-1986
United States	31.3	0.5	0.5	1.5
Germany	44.7	0.7	0.3	0.8
France	48.2	0.3	0.6	1.3
United Kingdom	41.9	1.0	0.2	0.5
Italy	38.9	3.9	2.4	6.2
Belgium	44.8	0.9	0.2	0.4
Denmark	58.0	0.3	0.3	0.6
Netherlands	52.8	0.6	0.4	0.9
Norway	56.3	1.0	0.3	0.5
Sweden	61.5	0.9	1.0	1.6
Iceland	32.1	2.8	3.9	11.0
Ireland	44.3	..	0.8	2.5
Greece	36.4	..	3.5	9.1
Portugal	38.0	..	4.2	11.9
Spain	35.9	..	1.8	5.9

1. Average of the change in the monetary base as defined in line 14 in IMF International Financial Statistics.
Sources: S. Fisher, "Seigniorage and the case for national money", *Journal of Political Economy,* 1982, Vol. 90, No. 2; F. Giavazzi, *The exchange rate question in Europe,* Centre for European Policy Studies, Feb. 1988, and *OECD Economic Survey of Iceland,* 1988.

b) Deficits, interest rates and crowding out

Since the late 1970s there has been a *prima facie* association between government debt accumulation and high real interest rates (Diagram 5.7). This correlation has had an important influence on fiscal stance, even though the degree of causality is subject to dispute. High long-term interest rates may be traced in part to a tightening of monetary policies in the early 1980s. By the end of the 1970s monetary targeting had begun to have an important bearing on the setting of policies in OECD countries, particularly in *Germany, Switzerland, the United Kingdom* and *the United States*. However, the fact that long-term yields have remained high in real terms is difficult to explain in terms of expected short-term rates.

Empirical evidence as to whether persisting high real bond yields partly reflect the "crowding out" effects of government budget deficits[20] is provided by pooled time-series/cross section regression estimates reported in the 1988 *OECD Survey of Belgium* (Table 5.20). The budget deficit/saving ratio (which by 1983 averaged 50 per cent for the major seven OECD economies (Table 5.21)) emerges as a significant explanatory variable, a 1 percentage point increase in the ratio raising the long-term interest rate by between 5 and 7 basis points. For the OECD excluding the

Table 5.20. **Government deficits and interest rates**[1]

t-statistics in brackets

	Constant	Price expectations (PE)	Potential growth rate (GPOT)	Public debt (DT)	Budget deficit (DEF)	Budget sector (PUB)	Current account (CUR)	US bond rate (IUS)	Standard error
Including the United States									
A.1	0.516	0.462	1.564	0.28	− 0.071	..	− 0.030	..	1.359
	(3.16)	(12.43)	(5.90)	(1.87)	(− 2.69)		(− 0.45)		
A.2	0.213	0.377	0.147	1.869^2	− 0.059	..	− 0.076	..	1.232
	(1.37)	(10.30)	0.50	(6.67)	(− 2.40)		(− 1.3)		
B.	0.094	0.374	0.420	..	− 0.045	0.152	− 0.050	..	1.192
	(0.6)	(10.69)	(1.60)		(− 2.56)	(7.49)	(− 0.87)		
Excluding the United States (with IUS as an explanatory variable)									
C.	..	0.329	0.140	..	− 0.045	0.069	− 0.053	0.433	1.033
		(11.76)	(0.69)		(− 3.12)	(4.00)	(− 1.04)	(7.76)	

1. *Definition of variables.*
   Dependent variable: long-term interest rate on government bonds;
   PE: Current rate of increase in the consumer price index;
   GPOT: Potential GDP growth rate estimated by joining up cyclical peaks;
   DT: Five-year average (t − 2 to t + 2) of gross public debt/GDP;
   DEF: Five-year average (t − 2 to t + 2) of the government borrowing requirement/domestic private saving;
   PUB: Five-year average (t − 2 to t + 2) of public expenditure excluding interest/GDP;
   CUR: Current account balance divided by GDP;
   IUS: Long-term interest rate on US private bonds (AAA Corporate Bond Rate).
2. Log of DT.
Source: OECD Survey of Belgium, February 1988.

United States the coefficient falls to 0.045, explaining one-third of the 1½ percentage point increase in bond yields from 1979 to 1983. U.S. bond yields explain a further third of the increase, indicating that the determinants of U.S. bond yields – including, perhaps, the federal deficit – are important concerns for the OECD area at large.

Because of the effects of high U.S. interest rates on rates in the OECD area at large, European governments have been vocal in calling for U.S. federal deficit cuts as a means of achieving a general reduction in interest rates. But the link between the budget deficit and high U.S. interest rates has been difficult to demonstrate empirically. On the one hand, research tends to generate links between *structural* (i.e. cyclically-adjusted) budget deficits and interest rates which are consistent with the conventional view that the deficit adds to credit market pressures (Congressional Budget Office, 1987; Barth *et al*, 1984). But results can be altered by changes in specification and research based on correlations between *actual* deficits and interest rates is inconclusive. On this basis, the idea of a link between the Federal deficit and

Table 5.21. **General government deficits and private saving**

Deficit [+] as a per cent of net private saving

	1982	1983	1984	1985	1986	1987	1988
United States	63.7	65.5	40.8	57.7	64.0	55.5	46.2
Japan	25.4	26.6	15.2	6.1	7.9	2.4	1.6
Germany	45.2	32.6	24.5	15.4	13.4	17.7	17.3
France	44.6	52.0	47.9	48.6	42.3	42.1	23.6
United Kingdom	34.6	45.6	43.2	32.9	33.1	19.8	5.6
Italy	62.9	59.1	61.5	69.0	61.5	67.6	66.6
Canada	52.3	58.4	48.7	54.8	53.0	44.4	31.8
Average for major seven countries	47.6	49.2	37.6	40.8	40.5	35.5	28.0

Source: OECD Secretariat estimates.

interest rates has been questioned, particularly by the U.S. Treasury (United States Treasury Department, 1984).

One reason for the failure of researchers to agree may be that the *stock of debt* may matter for interest rates as much as the deficit itself. Portfolio balance principles – the wish of financial investors to hold a balanced portfolio of bonds, equities, money etc. – suggest that increases in debt/GNP ratios (or debt/wealth ratios) could affect interest rates[21]. In this case, the failure of bond yields to respond to falling structural deficits may be due to the fact that debt/GNP ratios have, in most cases, continued to rise. In the cross-section analysis mentioned above, the government debt emerges as a significant determinant of interest rates, although a public sector size variable works just as well (Table 5.20). One presumption might be that the higher the public debt or public expenditure burden, the higher the inflation-risk premium demanded by savers before they will invest in bonds.

c) *Budget deficits and private saving*

Governmental concern about the crowding out effects of deficits have been conditioned, in part, by the amount of domestic saving available to finance government borrowing. The high rate of private saving in Japan, for example, has reduced worries that fiscal deficits will induce inflation and crowding out (Ishi, 1986), while the problem of the federal deficit has been exacerbated by a fall in the U.S. personal saving ratio (OECD, 1988d). This has not seriously deterred business fixed investment in the United States: capital inflows (i.e. foreign – particularly Japanese – saving) have substituted for the domestic saving shortfall. But the federal deficit has made substantial demands on the pool of world savings. How serious such demands have been from the point of view of reducing private investment is a matter of debate. The evidence cited in the previous Section points to the probability that personal saving is quite interest-rate sensitive, so that fiscal deficits displace private consumption in the first instance, with only a limited effect on interest rates and a partial impact on interest-sensitive investment.

An extreme version of the above argument would be that budget deficits wholly displace private consumption, at no cost in higher interest rates. According to this view, taxpayers "discount" the future taxes which governments will eventually have to levy to pay for increased interest payments on their debt, by saving today an amount equal to the deficit. In this sense deficits are equivalent to future tax increases and government debt is not a net addition to wealth. Portfolio disturbances cannot therefore occur. Instead, deficits distort resource allocation in the same way as taxes already levied (the difference between the two lies only in uncertainty as to how the future tax will be imposed). Raising taxes to cut deficits is thus of no long-run benefit.

The validity of the tax discounting proposition depends on several rather strong rationality assumptions with rather weak intuitive appeal: that households anticipate the future tax liabilities generated by government debt; that the net return on government spending, social and economic, is zero (so that no government income is generated to offset interest payments); and that households are averse to passing on the burden of taxation to future generations. Empirically, the theory has been difficult to verify either through the interest rate equations discussed above or through work on consumption functions. Recent research into consumer behaviour at the OECD concludes that the full tax-discounting hypothesis does not receive much support from the data[22]. In the majority of countries studied, the tax-discounting factor appears to be close to zero, although for the *United States*, *Canada*, *Italy* and *Belgium* there is evidence of a small amount of discounting. Nevertheless, a link between higher government dissaving and greater private saving cannot be wholly ruled out, either directly (it is probably more important the larger is the outstanding debt/GNP ratio and the greater the public debate on the need for tax increases to reduce it), or more importantly, via the effects of interest rates on private saving.

d) The "stock effects" of deficits: debt and debt interest payments

Irrespective of whether deficits crowd out consumption or investment, higher real interest rates have greatly complicated the task of public sector management, because of growing public debt service commitments. In *Japan,* interest payments had reached nearly 14 per cent of general government expenditures by 1986, compared with under 4 per cent in 1970, while in the *United States* they grew from 8 to 16 per cent of federal outlays (Table 5.22). In several OECD economies (including the United States in the 1984 to 1985 period (OECD, 1985b)) there has been concern about the potentially explosive nature of feedbacks between deficits, interest payments and interest rates. Borrowing to finance interest payments creates an unstable situation where deficit- and debt-GNP ratios can expand indefinitely.

To prevent such an occurrence it is sufficient to stabilize the deficit/GNP ratio. In this case, the rate of increase in debt cannot permanently exceed the growth rate of the economy, which sets a ceiling for the debt/GNP ratio[23]. The ceiling may of course

Table 5.22. **Gross interest paid on public debt**

Per cent of general government expenditure

	1970	1975	1980	1983	1986	1988[1]
United States[2]	8.0	7.4	10.2	13.3	15.7	15.7
Japan	3.6	4.5	9.9	12.7	13.9	13.7
Germany	2.5	2.8	4.0	6.3	6.4	6.2
France	2.3	2.9	3.2	5.0	5.6	5.5
United Kingdom	9.4	8.9	10.9	10.4	10.4	9.8
Italy	5.5	9.3	13.0	15.6	16.6	16.5
Canada	10.8	9.9	13.9	16.0	18.8	19.4
Total of above countries	4.1	4.5	6.3	8.2	9.0	9.0
Total of above countries less United States	4.8	5.6	8.6	10.6	11.4	11.3
Australia	9.3	6.6	7.3	8.2	10.8	9.7
Austria	2.5	2.9	5.2	6.1	7.1	8.2
Belgium	8.3	7.9	11.6	16.5	20.4	21.2
Denmark	3.1	2.5	7.0	13.1	15.8	13.2
Finland	2.7	1.8	2.9	3.8	4.1	4.1
Greece	3.5	4.5	7.3	8.9	12.5	18.2
Ireland	8.8	9.1	12.6	16.8	18.3	..
Netherlands	7.6	7.2	8.5	11.7	13.4	13.5
Norway	4.4	4.6	8.1	8.6	10.8	9.8
Spain	2.5	1.9	2.3	3.4	9.2	9.4
Sweden	4.1	4.4	6.8	11.0	12.0	10.1
Turkey	..	2.4	2.2	3.7	13.3	..
Total of smaller countries	5.4	4.7	7.2	10.0	11.6	11.3
Total of above countries	4.3	4.5	6.4	8.2	9.3	9.3
Total OECD less United States	5.0	5.4	8.2	10.2	11.5	11.3

1. Forecasts.
2. Federal government.
Source: OECD Secretariat estimates.

be too high to be financed properly and may be unacceptable on these grounds, although "optimal" public debt or debt service ratios are probably positive. However, to sustain a given deficit/GNP ratio, non-interest spending has to be cut back (or taxes raised) by at least as much as interest payments rise. This has interesting implications for the longer-run (in)effectiveness of fiscal deficits in sustaining demand, in that, depending on the interest rate, a persistent deficit will always lead to the displacement of non-interest spending[24]. Where the interest rate equals the growth rate, for example, the deficit will eventually be wholly composed of interest payments.

Where interest rates exceed the growth rate of OECD economies, which has been the case during the 1980s, matters are more complicated, since stability implies the need for a "primary surplus": i.e. a surplus in the budget balance excluding interest payments. Hence, if government debt accumulation leads to both higher interest rates and debt service costs, the medium-term effects of deficit-finance on economic activity may be negative. The primary deficit will eventually have to fall, leading to a withdrawal of fiscal stimulus insofar as this is measured by the structural deficit net of interest payments (Price and Muller, 1984)[25]. Even where budgetary policies have been framed in the belief that short-term deficit finance may be beneficial (especially if financed from abroad) the combination of rising public debt levels and high interest rates has necessitated subsequent fiscal restraint to prevent debt service ratios rising above acceptable levels.

Stabilizing debt/GNP ratios

The dilemma caused by rising debt service costs has provided the background to the medium-term budgetary strategies of budget consolidation described in *OECD Economic Surveys* and outlined below. While OECD budgets are, on average, in approximate balance excluding interest payments and fiscal stance has been consistently restrictive for some time, many OECD economies are in the position where, unless the budget deficit/GNP ratio is reduced or interest rates fall, the proportion of interest payments in total expenditure will continue to rise. Debt dynamics thus continue to impose restrictive fiscal policies on the OECD area at large.

Several countries, including the *United States* and *Japan,* are in a position where the general government deficit is now small enough for the net debt/GNP ratio to begin to decline, while in *Denmark, Sweden, Finland, Norway* and *Australia* the ratio is falling quite rapidly (Table 5.23)[26]. This would also now be true of the *United Kingdom*, where recent years have seen a net repayment of debt. In the *United States*

Table 5.23. **Stabilizing general government debt/GNP ratios**

	Net general government debt		Budget deficit (+)		Medium-term trend in debt/GDP ratio under current tax law and spending plans	Memorandum item:
	1976	1987	1988	Deficit required for stability[1]		General government debt held abroad 1987
	% GDP/GNP					% GNP/GDP
United States	24	30	2.7 >	2.1	Decreasing	6.7
Japan	2	26	0.2 <	1.4	Decreasing	—
Germany	5	23	2.0 >	0.8	Increasing	3.3
France	11	27	1.6 >	1.0	Increasing	0.8
United Kingdom	56	43	−0.3 <	3.0	Decreasing rapidly	5.0
Italy	53	89	10.0 >	5.3	Increasing rapidly	2.0
Canada	5	36	3.3 >	2.5	Increasing	18.3
Australia	28	25	−1.2 <	2.0	Decreasing	5.4
Austria	27	52	3.6 >	1.4	Increasing rapidly	10.0
Belgium	50	117	7.0 >	3.6	Increasing rapidly	21.8
Denmark	8	25	−1.2 <	0.5	Decreasing	18.4
Finland	10	1	−1.2 <	0	Decreasing	7.8
Greece	22	61	13.0 >	5.0	Increasing rapidly	22.9
Iceland	40[2]	43	0.5 <	0.8	Decreasing	28.0
Ireland	..	126	5.4 >	4.7	Increasing	75.0[3]
Netherlands	20	54	5.9 >	1.5	Increasing rapidly	—
Norway	4	−19	−2.3 <	−1.1	Decreasing	2.2
Portugal	..	72	7.5 >	4.3	Increasing	35.0[3]
Spain	2	30	3.3 >	2.1	Increasing rapidly	1.7
Sweden	−30	11	−3.7 <	0.2	Decreasing	14.2
Total of above countries	20	34				

1. Calculated as the 1987 debt ratio multiplied by $g/(1+g)$ where g is the nominal growth rate in the OECD medium-term reference case. Foreign debt is multiplied by the real growth rate. The sustainable deficit is greater, the higher is the growth rate of potential output and (in the case of domestic debt), depends on the acceptable rate of inflation in the medium term.
2. Including state enterprises, 1978.
3. Total net external indebtedness.
Source: OECD Secretariat estimates.

the general government debt/GNP ratio is expected to fall even if no additional action were taken (which would contravene the Balanced Budget Act), while the federal debt ratio could begin to stabilize by 1990 if interest rate trends are not unfavourable. Similarly, the *Canadian* medium-term "Agenda" still aims to stabilize the federal debt to GNP ratio (at about 56 per cent of GNP) in the early 1990s.

But other countries, even where they have been relatively successful in cutting their deficits, need to make further progress for debt/GNP ratios to stabilize. In the *Netherlands*, for example, the goal for deficit reduction pursued in the 1982-86 period appears to have been achieved, and the 1986-90 goal is a further progressive cut in the deficit (OECD, 1987d). However, by 1987, the net public sector debt ratio had reached some 50 per cent of GNP. It is expected to continue to rise, illustrating the difficulty of eliminating imbalances once these begin to gain momentum. Similarly, in *Italy* the budget deficit is too high to stabilise the already high debt/GNP ratio, while in *Belgium* the ratio now exceeds 100 per cent and is projected to increase further in the absence of more discretionary measures to raise taxes (OECD, 1988b).

In *Ireland*, the 1982 and 1984 medium-term plans for reducing the government borrowing requirement were not realised and by 1986 the general government debt/GNP ratio had reached 140 per cent – the highest in the OECD area (OECD, 1987f). The budget deficit needed to be reduced by 4½ to 5 per cent of GNP in order to stabilize the debt/GNP ratio at this level, which would still imply a deficit of 8 per cent of GNP. Recognising that a reduction in the ratio was required, the authorities announced a medium-term borrowing target of 5 to 7 per cent of GNP in late 1987, to be reached by 1990. *Portugal*, which has one of the largest budget deficits in the OECD area, also faces difficulties in stabilizing the government debt/GNP ratio, which has reached 72 per cent. A medium-term objective of reducing the general government deficit to 4½ per cent of GNP has been set in order to meet that goal (OECD, 1988a). In *Greece*, a similar situation obtains. The government debt ratio has increased rapidly and the widening gap between expenditures and receipts has been ascribed in part directly to growing interest payments. The 1985-87 Stabilization Programme, by focusing on a steady reduction in public sector borrowing, has reduced the risk of an explosive debt spiral, but much still remains to be done, implying severe cuts in the non-interest component of public spending (OECD, 1987c).

Controlling external indebtedness

In a number of OECD economies government borrowing has been associated with a build-up in overseas indebtedness (Table 5.23), either directly or indirectly because domestic saving has been insufficient to meet the capital needs of industry and government, so forcing the private sector to borrow abroad. In *Ireland* net external debt has reached 80 per cent of GNP, most of it associated with government borrowing. In *Greece* it has reached 50 per cent and other highly-indebted OECD countries include *New Zealand, Portugal, Turkey* and *Iceland*, where foreign debt increased particularly rapidly in the first half of the 1980s. The recent real appreciation of the Icelandic krona, together with rapid GDP growth, have since reduced the external debt/GNP ratio, but net interest payments abroad are still equal to 3¼ per cent of GNP, implying that a trade surplus of that amount is needed to balance the current account (OECD, 1988j). Because the average real rate of interest on foreign loans is nearly 4 per cent, while the potential growth rate of the economy is no more than half this, a persistent trade surplus of ¾ per cent of GNP is needed just to prevent the external debt/GNP ratio from increasing. Since countries which have borrowed in foreign currency cannot use exchange rate depreciation to improve the trade balance[27], just to stabilise the external debt ratio requires severe constraints on the growth of domestic demand – a situation which acts as a similar constraint on fiscal stance and living standards in the other heavily-borrowed economies mentioned above.

Questions about the sustainability of the *United States* federal deficit have focused on both the domestic and external dimensions. Until 1985 the domestic problem was the dominant one. The FY 1986 "current services" baseline projected Federal deficits of the order of 5 per cent of GNP indefinitely. At best, if left uncorrected, this would have implied a substantial increase in the debt interest/GNP ratio, with corresponding cuts in non-interest spending. At worst it could have implied an explosion in debt – a prospect which did not seem remote to legislators as they fought to contain spending as interest rates rose in 1984 (OECD, 1985b and 1986a). With reductions in the growth of defence spending and lower long-term interest rates, the danger of such an explosion abated. The Federal net debt/GNP ratio is now projected to stabilize over the next few years, even under the relatively cautious growth assumptions contained in the CBO baseline (Congressional Budget Office, 1988a), although net Federal interest payments will continue to rise as a proportion of outlays.

As the domestic sustainability problem has eased, attention has shifted to the external problem. The Federal deficit has been accompanied by a shift in the net overseas debt position of the *United States* from a net creditor to a net debtor and despite the prospective stabilization of the Federal debt/GNP ratio, the net international investment/GNP ratio is likely to become increasingly negative (OECD, 1988d). This trend is not just a matter of Federal debt accumulation; the halving of the household saving rate between 1981 and 1987 has also been a factor. Nor is it a matter of direct Federal government borrowing abroad, since only 6 per cent of Federal debt is currently held directly by foreigners (16 per cent including official holdings[28]). But by absorbing the bulk of private saving, the Federal deficit remains responsible for a substantial part of the build-up in foreign debt. Like other indebted economies, domestic demand will need to grow slower than GNP to control the debt build-up. However, since United States external debt is exceptionally denominated in its own currency the overseas debt/GNP ratio could be reduced by an expansionary monetary policy and dollar depreciation (OECD, 1988d, p.71). The Federal deficit thus remains a source of potential inflation and interest rate pressure, via possible weakness in the dollar.

The longer-term: the impact of growing social security commitments

Meeting the pension and health obligations of the social security system without raising tax rates, reducing benefits or increasing budget deficits will become increasingly difficult in many OECD countries as the proportion of the population dependent on state pension systems increases (Table 5.24). For the OECD as a whole, the effect of demographic changes could be to raise pension expenditures by about 5 per cent of national income by the year 2020 (OECD 1988f/g), with social

Table 5.24. **Age dependency ratios**[1]

	1980	2000	2020	2040
Australia	14.8	17.5	23.6	32.1
Austria	24.2	22.6	30.4	40.8
Belgium	21.9	22.0	26.9	36.0
Canada	14.1	19.0	28.9	37.8
Denmark	22.3	21.5	30.5	42.1
Finland	17.7	21.2	34.8	38.8
France	21.9	23.3	30.6	38.2
Germany	23.4	25.4	33.5	48.2
Greece	20.5	22.6	27.4	34.0
Iceland	15.8	16.1	20.9	33.2
Ireland	18.2	16.9	18.7	27.1
Italy	20.8	22.6	29.3	41.0
Japan	13.5	22.6	33.6	37.8
Luxembourg	20.0	25.5	31.9	36.4
Netherlands	17.4	19.7	28.9	42.0
New Zealand	15.4	16.3	23.0	35.8
Norway	23.4	22.8	27.9	38.2
Portugal	16.1	20.8	23.7	33.1
Spain	17.2	21.8	25.3	38.2
Sweden	25.4	25.1	33.1	37.4
Switzerland	20.8	25.0	39.9	49.9
Turkey	8.5	8.0	10.3	15.9
United Kingdom	23.2	22.3	25.5	33.1
United States	17.1	18.2	25.0	32.3
OECD average	18.9	20.8	27.6	36.6

1. Population 65 + /population 15-64 x 100; 1980 actual ratios; 1990 to 2040 projected ratios.
Source: OECD Social Data Bank.

security budgets in *Japan, Germany, France, Italy, the Netherlands* and *Switzerland* likely to experience the most severe pressures because of a rising age dependency ratio (Table 5.25). In a number of other OECD countries (such as *Germany* and *France*), there are explicit mechanisms for adjusting social security contributions to keep the funds on a pay-as-you-go basis. The extent of the future increase in government liabilities could be measured in terms of the contribution rates which will be needed to balance the social security funds on a pay-as-you-go basis. These are likely to be very substantial during the first decades of the next century in some cases.

However, in many economies, social security payments have become increasingly dissociated from contributions. In countries such as *Greece*, this has been one of

Table 5.25. **The influence of demographic change on the share of pension expenditure in national income**[1,2]

1984 - 2040

	1984	2000	2020	2040
Australia	6.0	6.7	9.1	12.4
Austria	16.5	17.6	23.7	31.7
Belgium[3]	14.0	13.8	17.0	22.7
Canada	6.1	7.6	11.6	15.2
Denmark	10.1	9.5	13.5	18.7
Finland	8.5	9.7	16.0	17.8
France	14.3	16.5	21.6	27.0
Germany	13.7	16.4	21.6	31.1
Greece	10.8	13.0	15.7	19.5
Ireland	6.7	6.2	6.8	9.9
Italy	16.9	19.7	25.6	35.7
Japan	6.0	9.4	14.0	15.7
Netherlands	12.1	13.4	19.6	28.5
New Zealand	8.9	9.3	13.0	20.3
Norway	9.6	9.0	11.0	15.0
Portugal	8.2	10.6	12.1	16.9
Spain	10.0	11.7	13.6	20.4
Sweden	12.9	12.1	15.9	18.0
Switzerland	8.8	10.6	16.9	21.1
United Kingdom	7.7	7.5	8.6	11.2
United States	8.1	8.2	11.3	14.6
OECD average[4]	10.3	11.4	15.1	20.2

1. The projections show only the impact of demographic change. They assume constant benefit levels per beneficiary relative to national income per worker, constant labour force participation rates and constant proportions of elderly people in receipt of benefits.
2. OECD medium fertility variant.
3. Expenditure ratio for 1983.
4. Arithmetic mean.
Source: OECD 1988f.

the main reasons behind the deterioration in the public accounts. Pensions have grown from 7.3 per cent of GNP in 1979 to over 13 per cent. The number of pensioners has increased rapidly and the deteriorating ratio of contributors to beneficiaries has brought serious financial difficulties. Rising dependency ratios are thus likely to put increasing strain on budget deficits. One way of looking at this would be to calculate the present value of future social security liabilities at current real rates of benefit (in terms of the growing actuarial deficiency at a time when the funds should be accumulating increasing surpluses to prepare for the pay-out of future benefits from future investment income). If such "liabilities" were added to the measure of outstanding government debt conventionally used, debt/GNP ratios so-measured would appear to be much higher, and increasing faster, than would appear from the calculations given in Table 5.23. (But if the definition of debt is expanded in this way, there could also be an argument for drawing up a full government balance sheet which allows the calculation of government net worth).

In anticipation of future liabilities some economies, such as the *United States, Japan* and *Sweden* are accumulating surpluses in the social security funds. However, building up surpluses is of little long-run advantage if they are used to finance government consumption, as appears to be currently the case in the *United States*. Net contributions are scheduled to increase from $40 to $100 billion a year by FY 1993 (OECD, 1988d), but the Balanced Budget Act allows these surpluses to count towards meeting its deficit targets: i.e. they can be used to offset the deficit on ordinary government spending. It is as a result of the surpluses that the net government debt ratio will stabilize and then begin to fall (Table 5.23). But the gross debt/GNP ratio, which includes federal government liabilities towards the funds, will continue to rise because interest will be accruing at least as fast as GNP is growing and probably faster. Contributions will have to be paid back with interest when the contributors retire, so that when the funds are depleted in the 2020 to 2040 period, the need to raise taxes or run further deficits will re-occur. If interest has to be paid out of future tax revenues a fund used to finance government consumption is little different from a pay-as-you-go scheme (Munnel, 1985).

Conclusions

Progress towards better fiscal balance has been significant but partial and much remains to be done. The principal achievements have been:

   i)   Public expenditure has begun to fall as a ratio of GNP. Some of the factors which made for a faster-than-average public sector growth in earlier years have been checked as public sector pay and recruitment have been more closely controlled and greater efficiency imposed on public sector operations;

ii) Although the tax burden has not fallen, tax reforms, proposed and implemented, have meant that important progress has been made towards a more neutral, and allocatively more efficient, tax structure in many countries, reducing marginal rates of income tax and reducing disincentives to work, harmonising post-tax yields on capital and spreading the net of indirect taxes;

iii) Fiscal restraint has succeeded in reducing budget deficits relative to GNP from their peaks in the early 1980s, and in some countries the debt/GNP ratio has begun to fall.

However, personal tax rates still remain high in some countries and the scope for broadening the tax base by eliminating tax expenditures and increasing the scope of indirect taxes has not been exhausted. In several economies the introduction of a general consumption tax has proved infeasible so far, while the international harmonisation of company tax regimes is some way from being achieved.

In many OECD economies, particularly the smaller ones, debt/GNP ratios continue to rise, heavily constraining public sector choices. Even in those economies where debt/GNP ratios have stabilized, budgetary pressures may build up because of prospective deficits in social security funds. Increased debt interest payments have accounted for the growth of the public sector resource share in the 1980s, and pressure from this source is likely to remain a constraint on public-expenditure planning for some time to come. Though progress has been made towards better overall budgetary control, and the importance of medium-term planning has been widely recognised, real rates of interest remain higher than prospective growth rates. High government indebtedness will ensure that debt interest payments will grow as a proportion of revenues, restricting the scope for further reductions in taxation and hence making it inevitable that financing the government sector will remain a problem – both economic and financial – for some time to come.

Notes

1. The following *OECD Economic Surveys* contain special reviews of the public sector:

Australia	June 1985
Italy	April 1985
New Zealand	May 1985
Japan	July 1985
United States	September 1985, 1986, 1988
Canada	July 1986
Turkey	May 1987
Norway	December 1987
Belgium	January 1988
Luxembourg	January 1988
Portugal	January 1988
Switzerland	March 1988
Denmark	July 1988

   Public sector developments are also discussed extensively in the following *OECD Economic Surveys*:

New Zealand	1987
Greece	1987

2. The recognition of a secular tendency for the relative price of public services to increase has been part of public expenditure planning in the United Kingdom since the early 1960s. It has received more general expression in the theory of unbalanced productivity growth put forward by Baumol. Because of the assumption of zero productivity growth usually used when estimating government output (output is usually measured by manpower inputs), prices in the government sector increase at a rate $\delta P_g/P_g = \delta wr/wr$ percent per annum, (where P_g = the price of public services and wr is the wage rate increase in the private and public sectors). Assuming profits rise in line with unit labour costs, prices in the enterprise sector rise by $\delta P_{ng}/P_{ng} = \delta wr/wr - \delta q$, where δq is productivity growth. The relative price of public services would then rise by $\delta wr = \delta q$ per cent per annum if wages rise at the same rate in both sectors.

3. Real welfare spending (w) can be divided into three components:
   $$w = p^e.(n/p^e).(w/n),$$
   where p^e is that part of the population entitled to benefits (the dependency factor); (n/p^e) is the "take-up" or "eligibility" ratio; and (w/n) is the amount of real benefit per recipient (often called the "generosity ratio"). Table 5.5 gives a breakdown along these lines.

4. OECD (1985b). Until the mid-1960s most federal regulatory actions were "economic" – i.e. aimed at controlling monopoly power, market collusion, restraint-of-trade and anti-competitive behaviour or, in the case of financial regulations, at promoting financial stability. From the late 1960s concern over environmental issues, occupational hazards, auto safety and consumer issues led to special regulatory agencies which imposed significant costs on the economy. Moves to control the issuance of new regulations began in the 1970s, and from 1981 all agencies have to have their cost-benefit analyses approved. Moreover, Congress has passed a "Paperwork Reduction Act" which requires that any federal form for collecting information be subject to approval.

5. For recent surveys of tax reform trends, see Pechman (1988); the symposium on tax reform in *The Journal of Economic Perspectives*, Summer 1987; and Hagemann *et al.*, (1988).

6. Fiscal drag occurs where taxes grow faster than income, which has the effect of automatically raising the average rate of tax. For an income tax system of the form $t = ay^{\beta} p^{\eta}$, where the real income elasticity β and inflation elasticity η approximate to the progressive structure of the income tax system, the automatic change in the average rate of tax (t/yp) which occurs as a result of inflation ($\rho = dp/p$) is defined by $\rho(\eta - 1)$:
    i.e. fiscal drag is greater the greater is the elasticity of the taxes with respect to inflation. The object of indexation systems is to achieve a system where $\eta = 1$.

7. Tax expenditures can take various forms (exemptions, allowances, tax credits and special reliefs) and can be measured in several ways. The most common method of calculation is on a "tax foregone" basis, which relies on evaluating the relief at the marginal tax rate to which it would be subject. This can be a very inaccurate. Because the tax relief affects the amount of resources flowing into the activity receiving relief (i.e. it artificially raises them), the revenue loss can be grossly overstated – by about 40 per cent, for example, in the case of itemised deductions for charitable contributions. (See Stiglitz and Boskin (1977).

8. In its simplest form the *marginal excess burden* (meb) is defined as:

    $$\delta y/\delta t = (\delta y/\delta\tau)(\delta\tau/\delta t) \qquad ....\text{(marginal excess burden)};$$

    where $\delta y/\delta\tau = (\delta u/\delta\tau)/(\delta u/\delta y) = \theta \qquad ....\text{(utility function)};$

    and $\delta\tau/\delta t = \beta/y \qquad ....\text{(marginal tax rate function from } t = ay^{\beta});$

    The marginal excess burden here measures the welfare loss (δy) per unit of additional revenue (δt) arising from the loss of utility (δu) caused by an increase in the marginal tax rate δ. This "model" leads to a definition of the marginal excess burden in terms of the elasticity of the tax system (β):

    $$\delta y/\delta t = \theta\,\beta/y; \text{ or alternatively } \theta\,(\delta\tau/\delta t),$$

    where $\delta\tau$ is the change in the marginal rate needed to raise revenue equal to δt (cf. Hansson 1986). The *marginal cost of funds* (mcf) is (1 + meb) and measures the cost of raising an extra unit of revenues (δt) plus the indirect welfare loss, expressed as a proportion of taxes raised.

9. In terms of the model set out in the preceding note, the marginal cost of raising $1 via an increase in labour taxes would be:

$$\$mcf \; = \; 1 + [(\delta y/\delta l)(\delta l/\delta \tau)\tau]\delta \tau/\delta t.$$

The first term is the marginal productivity of labour and the second the responsiveness of labour to the marginal tax rate.

10. Hausman (1985) found that in the case of the United States a 30 per cent cut in taxes would increase the prime-age labour supply by between 1 and 4½ per cent and female participation by nearly 10 per cent. Ashworth and Ulph (*Taxation and Labour Supply,* 1981) estimate that a halving of the U.K. standard rate (from 30 to 15 per cent) would have increased male labour supply by nearly 2 per cent. Blomquist (*Journal of Public Economics,* 1983) estimates that taxes on labour in Sweden reduce adult male participation by 13 per cent and that a revenue-neutral change to a proportional rate of tax would increase labour supply by 7 per cent.

11. According to the life-cycle theory of consumer behaviour, individuals plan their consumption in accordance with expected lifetime resources, which include both the present value of the stream of future income and the market value of current assets (See Ando, A., and Modigliani F., "The life-cycle hypothesis of saving", *American Economic Review,* 53, 1963; Summers (1981)). This theory, on certain simplifying assumptions, suggests an aggregate saving function of the form where interest rates affect saving via incentive-, income- and wealth-effects:

$$S_t = \alpha_y (y^*) + \alpha_r(r - \tau - i^*) - \alpha_w(w^*)$$

where s is the saving ratio; y^* is discounted present value of real disposable after-tax income; r is the rate of interest;
τ = the effective marginal rate of tax on investment income; i = the rate of inflation; w is the real market value of current net household assets divided by income and $*$ denotes expected values.

Since the expected present value of household assets falls if interest rates rise (i.e. w^* is a function of $1/(1+r)$, which falls as r rises) any increase in saving due to the greater interest rate incentive to save is likely to be reinforced by the need to save more to restore the previous value of household assets. Conversely, a tax imposed on investment income lowers the opportunity cost of present consumption, causing the saving rate to decline, but since its effects on asset values will be negative (in this case w^* is determined by $[r(1-\tau)]/[1+r(1-\tau)]$, which declines as tax rates rise), a tax increase may raise saving. For a discussion see R.E. Brinner and S.H. Brooks "Stock prices", in Aaron and Pechman (1981).

12. *OECD Economic Survey of the United States 1988,* Annex I. The relative importance of wealth effects compared to substitution effects is confirmed by Summers (1981) and Boskin (1978), who estimate the direct interest-elasticity of saving at about 0.4 and the elasticity of saving with respect to wealth at 2.8. Thus, if the interest elasticity of wealth is one (as it would be if it were held in the form of undated stocks), the full elasticity would be nearer to 3.

13. The quantitative importance of disaggregation is illustrated in OECD 1987a. By one estimate disaggregation from 2 to 19 production sectors increases the estimated welfare gains by nearly 60 per cent.

14. See *Economic Report of the President*, January 1987, p.92 and Boskin (1988).

15. Ballard *et al* (1985) and Hansson (1986).

16. The *net* marginal cost of funds depends on the degree of complementarity between public and private goods. Models used to calculate marginal excess burdens assume that governments use revenues to provide transfer payments or other spending which have at best a zero economic rate of return. If allowance were made for complementarity, marginal excess burdens would be lower.

17. For instance, the replacement of selective employment tax (SET) and purchase tax by VAT in the United Kingdom in 1973 reduced economic efficiency because the capital market distortions caused by SET offset other distortions from capital income taxation (OECD, 1987a).

18. The "inflation tax" is essentially a wealth transfer from lender to borrower which arises because real yields on government debt are negative – i.e $r_d = i/d - p < 0$ (as in Diagram 5.7), where i = interest payments on government debt (d) held by the public (including the central bank) and p is the rate of inflation. The inflation tax, can then be defined:

$$t_l = -r_d d;$$
or $-r_d d/y$ in terms of GNP (Diagram 5.7)

19. Seigniorage (the narrowest definition of which is the profit accruing to the government by issuing coins at a value above their intrinsic cost) can also apply to the issue of central bank debt as a whole. It is defined as the change in the real value of central bank liabilities arising from inflation. It is a special form of "inflation tax", because it relates to monetary debt and is imposed on holders of money balances. It arises because the central bank pays no (or inadequate) interest on currency and reserves to compensate for inflation. The seigniorage tax rate may be defined as the change in the monetary base over GNP, on the basis that this determines inflation over the longer run $(\delta m_b/m_b = p)$ and interest paid on reserves is zero. By issuing monetary assets at a rate equal to (identical with) the inflation rate, the central bank is "taxing" money holders at that rate. Monetary base expansion (because of central bank credit to the government) was very high in the mid-1970s, particularly in Germany, the United Kingdom and Italy and continued to be significant in Italy, Portugal and Iceland (See *OECD Economic Survey of Iceland*, 1988).

20. "Crowding-out" is analogous (in a longer-run context where money is not a determinant of real growth) to the marginal excess burden imposed by capital taxes. Similarly:

$$\delta y/\delta b = (\delta y/\delta k)(\delta k/\delta b) = r(\delta k/\delta b);$$

where $\quad \delta k/\delta b = (\delta k/\delta r)\,(\delta r/\delta b) = \alpha_k(\delta r/\delta b) \quad$ ...(crowding out)

$\qquad \delta r/\delta b = -\delta r/\delta(s-i) = -1/(\alpha_r - \alpha_k) \quad$ ...(saving/investment balance)

and $\quad \delta k/\delta b = -\alpha k/\,(\alpha_r - \alpha_k) \quad$ ...(crowding out).

Crowding out here measures the decline in the capital stock (δk) per unit of additional government borrowing (δb) arising from the substitution of government consumption for private investment. Since b = s – i, an initial increase in government borrowing will displace investment to the extent that private saving does not rise to compensate. If saving is interest elastic $(\delta s/\delta r = \alpha_r > 0$ as in note 11) then private consumption rather than investment would be displaced by government spending.

213

21. Arguments that the stock of debt matters for the determination of interest rates are normally derived from "portfolio balance" models, where the interest rate is affected directly by the supply and demand for bonds relative to other financial assets. In this case, an increase in government debt (δd) has its first impact on interest rates (r_b = government bonds; r_k = corporate capital) via the portfolio disturbance caused by increasing the ratio of government debt to total financial wealth (w). This discourages investment but raises saving by an amount $\alpha_r . r_k$, which represents an increase in wealth. This serves partly to finance the resultant deficit. Unlike the previous saving-investment model, the portfolio one shows interest rate changes depending on b (the budget deficit) rather than (δb) (changes in the budget deficit). The rates will remain higher because of the outstanding stock of debt.

22. See G. Nicoletti (1988) and OECD (1988b). A model of consumption behaviour based on the life-cycle hypothesis is used, with tests carried out to determine the impact of government bonds on consumption (zero = full discounting; 1 = no discounting) and whether the deficit should be subtracted (1 = full discounting; zero = no discounting).

23. With the deficit/GNP (b/y) ratio fixed, the debt/GNP ratio (d/y) would stabilize at a ceiling of (b/y)/u, where u = the growth rate of GNP. The intuition behind this equilibrium is that at that point $b/d = u$ (i.e the rate of growth in debt would equal the growth rate of nominal GDP). For an exposition of public sector debt dynamics, including an analysis of the impact of taxes on interest receipts, see OECD (1987f).

24. In the long run, the budget deficit will be composed of debt interest payments to an extent determined by the ratio of the real rate of interest (r_d)*100% to the budget deficit ratio (b/y) – a situation relevant to OECD economies at the moment. This occurs because interest payments (i) would eventually equal $r_d d = (r_d/u)(b/y)$, where interest payments are a proportion (r_d/u) of the deficit. So long as $r_d = u$ equilibrium is achieved where the budget deficit is wholly composed of interest payments; i.e. $i/y = r_d d = b/y$; where $r > g$ the net of interest deficit will be lower when equilibrium is reached.

25. This interest burden constitutes obligatory public spending and to keep the budget deficit constant the tax/GNP ratio would have to be raised (or spending cut) by an amount equivalent to the increase in debt interest; the resultant long-run change in the net-of-interest government deficit (often used as an indicator of fiscal impulse – see Table 5.18) would then be (b/y)($1-r_d/u$). The long-run fiscal impulse thus depends on the rate of interest.

26. *Gross* debt relates to the total financial liabilities of the general government, including borrowings from the central bank (see note on seigniorage above); *net* debt equals gross debt less the government's financial assets, including those held by social security funds (which may be misleading, as is particularly the case in Japan, since the assets in the social security accounts have a counterpart in future government pension liabilities).

27. One of the advantages of a firm currency policy to countries with large foreign currency debt is that it reduces the resources needed to service external debt. This alters the perspective of economic policy-making, since any depreciation engineered to improve the trade balance could adversely affect real foreign debt exposure.

28. This is a smaller proportion of foreign holders than is the case in Germany, where there has been a sharp increase in government debt held abroad, from 5 per cent in the early 1980s, to 15 per cent. See OECD 1987e, pp.18-19.

Bibliography

Aaron, H. and J. Pechman (Eds), 1981, *How Taxes Affect Economic Behavior*, The Brookings Institution, Washington.

Auerbach, A.J (1987), "The Tax Reform Act of 1986 and the cost of capital", *Journal of Economic Perspectives*, Summer.

Ballard, C.L., J.B. Shoven and J. Whally (1985), "General equilibrium computations of the marginal welfare costs of taxes in the United States", *American Economic Review*, Vol. 75, No. 1 (March).

Barth, J.R., G. Iden and F.S. Russek (1984), "Do Federal deficits really matter?", *Contemporary Policy Issues*, Vol.III (Autumn).

Boskin, M.J. (1988), "Tax Policy and Economic Growth: Lessons from the 1980s", *Journal of Economic Perspectives*, Fall.

Chouraqui, J-C., B. Jones and R.B. Montador (1986), "Public debt in a medium-term perspective", *OECD Economic Studies* No. 7 (Autumn).

Chouraqui, J-C. and R.W.R. Price (1984), "Medium-term financial strategy: the co-ordination of fiscal and monetary policies", *OECD Economic Studies* No. 2 (Spring).

Congressional Budget Office (1983), *Revising the Individual Income Tax*, July.

Congressional Budget Office (1985), *Revising the Corporate Income Tax*, May.

Congressional Budget Office (1987), "Economic growth, capital formation and the Federal deficit" in *The Economic and Budget Outlook: Fiscal Years 1989-1993* (January).

Congressional Budget Office (1988a), *The Economic and Budget Outlook: Fiscal Years 1989 to 1993*, February.

Congressional Budget Office (1988b), *The Effects of Tax Reform on Tax Expenditures*, March.

French, M. (1988), "Efficiency and equity of a gasoline tax increase", *Finance and Economies Discussion Series*, no.33, Federal Reserve Board, July.

Hagemann, R.P., B.R. Jones and R.B. Montador (1988), "Tax reform in OECD countries: motives, constraints and practice", *OECD Economic Studies* No. 10 (Spring).

Hansson, Ingemar (1986), "Marginal cost of public funds for different tax instruments and government expenditures", *Scandinavian Journal of Economics* 86(2).

Hausman, J.A. (1985), "Taxes and labour supply", in Auerbach, A., and Feldstein, M. (Eds), *Handbook of Public Economics*, North Holland.

Hausman, J.A. and J.M. Poterba (1987), "Household behavior and the Tax Reform Act", *Economic perspectives*, Vol. 1, No. 1 (Summer).

Ishi, A. (1986), "Overview of fiscal deficits in Japan with special reference to the fiscal policy debate", *Hitotsubashi Journal of Economics*, 27.

Knoester, A. and N. van der Windt (1987), "Real wages and taxation in ten OECD countries", *Oxford Bulletin of Economics and Statistics* 49, 1.

McKee, M.J., J.J.C. Visser and P.G. Saunders (1986), "Marginal tax rates on the use of capital and labour in OECD countries", *OECD Economic Studies* No. 7 (Autumn).

Messere, K.C. and J.P. Owens (1987), "International comparisons of tax levels: pitfalls and insights", *OECD Economic Studies* No. 8 (Spring).

Munnel, A.H (1985), "Social security and the budget", *New England Economic Review*, July/August.

Musgrave, R.A (1987), "Short of euphoria", *The Journal of Economic perspectives*, Summer.

Nicoletti, G. (1988), "Private consumption, inflation and the 'debt-neutrality hypothesis'" *OECD Economics and Statistics Department Working Paper No. 50.*

OECD (1972), *Expenditure Trends in OECD Countries 1960-1980.*

OECD (1981), *The Welfare State in Crisis.*

OECD (1984), *Tax Expenditures. A Review of Issues and Country Practices.*

OECD (1985a), *OECD Economic Survey of Italy* (April).

OECD (1985b), *OECD Economic Survey of the United States* (September).

OECD (1986a), *OECD Economic Survey of the United States* (September).

OECD (1986b), personal Income Tax Systems under Changing Economic Conditions.

OECD (1986c), *An Empirical Analysis of Changes in Personal Income Taxes.*

OECD (1987a), *Structural Adjustment and Economic Performance.*

OECD (1987b), *OECD Economic Survey of New Zealand* (March).

OECD (1987c), *OECD Economic Survey of Greece* (May).

OECD (1987d), *OECD Economic Survey of the Netherlands* (May).

OECD (1987e), *OECD Economic Survey of Germany* (June).

OECD (1987f), *OECD Economic Survey of Ireland* (October).

OECD (1987g), *OECD Economic Outlook 39* (December).

OECD (1987h), *OECD Economic Survey of Belgium* (December).

OECD (1987i), *OECD Economic Survey of Norway* (December).

OECD (1987j), *Revenue Statistics of OECD Member Countries.*

OECD (1987k), *The Tax-Benefit Position of Production Workers 1983-1986.*

OECD (1987l), *The Control and Management of Government Expenditure*

OECD (1987m), *Taxation in Developed Countries.*

OECD (1988a), *OECD Economic Survey of Portugal* (January).

OECD (1988b), *OECD Economic Survey of Belgium* (January).

OECD (1988c), *OECD Economic Survey of Finland* (February).

OECD (1988d), *OECD Economic Survey of the United States* (February).

OECD (1988e), *OECD Economic Survey of Denmark* (July).

OECD (1988f), *Reforming Public Pensions.*

OECD (1988g), *Ageing Populations, The Social Policy Implications.*

OECD (1988h), *Revenue Statistics 1965-1987.*

OECD (1988i), *Historical Statistics 1960-1986.*

OECD (1988j), *OECD Economic Survey of Iceland* (October).

Pechman, J.A. (1987), "Tax Reform in Theory and Practice", *Economic perspectives*, Vol. 1, No. 1.

Pechman, J.A. (Ed.), (1988), *World Tax Reform: A Progress Report*, Brookings Dialogues on Public Policy, Washington.

Price, R.W.R. and J-C. Chouraqui (1983), "Public sector deficits: problems and policy implications", *OECD Occasional Studies* (June).

Price, R.W.R. and P. Muller (1984), "Structural budget indicators and the interpretation of fiscal policy stance in OECD economies", *OECD Economic Studies* No. 3 (Autumn).

Sandmo, Agnar (1976), "Optimal Taxation", *Journal of Public Economics 6.*

Saunders, Peter and Friedrich Klau (1985), "The role of the public sector: causes and consequences of the growth of government", *OECD Economic Studies* No. 4 (Spring).

Stiglitz, J. and M.J. Boskin (1977), "Impact of Recent Developments in Public Finance Theory on Public Policy Decisions", *American Economic Review, Papers and Proceedings*, February 1977.

United States Treasury Department (1984), *The Effects of Deficits on Prices of Financial Assets: Theory and Evidence*, Washington, D.C. (March).

United States Treasury Department (1988), "The direct revenue effects of capital gains", *Treasury Bulletin*, June.

Whalley, J. (1975), "A general equilibrium assessment of the 1973 United Kingdom tax reform", *Economica*, May.